IRELAND UNBOUND

A TURN OF THE CENTURY CHRONICLE

Also in this series:

Encounters with Modern Ireland: A Sociological Chronicle 1995–1996
Edited by Michel Peillon and Eamonn Slater
Dublin: Institute of Public Administration, 1998.

Memories of the Present: A Sociological Chronicle of Ireland 1997–1998
Edited by Eamonn Slater and Michel Peillon
Dublin: Institute of Public Administration, 2000.

Irish Sociological Chronicles
volume 3 (1999–2000)

IRELAND UNBOUND

A TURN OF THE CENTURY CHRONICLE

Edited by Mary P. Corcoran and Michel Peillon

INSTITUTE OF PUBLIC
ADMINISTRATION

First published 2002
by the Institute of Public Administration
57-61 Lansdowne Road
Dublin 4
Ireland

ISBN 1 902448 69 3
ISSN 1393-7464

Cover design by Corporate Graphics, Dublin
Front cover photograph by Theresa McNamee
Back cover photograph by Liam Devlin
Typeset in 10.75/13 New Century Schoolbook
by Computertype Ltd, Dublin
Printed in Ireland by Future Print, Dublin

Contents

Contributors

Derek CHAMBERS, Western Health Board
Peter COLLIER, Independent Researcher
Mary P. CORCORAN, National University of Ireland,
  Maynooth
Jane GRAY, National University of Ireland, Maynooth
Ellen HAZELKORN, Dublin Institute of Technology
Tom INGLIS, University College Dublin
Kieran KEOHANE, University College Cork
Aphra KERR, Dublin City University
Carmen KUHLING, University of Limerick
Katie LISTON, University College Dublin
Steve LOYAL, University College Dublin
Ciaran McCULLAGH, University College Cork
Colm MURPHY, Dublin Institute of Technology
J. Paddy O'CARROLL, University College Cork
Liam O'DOWD, Queen's University Belfast
Michel PEILLON, National University of Ireland,
  Maynooth
Stephen QUILLEY, University College Dublin
Perry SHARE, Institute of Technology, Sligo
Karen SUGRUE, University of Limerick
Hilary TOVEY, Trinity College, Dublin

Preface

This book, the third in the *Irish Sociological Chronicles* series, follows up the two earlier volumes which sought to broaden the appeal of sociology beyond the academy. Once again, the contributions contained here seek to place contemporary events, happenings and processes in an engaging sociological context. Volume 3 deals with 1999 and 2000, the turn of a new century for a country still coming to terms with changes wrought by unprecedented economic growth and social transformation.

The format of the book differs slightly from *Encounters with Modern Ireland* and *Memories of the Present*. As in the past, our call for papers produced a diversity of contributions which reflect on changes taking place in the fabric and quality of Irish life, the way we look at ourselves and the way we look at others. Mindful of the significance of the years chronicled – the turn, not only of the century, but of the millennium – we decided to commission essays from three of our fellow sociologists: Paddy O'Carroll, Liam O'Dowd and Hilary Tovey. Each has provided us with a critical commentary on Irish society, focusing on key transitions and changes as they see them.

The series, from its very start, aimed to contribute to the construction of intellectual tools through which our society could be viewed afresh. Several contributions in this volume draw on the intellectual insights of the French sociologist, Pierre Bourdieu, who died while this book was being completed. Indeed, this volume may be interpreted as an invitation to read and reflect on Irish society through the socially relevant perspective that was the hallmark of Bourdieu's work.

We would like to thank a number of people for their contributions to this work. Anthony Haughey facilitated us in consulting the archives of the DIT School of Media's Photography and Digital Imaging Studio. He helped us put together a series of images that relate to Ireland at the turn of the millennium and to produce the chapter entitled 'Transposition'. Both the DIT School of Photography and the photographers involved graciously allowed us to publish these images, and we thank them for that. The Institute of Public Administration, and principally Tony McNamara, continues to be supportive, for which we are extremely grateful. Our thanks also go to our contributors and our three essayists, whose cogent reflections allow us to approach, understand and deconstruct the processes through which Ireland has become unbound.

Boundaries and the Metamorphosis of Ireland

MICHEL PEILLON

In the contemporary world, it would be difficult to find an example of such deep, intense and rapid transformation as has occurred in Ireland. In less than a half-century, Ireland experienced a metamorphosis which propelled it out of the pre-industrial condition. While failing to generate an industrial order, it has, as a kind of unintended conse-quence, managed to establish itself as a post-industrial enclave within global capitalism. Despite the speed and the structural violence of such a process, this transformation has taken place without major social upheaval.

This third volume in the *Irish Sociological Chronicles* focuses on the years 1999 and 2000, a highly symbolic time in the history of Ireland. The significance of these two years relates to the coming of a new millennium, but also to the fact that they represented a peak in Irish economic growth and an apex in its newly found confidence. The first volume in the series, *Encounters with Modern Ireland*, highlights the configuration of social processes that are shaping Irish society. A series of circumstances allowed Ireland to bypass the industrial stage that it endeavoured to attain for so long, and ushered it into a post-industrial world, but not without distortions or unevenness. The second volume, *Memories of the Present*, revisits some of those processes. But it is also

1

concerned with the way the past and present in Ireland are linked through memories: how the act of remembering helps fix contemporary points of reference that sustain an identity and how, too, the present conditions of Ireland are constituted as something to be remembered. This third book, *Ireland Unbound*, is also about change in Ireland.

All societies experience change, and they do so in different rhythms. They contain within themselves sources of effervescence and are engaged in a continuous process of restructuring. Many of the changes Ireland is going through relate to the boundaries according to which Ireland is constructed and organised. These boundaries take many forms:

- They are found in the rules that regulate conduct, set the limits of acceptable behaviour, constrain the actions of individuals and groups and generally frame social life.

- They draw the contours of group identity and mark them out: for example nationals and immigrants, unionists and nationalists, occupational groups.

- They separate sectors and dimensions of social life that are differentiated and animated by respective dynamics: such as those of economy and culture or urban and rural worlds.

- They divide societies along many lines, according to which cultural differences and social inequalities are constituted and through which marginalisation and exclusion occur.

- They outline the physical setting in which social activities are embedded, such as the boundaries of localities which are shaped by global processes.

The transformation of Ireland, its metamorphosis, is effected mainly through a remodelling of its boundaries. This book examines what is happening to such boundaries, at the turn of the century.

2

The dissolution of boundaries

Ireland has changed, in the recent past, through the rapid evaporation of crucial boundaries and the crumbling of the institutional edifices that sustained them. In his contribution, Tom Inglis notes the collapse of the boundaries concerning bodily matters and pleasures. In the past, such desires and pleasures were fenced off by a series of rules and practices that, for all purposes, denied their reality. Not that such desires were ignored or entirely renounced. Irish people developed various ways of giving in to their desires and indulging themselves. Opportunities existed for letting go. These boundaries have, by and large, dissolved or collapsed to make room for an indulgence about food and drink, along with an exploration of sexual pleasures. But the rejection of the culture of self-denial, of all the practices that transformed the body into a forbidden object about which silence had to reign, is not accompanied by a renewed conception of the good life. This absence of boundaries, if it has to a large extent eradicated feelings of shame about bodily matters, has meant that limits have simply disappeared.

The dissolution of established boundaries is dramatically manifested by the growing incidence of suicide particularly among young men. Ireland has become, in the words of Kieran Keohane and Derek Chambers, a 'bewildering space'. The unbound subject evolves in a social world where ideals and points of reference belong to the past and haunt the present. Contemporary culture contains elements that once belonged to different worlds, but now co-exist in a curious mix. Features of reality have ceased to be either modern or traditional, either local or global, either rural or urban. Many young men have fallen victim to Ireland's ambivalent culture, one in which they can ascertain no clear identity.

Boundaries rarely vanish entirely. They leave traces behind and are often reconstituted in a different configuration. The grounds of normality have been shifting, no more so than in relation to sexuality. Karen Sugrue argues that

3

the outcry about an Ann Summers shop in Dublin was not really directed at its opening, but was fuelled by the failure to contain such a shop in an appropriate context: the back street. Instead the shop established itself on the main Dublin thoroughfare, a street invested with a high symbolic value. More space is now allowed for the expression of sexuality, but this remains in some ways problematic. It reconstitutes its own boundaries: so that, for instance, only some expressions of women's sexuality may be acknowledged in the social networks that form the basis for Ann Summers' popular house parties.

Ciaran McCullagh reminds us that criminals are rarely out of bounds: they accept the rules and norms that they breach and according to which they are declared criminals. They rely on a range of techniques in order to justify their criminal action, without rejecting the validity of such laws. However, the DIRT parliamentary inquiry found many financial institutions and their senior management in serious breach of the laws of the land. They were declared guilty of systematically facilitating tax evasion, yet they did not feel the need to offer justification for their actions. McCullagh points to the understanding, shared by tax officials and financial corporate heads, that the law could not be enforced. Well aware of the breaching of the law, they did not consider themselves bound by it; they had established different boundaries, which, according to the wisdom of this elite group, were more in tune with the technical requirements of competition in the financial market. Boundaries that are tailored to the preferences of a particular group provide an escape from normal constraints. They too manifest the weakening power of those rules which, in society at large, bind people together.

Melanges

The weakening or dissolution of boundaries triggers a range of phenomena. For instance, weak boundaries are easily crossed. They allow areas of activity to mix together and

4

elements of reality that belong to different worlds or orientations to stand side by side. The disappearance of boundaries may also accompany the merging, or fusion, of two areas of social activity.

The development and popularity of organic food point to a crossing of boundaries. Organic food has moved from the margins, where it was so long confined, to the mainstream. The production of this organic food is nowadays sponsored by supermarkets, on whose shelves it enjoys a prominent place. It is promoted by state agencies and attracts European subsidies. This crossing has to a large extent been accelerated by an excessive manipulation and alteration of foodstuff. Perry Sharc develops the view that organic food, if it has developed by crossing boundaries, must now build its own boundaries, in the form of regulations that consumers can trust.

Stephen Quilley looks critically at the way many people are pushed to the outer suburbs of Irish cities. He argues that a national commitment to the bungalow has transformed the process of urbanisation into the suburbanisation of the countryside. He regrets the lack of both an urban policy and an embracing of urban living. The bungalow became a symbol of modernity, one that stood for the alleviation of poverty and overcrowding, for brightness and convenience. As a form of housing, it reconciled rural and urban living around variations of dispersed habitat. The bungalow is located at the intersection of the urban and rural worlds, in a kind of transitional space. Quilley stresses that rural thinking continues to dominate urban living, and this constitutes the most fundamental impediment to the emergence of sustained urbanism. He wants to reverse the link between the urban and the rural: rather than shape cities according to rural mentalities, the countryside is, for him, best fashioned and appreciated through urban eyes and priorities.

Boundaries that are easily crossed, sooner or later bring together elements that were previously clearly separated. We 'live in an in-between world' according to Carmen

Kuhling and Kieran Keohane, one in which the boundaries between what is global and local, communal and societal, traditional and modern, collective and individual have to a large extent dissolved. They now co-exist in a melange of sorts. This hybridisation of Irish life is well illustrated by the replacement of heroes, standard bearers of the group, by celebrities: individuals who, through their success, become objects of desire. Celebrities are presented and constructed in a particular way in Irish popular culture, as exemplified by weekly journals such as the *RTÉ Guide*. Celebrities embody and express core values of the modern world, but they are also made to uphold the values of the traditional Irish community. They act in that sense as markers and upholders of the symbolic boundaries of the Irish community. Irish celebrities, although at ease in a global world, espouse the values of the local, which are always seen as superior to the global. Celebrities are then located at the meeting point of global individual success and local values. They form one of the sites where the local is globalised and the global localised.

The crossing of boundaries may produce a dramatic outcome: a fusion between features that were quite clearly set apart. Ellen Hazelkorn and Colm Murphy examine the constellation of features leading the project of urban regeneration in Dublin known as the Digital Hub, which centres on the promotion of the new multimedia industry. This industry relies on digital technology to create products with a high cultural content. The boundary between economy and culture has long been undermined, with many cultural features assuming the form of commodities. The point is not that culture is nowadays commodified, but that culture has become a crucial ingredient in the production of commodities. The close association of commerce and culture was previously driven by consumption; but the coming together of economy and culture in the multimedia industry is production driven. The fusion of commerce and culture occurs within the process of production itself. But the story does not stop there, for economic development on the basis

6

of a marriage of digital technology and culture is further linked with an urban renewal project. Art and culture are used to attract a particular type of business and the very flexible labour force which it employs: an industry that is sensitive to the cultural profile of its working environment and to the quality of life that this environment offers to the labour force.

The crossing of boundaries, the intermingling and fusion of separate areas of social life may even underpin the longer project of state building and social formation. Paddy O'Carroll, in a bold overview of the twentieth century, identifies three main processes that have shaped Irish society. The first relates to an early endeavour to ensure the legitimacy of the political regime in southern Ireland, a difficult task when a significant part of the territory of the island had been partitioned. The second refers to Ireland's sustained effort to develop its economy, with rather mixed success until the 1990s. Finally, he points to the more recent emergence of numerous social movements and their demands for a more open and transparent public sphere. The two processes of political legitimation and economic development, once distinct, are now intertwined. The modalities of wealth creation and wealth distribution are highly contested, and are legitimised with increasing difficulty. The blurring of the boundary between political legitimation and economic development brings the two issues together within a public space, which, it is urged, must become more democratic and open to debate. This, O'Carroll claims, is the main agenda for Ireland moving into the twenty-first century.

Uneasy interfaces

When the boundaries that set apart areas of activity dissolve, they are replaced by an uneasy interface: a direct point of contact where elements that are still differentiated come to confront each other in a very immediate and tension-filled way. The development of the multimedia industry revolved to a great extent around the demarcation of two dynamics, and consequently two institutional spheres. According to Aphra Kerr, these two ways of defining and constituting the multimedia industry were competing with each other. One focused on the cultural content of the products and services generated: on the production of information, knowledge, images, ideas and so forth. But another way of developing took precedence, one promoted by the main software companies, and the emphasis was soon set on transmission rather than content, on technology rather than culture. The multimedia industry is located in that sense in a strategic position: one in which culture and economy are brought closer together, but also one in which a clear boundary between these two elements has been replaced by an uneasy interface. In Ireland, the dominance of an economic–technological definition of the multimedia industry actually led to a failure of a marketing strategy of localisation: one in which cultural content is marketed throughout the world, after some minor local adjustment. The standardisation of cultural content simply did not work, even when the adequate technology was in place.

The interface between urban and rural is also contentious. The countryside has ceased to be a social world apart, if it ever was. The rural world was to a great extent equated with agriculture, while nowadays most country people are not wholly engaged in agricultural work. It is not simply that the boundaries between rural and urban worlds are dissolving, but that they are turned into a site of struggle. Hilary Tovey contends that this struggle involves converting the rural into an urban game. The struggles over the meaning of space entail the replacement of the rural by the urban: that is, the progressive assimilation of the country-side into a perspective dominated by the viewpoints and interests of those who reside in towns and cities. It nonetheless involves an interaction between rural and urban viewpoints, one which is framed by a pattern of dominance. This interaction is well illustrated by all those who cross the rural–urban boundary (at weekends or holidays mainly) and regularly move from one setting to another. The rural, as a particular domain of social life, is characterised by a distinctive logic and remains autonomous, contained within loose boundaries, but urban interests and perspectives acquire an increasingly dominant position within it. This points to a paradox: boundaries do not necessarily disappear when they are crossed, instead they may become problematic and contentious in an uneasy interface.

The emergence of immigration has brought to the fore some of the boundaries through which Ireland has been constituted. Immigration has activated existing, but largely latent, boundaries and transformed them into sites of tension and struggle. Steve Loyal examines how these tensions have been exacerbated by the decision to grant a right-to-work amnesty for a limited group of asylum seekers. Nationalism articulates, almost by definition, an ideology of boundaries; national citizenship defines the rights of those within, while denying them to those who remain outside. These boundaries are closely policed by a range of regulations that determine the conditions under which outsiders may come in. They are also sustained by unsympathetic state practices and through expressions of racism directed at asylum seekers in their daily lives. This closure of Irish society is confronted by an opposite trend, that of its opening. The right of asylum seekers to work is promoted by many who articulate the needs of the Irish economy for a growing labour force. The way Ireland has linked with global capitalism requires the dissolution of this kind of boundary. The tension between closure and opening, between upholding and dissolving boundaries, has crystallised around the right to work of asylum seekers.

The phenomenal transformation of Dublin has also brought about, in a very concrete way, a replacement of established boundaries by a confrontational edge. Mary Corcoran retraces the clash that took place over the proposed development of Spencer Dock. This project of urban renewal has mobilised two radically opposed viewpoints about the nature of cities and the fabric of urban space. One, championed by local neighbourhoods, views the city in terms of highly personalised urban villages. The other, promoted by developers, pushes a dense urban architecture geared to a cosmopolitan lifestyle. These two viewpoints clashed in the Spencer Dock project, mainly because it proposed to place opposite one another, in a direct and immediate way, two different types of urban organisation and living. They were juxtaposed without any kind of transition; they were face to face as two incompatible social universes.

Resilient boundaries

Not all boundaries are dissolving or shifting, far from it. Many persist and are even reinforced. The persistence of boundaries does not depend on inertia. Rather they have to be maintained, and this requires a great deal of work and activity. Peter Collier chronicles the transformation of offshore fishing in Ireland, focusing on a particular fishing port. Only a small number of individuals are involved in the fishing industry. Most of the fishing entrepreneurs and workers came from a class of landless workers, and fishing gave to some of them the prospect of crossing the deep social boundaries that separated them from the world of small property enterprise. They have developed, in their work mainly, a range of practices and dispositions that to a large extent set them apart and define their identity. They have upheld these dispositions in an environment that is rapidly changing. In other words, they have responded to these changes according to their 'habitus', through which they are marked as a group, and in order to sustain their identity. The author points to the unrelenting increase in the size of fishing boats. This increase is not so much accounted for in terms of greater productivity as it is by an adaptation to the changed circumstances of fishing according to dispositions that have been traditionally associated with fishing.

Boundaries do linger, although such lingering does not occur without a purpose. Katie Liston develops the view that sport works as a site for the demarcation of masculinity and femininity, that it generates practices that are gendered and reinforces this boundary. Sport is a male preserve; that is to say an area of activity where male values prevail: values of physicality, endurance, aggression, and also of camaraderie. Femininity is not easily reconciled with sport, and particularly team sport, because femininity is not constructed around male values. When women display physicality, fitness, endurance and aggression, their performance is not highly valued and their sporting achievements are not well rewarded. The difficulty women face in converting their sporting prowess into material, political and social rewards constitutes one of the mechanisms through which boundaries between masculinity and femininity are maintained.

Some of the boundaries that structure our social world persist long after they have lost their *raison d'être*, mainly because they are deeply rooted in a pattern of power. Mostly, such boundaries are contested, but some generate little or no resistance. Clear boundaries have been drawn around childbirth; not so much the physical boundaries of the maternity hospital, but the practices and ideas that govern childbirth have been heavily institutionalised. Jane Gray argues that the childbirth regime which dominates in Ireland, that of active labour, is not in practice women-centred. On the contrary, it is overseen by specialist obstetricians, who act as the gatekeepers of institutionalised practice. Such boundaries are maintained, mainly because they protect the power of the medical specialists over all those involved in the process of giving birth, particularly mothers. Gray reflects on the strength of these boundaries, a strength that is manifested by the lack of challenge to this childbirth regime and the compliance displayed by mothers.

The boundary that separates unionists and nationalists has also demonstrated high resilience. This line is not easily crossed and seems to crystallise all the tensions of Northern Irish society. Liam O'Dowd records the persistence of this boundary through the ideologies of the two groups it keeps apart, but he also emphasises the profound transformation that has taken place. In the 1950s, Northern Ireland as a political entity within the UK was secure, and the power of unionists within it well established. They could claim to embody British modernity in an Irish context. The nationalist project was seriously undermined by what was widely perceived as the failure of the Irish state: economic stagnation, high levels of emigration, rural decline, cultural rot and no headway in ending territorial partition. The boundary that split Northern Irish society in the 1950s has not weakened or disappeared. It still keeps the two communities well apart, but its meaning has drastically changed. The nationalist ideology has moved to the fore, fed in the 1990s by economic success, an expanding population, the end of mass emigration, a high cultural profile and an eager embracing of modernity in southern Ireland, as well as power-sharing in Northern Ireland. O'Dowd endeavours to account for this extraordinary reversal: one in which a crucial boundary persists, but in a way which radically alters the relations between the two groups which it keeps apart.

The focus on boundaries throughout this volume directs our attention to some of the mechanisms through which change in Ireland is taking place. The dissolution, blurring or even strengthening of particular boundaries, and the merging or clash which develops in the aftermath of such changes, all point to deeper forces and processes that are fundamentally altering the very structure and dynamic of Irish society. The reproduction or dislocation of boundaries represents a crucial moment in this transformation.

Transposition

VARIOUS

Robert Redmond

Armelle Skatulski

Armelle Skatulski

Sandra Erckhardt

16

Sandra Erckhardt

17

Phil Voon

Isabelle Quinn

Vanessa Fay

Karl O'Keeffe

21

Deirdre Molloy

PART 1

THE DISSOLUTION OF BOUNDARIES

CHAPTER 1

Pleasure Pursuits

TOM INGLIS

I rish people have taken to pampering themselves. It is now right and fitting to want and have the best. The consumer culture has been egged on by advertisers. In the television advertisement, the beautiful woman looks straight into the camera and tells the world she does not need to justify spending money on herself: 'I'm worth it'. There is no sense of shame about this woman; she is an icon for being self-confident in self-indulgence and she is far removed from the female icons of Catholic Ireland. She has replaced the idol of the demure Irish colleen on whose lips, and in whose heart, mind and body, was ingrained the belief: 'Lord, I am not worthy'.

There is no shame in wanting to look young, healthy and beautiful. In 2000, one of Dublin's leading department stores advertised a skin cream at £950 (€1,206.25) for a 500ml jar. Such care for the body is part of a general trend: between 1990 and 1999, the total amount of money spent in the Irish Republic per year on personal care rose from €373m to €1,092m, an increase of 193 per cent. This new self-confidence, the growth in gyms and fitness regimes and the general care for health and beauty suggest that economic prosperity has led to a new form of self-indulgence.

While some have taken to making and keeping the body beautiful, others have taken to eating, especially eating out, in a big way. In the 1990s the total amount spent per year

25

going out for something to eat or drink rose from €2.5bn to €5.6bn, an increase of 124 per cent. Despite all the advice about staying fit, trim and healthy, Irish people seem to be getting fatter by the day. Two-thirds of Irish men and over half of the Irish population are now overweight. During the 1990s the average weight of Irish people increased by one stone. This has been linked to an increase in both alcohol consumption and eating out.[1] Not only is the Irish 'couch potato' getting fatter, but for stimulation he or she still turns to the old reliables: drink and tobacco. During the 1990s the total amount spent on alcohol per year rose from €504m to €1,079m, an increase of 114 per cent. And again, despite all the warnings about the dangers of smoking, the amount of money spent on tobacco rose by 98 per cent, from €771m to €1,526m.[2]

Fast food

The traditional fish and chip shop has given way to a plethora of hamburger joints, ethnic takeaways and fast-food restaurants. By the end of 2000 there were fifty-seven McDonalds restaurants in Ireland. Much of what is offered in fast-food restaurants may be seen as fancy fodder. Ritzer argues that these restaurants have reduced our engagement with and appreciation of food to a bureaucratic exercise that epitomises the rationalisation of Western life. What is important in these restaurants is not the taste or the quality of the food, but that it is produced in a highly regulated, calculable, predictable and efficient manner. Potatoes are cut to the exact same thickness and fried at the exact same temperature. The number of fries that will fit into a regular container can be calculated precisely. The food will always

---

[1] *The Irish Times*, 8 August 2000.
[2] *Annual Household Budget Survey Results 1990–99*. As these figures to not take inflation into account, some of the increased expenditure could be due to an increase in prices and/or taxes. My thanks to Brian King for providing these figures.

taste the same, and it will always be in your hands within five minutes of arriving inside the door. Ritzer claims that fast food limits, if not destroys, 'the human craving for new and diverse experiences'.[3] This may be so, but fast food has made eating out more democratic and informal.

It used to be that eating out meant going to restaurants or hotels. Such meals were expensive and formal. Dining out was an activity confined to special occasions and the middle and upper classes. It may have been enjoyable, but it could also be a nightmare. To avoid shame and embarrass-ment it was necessary to embody a strict etiquette. Eating out was an opportunity to display good manners. Now all sorts and classes of men, women and children can indulge in the pleasure of eating out. At the same time, the enjoyment of eating has been liberated from the rigidity of strict Victorian protocols. And while Ritzer may be right about America, it could be argued that in Ireland the availability of fast food has broadened rather than limited people's taste buds.

Look what has happened to the sandwich. The plain and simple 'hang' sandwich has disappeared from the Irish landscape. Fillings have multiplied. Ham is no longer just ham, it is either boiled, smoked, baked or Parma. Beef has become corned, spiced or pastrami. Then there are choices to be made about garnishes, whether the sandwich is to be spread with mayonnaise (full fat or low calorie) or mustard, whether lettuce is to be included and, if so, which type. And whether these fillings are to be placed in French, Italian or Irish bread and, if the latter, whether this is to be white, brown, wholegrain or rye.

Indeed there is plenty of evidence that Irish people are becoming more rational, circumspect and educated about the pleasures of food and drink. They want to explore different tastes, products and services, and to eat and drink

---

3 George Ritzer, *The MacDonaldization of Society,* California: Pine Forge Press, 1993, p. 139.

in new places. Besides fast-food restaurants, there has been a dramatic rise in the number of designer pubs, cafés, ethnic restaurants and delicatessens. People have begun to read, talk and share information about dishes and restaurants that they have discovered. Devotees of food sometimes behave as if they were members of a religious sect, meeting to eat and discuss the latest find or taste sensation. They make pilgrimages in search of handmade gnocchi, wild boar sausage, fresh crayfish and authentic sushi. Even drink tastes have expanded: people talk about their favourite cocktails, Belgian beers or small vineyards in the South of France that produce the most exquisite Viognier. For many, salvation is not about life after death, it is discovering heaven on earth. Being blessed is being able to indulge in fine food and drink all day, every day.

We are led into the promised land by a whole host of wine connoisseurs and celebrity chefs. They have become our modern day Eves. These masters of self-indulgence sigh, eulogise and go into paroxysms of pleasure about the wines they drink and the dishes they create. Turn off the television and open a magazine and, alongside photographs of scantily clothed women, there are pictures of sumptuous dishes ready to be devoured. We are encouraged to let go, give in to our desires, and allow pleasure to reign free. Readers move from looking at or drooling over beautiful women to salivating over exotic dishes.

Giving into bodily pleasures is obviously nothing new. What is new is the frank, open, public display of such self-indulgence. Private passions have gone public. Developing our own particular tastes, preferences and pleasures has become part of what we are. Announcing and pursuing these pleasures, and sharing them with others, has become part of an intimate disclosure, a way of creating, developing and communicating a sense of self.

The transformations taking place in the sense of self in Ireland can be linked to the modernisation of Irish society during the last half of the twentieth century and, more specifically, to the rapid economic growth of the 1990s.

Europe and transnational corporations literally entered into our society and homes and, through jobs, prosperity and consumer choice, helped create a new sense of self. We became consumers, increasingly consumed with ourselves. Indeed given that economic growth is heavily dependent on consumption, this increase in self-indulgence could be seen as central to proserity and the accumulation of wealth.[4] In this way, the rejection of the traditional sense of self engendered through Catholic Church teaching was central to the modernisation of Irish society. At the heart of this rejection was a turning on its head of the notion that self-indulgence was a sin. Indulging the self became an un-ashamed pleasure.

But appearances can be deceiving. The process of pursuing pleasures and indulging the self has been fraught with contradictions. Irish people are ambivalent and incon sistent when it comes to pleasure. We encourage people to be expressive, assertive and self-confident in announcing and fulfilling their desires and pleasures. But we do not teach our children about pleasures, how they can be realised and developed and how they have to be balanced with duties and responsibilities. Instead, through generations of embodied Catholic Church teachings, our disposition and reaction to their taking pleasure is often negative, while our reaction to their humility and practice of self-denial is often positive.

The legacy of self-denial

The past was a different place in Ireland. Of course people took pleasure in their bodies, in caring for themselves and in indulging in food, drink and sex, but there was not the same discourse, language or competency in talking about these pleasures. Self-indulgence was a sin and pleasure had to be

---

4   For an elaboration of this argument see Michel Peillon, 'Carnival Ireland', in Eamonn Slater and Michel Peillon (eds), *Memories of the Present*, Dublin: IPA, 2000, pp. 133–42.

legitimated within an overall habitus of self-denial.[5] Taking pleasure in food and drink had to be justified within the rhetoric of an unusual, unexpected or special occasion: someone's funeral, birthday or anniversary. People worked within a culture of making good excuses for letting go and indulging themselves. They talked about food and drink being forced on them, as if they had no choice or control. It was others who insisted that they should enjoy themselves; after all, self-indulgence was immoral. This gave rise to some very peculiar, but complex, social rituals.

When offered food and drink, the custom was to refuse politely, this indicated that one knew the logic and rules under which the offer had been made: food and resources were scarce, but it was necessary to make an offer. It showed a willingness to sacrifice the self for the greater need of others, to be humble and to deem oneself unworthy. The logic and practice of the game of social offering was learnt at home as part of the larger, wider game of self-denial. The host was expected to repeat the offer a second, third or fourth time. At some suitable stage there was a shift and it became honourable and polite to accept the offer and, at the same time, to emphasise how small the offering should be. It was an art of life at which the Irish became particularly skilled. It was sometimes a rude awakening when these skilled practitioners went abroad and the first refusal was taken as a real announcement of what one wanted.

To understand the change in the pursuit of pleasures in Ireland, it is necessary to go back and examine the culture that venerated the plain and simple, of people taking what they were given, being grateful for small mercies, and making do. We have to go back to the days when the

---

5 Following the work of sociologist Pierre Bourdieu, 'habitus' can be understood as the inherited, embodied, predisposed, but nevertheless flexible and transposable, ways that people have of reading, understanding and relating to the social environments in which they operate. See Pierre Bourdieu, *Pascalian Meditations*, Cambridge: Polity Press, 2000.

pleasure of drinking was a male pleasure, when drinking and eating were seen as separate pleasures, and when self-elimination in drink was accepted, but self-assertion was treated as a mortal sin.

Drinking but not eating

We have come a long way from the days when going out for most people revolved around men going to the pub. Pubs acquired a unique place in Irish society as a sanctuary where men could take refuge from the rigours and confines of domestic life. Pubs developed their own culture: ways of greeting, talking, interacting and behaving.[6] Seemingly informal, there were strict orthodoxies about drinking and eating. Some hardened drinkers saw eating as a sacrilegious act that threatened the purity of the pub. However, over the years concessions began to be made. Pubs began to provide a small selection of sandwiches, often just ham, chicken or cheese. The sandwiches were not treated as culinary delights but as 'blotting-paper' to soak up the alcohol. At the base of hard drinking is a collective ritualised practice of self-elimination – the drinker sublimates himself through drink and this eases surrender within the group. The sublimation of self was a social requirement in a culture of poverty.

Bourdieu has suggested that what characterises peasant and working-class culture is an attitude of 'simple modest taste', getting by and making do. All pretensions are forbidden. There is an insistence on conformity, which, if resisted, is met by calls to order such as: 'who does he think

---

6 Although McNabb drew attention to the importance of the pub in Irish social life, and Cassidy has done some important work, we still await a major social study and history of this important social institution. See Patrick McNabb, 'Social Structure', in Jeremiah Newman (ed.), *Limerick Rural Survey*, Tipperary: Muintir na Tíre, 1964; and Tanya Cassidy, 'Just Two Will Do', in Michel Peillon and Eamonn Slater (eds), *Encounters with Modern Ireland*, Dublin: IPA, 1998, pp. 165 74.

he is?' or 'that's not for the like of us'. The emphasis on making do, of limiting choice to the necessary, is, Bourdieu argues, linked to a preference for strong, plain food, which in turn can be linked to the type of diet necessary to produce the muscle that often constitutes labour power.[7] In such a culture the emphasis is quantity rather than quality. But in Ireland, particularly among male drinkers, a culture emerged of quantities of plain drink and of not mixing food and drink. The pattern of drinking heavily and then looking for food has not changed, except that more women are following this form of self-indulgence. It is a practice that has its origins in the culture of scarcity and self-denial. What has changed is the number of opportunities in towns and cities to avail of quick and easy food after a drink. But what happens when many young people leave the cocoon of ritualised self-elimination, sodden with drink, and enter into a competitive search for fast food? Not mixing food and drink can be an explosive mixture.

The problem of people not knowing what they want, of making do, of practising self-denial and eliminating themselves in drink, is part of a wider problem of cultural ambivalence about pleasure. Many Irish people think of pleasure as a sin and of events where people let go and indulge in bodily pleasures as an occasion of sin. They have grown up in a culture of not knowing and not being able to announce their pleasures. Priests, parents and teachers have given ambiguous, mixed messages about pleasures. Coming out of a culture of poverty, scarcity and self-denial, they are effectively handicapped when it comes to knowing and appreciating pleasures and how to balance them with duties and responsibilities. Young people are living in a cultural limbo, or a state of anomie. Many have rejected the ethical principles and practices of the culture of self-denial, but they have not replaced it with any other system of

---

7 Pierre Bourdieu, *Distinction*, London: Routledge and Kegan Paul, 1984, pp. 380–1.

ethics. They are caught at the crossroads of change in Irish culture, between Catholic fundamentalism and postmodernism. The problem with the relativism of postmodernity is that it makes all ethical packages look the same. If they are to avoid complete hedonism, they have to choose and develop their own self-control, their own ethical lifestyles.

Division, ambiguity and ambivalence

Irish people have always tended to be divided on, and to have an ambivalent attitude to, pleasure. In the field of sex, there were celibates and non-celibates. The symbolic domination of celibacy within the Catholic Church led to ambiguity and ambivalence about sex among non-celibates. Was it right to pursue sex as a pleasure? Do women enjoy sex? These ambiguities were not resolved in the silence about sex imposed by celibates.

Similarly, the field of drink tended to be divided between those who did and those who did not: drinkers and pioneers. Pioneers wore a pin as a sign that they abstained from drink, not so much as an indication of their moral superiority, but more so that people would not offer or push drink on them. Drink was both a pleasure and a curse, but the tirades against alcohol led to ambivalent attitudes and ambiguity as to whether it was a good or bad thing. Like sex, children had to be shielded from this evil pleasure, and those who drank did so in the private, almost secret, world of the pub. It had to be a rare occasion to drink at home.

The divisions, ambiguities and ambivalent attitudes could be linked to the 'all or nothing' way Irish people drank. People moved from being completely sober to being completely drunk, often very quickly. It was as if one drink was enough to break through the moral damn of restraint, the floodgates opened. Self-indulgence merged into self-elimination.

Pleasure was wrapped up in a language of repression. Drink, like sex, was an occasion of sin. If we go back into the archives to find who wrote what about pleasure, we can find

33

numerous diatribes about the evils of sex and drink, but very few about its pleasures. One of the consequences of this was that people drank, but did not discuss their drinking. People had sex, but did not discuss their desires, preferences or sexual orientation. People ate, but did not discuss food. This cultural incompetence to write and talk about pleasure, led to a particular approach to sex, food and drink. Food was seen and treated as fodder. It was talked about in terms of quantity more than quality. Among males – and it must be remembered that in most societies male pleasure has always tended to come first – size mattered most. When men went out for a meal, it was the size of the serving, particularly of the meat, which caused concern. Sex was seen in terms of conquests and frequency. It was the same with drink. It was not the taste, but the quantity that was consumed that mattered. In a culture where quantity domi-nates quality, where the self and pleasure are eliminated, it may not be surprising that young people learn to sublimate if not eliminate themselves in drink. Drinkers talk of 'losing the head', 'being absolutely smashed' or 'totally arseholed'. It may be a source of ridicule, but there is no real loss of honour or self-respect.

The absence of a discourse or competence to talk about oneself and one's pleasures can be linked to the culture of self-denial and mortification. At the heart of Catholic Church teaching there has always been great value put on self-emptying or selflessness. The body, the source of temptation and evil, had to be denied and mortified. People like Blessed Matt Talbot were venerated. He fell into the depraved world of drink, but through prayer and self-mortification, particularly the embodiment of a series of penitential practices that emulated the life of the early Irish monks, he saved his soul and became a model for all Irish drinkers. This ethical lifestyle can be traced back to the early days of Christianity and the emergence of a system of ethics revolving around sin and self-mortification.

In Ireland the culture of making do and self-denial was not just a working-class phenomenon, it was universal or

34

catholic. Recent changes in Irish culture can therefore be characterised as a shift from a culture of self-denial to one of self-indulgence. But whereas the culture of self-denial had well-defined values, beliefs and practices, which were inculcated, monitored and evaluated in confession by priests, Irish people are on their own when it comes to knowing, understanding and appreciating pleasures. Many young people have torn up the Catholic guide to living a good life and turned to an ancient Greek notion that it is up to each individual to construct an ethical life based around duties, responsibilities and pleasures. For the ancient Greeks, not paying attention to one's pleasures was as unethical as not fulfilling one's duties and responsibilities.[8] In a world of plenty, it may be that Irish people need pleasure counsellors, rather than priests, to offer guidance as to how to live an ethical life that balances pleasures with responsibilities. It would certainly make a change to sit down and critically reflect with someone about one's pleasures rather than to kneel down and confess one's sins.

---

8 See Michel Foucault, *The Use of Pleasure, Volume 2. The History of Sexuality,* London: Penguin, 1987.

CHAPTER 2

Understanding Irish Suicides

KIERAN KEOHANE AND DEREK CHAMBERS

Suicide in Ireland rose dramatically in the 1990s. The increase is especially marked amongst men in their twenties and there is some evidence to suggest that the rise has been greater in rural areas.[1] The grim statistics are well known, and tragic stories of Irish suicides have become all too familiar. The public discourse on suicide in Ireland has been mostly informed by medical and psychological explanations, which analyse the epidemiology of suicide in terms of risk factors, linking suicide with alcohol and substance abuse, with mental illness such as depression, and with stress associated with transition to adulthood and role adaptation. Such an approach, while useful in understanding individual cases, has not contributed significantly to our understanding of why the overall pattern of death by suicide in Ireland changed over the final decades of the twentieth century.

Here we offer a sociological interpretation of Irish suicide, one that collects the medical and psychological discourses in terms of a broader historical and cultural explanation. The explanation is based on a number of case profiles, compiled

---

1   M. J. Kelleher, D. Chambers and P. Corcoran, 'Suicide and Religion in Ireland: An Investigation of Thomas Masaryk's Theory of Suicide', *Archives of Suicide Research,* vol. 5, 1999, pp. 173–180.

by Irish coroners, that we interpret within a sociological framework of transformation in Irish society.[2] In these 'sociological autopsies',[3] we show that the causes underpinning the increase in suicide in Irish society stem from the historical experience of cultural collisions: collisions between the vestiges of traditional community and accelerated modern society, the rural and the urban, the local and the global; and collisions that impact traumatically on the life histories of individuals. Suicides, we argue, are to be understood as the casualties of Ireland's collision culture.

Durkheim's typology of suicide

In a classic sociological study, Durkheim identifies four different types of suicide: 'altruistic' and 'fatalistic', which he associates with pre-modern, traditional community, and 'egoistic' and 'anomic', which are more characteristic of modern society.[4] The latter are particularly useful in developing a sociological explanation of suicide in a contemporary Irish context. In modern societies people lead highly individualised lives and, as a result, they may be insufficiently integrated into normal collective life. Excessive individuation may lead to egoistic suicide, such as the high-profile suicides of rock stars and other celebrities. More mundane and, sadly, very familiar examples of egoistic suicide may be those related to pressures and anxiety generated by expectations that we be 'stars' ourselves, for example in examinations or career performance.

Anomic suicide is also associated with the conditions of modern society. This type of suicide occurs most frequently

---

2   Identifying details of the cases have been omitted and disguised to ensure anonymity.
3   D. Chambers, 'A Sociological Account of the Rise in Irish Suicide: Suicide as a Symptom of the Celtic Tiger', unpublished MA dissertation, Department of Sociology, NUI Cork, 1999.
4   E. Durkheim, *Suicide*, New York: Free Press, 1951, pp. 152–277.

in times of moral confusion due to rapid social change, when moral and regulatory frameworks and institutions are unstable. Anomic suicide is symptomatic of insufficient moral regulation, arising not only from the decline of an agreed source of moral authority, but also from the proliferation of competing moralities. The normative confusion created is characteristic of modern life, and especially of periods of rapid transformation. In modern society suicide rates increase during periods of economic recession as well as during economic booms, both of which are times of instability. In contemporary Ireland anomic suicide is related not only to the boom, but also to the decline of Catholicism as a unifying moral framework, fundamental transformations of gender roles and family life and the rise of secular moralities of affluence.

Durkheim's *Suicide* is part of a broader analysis of the social transformation of the nineteenth century, with the emergence of a secular, urban, industrial society, and the tension between the new society and the vestiges of the pre-modern, religious, rural and agrarian community. Durkheim draws up the characteristic and distinguishing features of pre-modern community and modern society.[5] In a traditional community there is an undifferentiated division of labour, whereas there is a high degree of occupational specialisation in the modern society, with the corollary that one's resemblance to others is valued in the former, whereas one's specific and peculiar difference from others is valued in the latter. Traditional communities are integrated by the principle of mechanical solidarity: the individual resembles the other members of the collective not only in terms of labour and occupation, but through a shared body of beliefs, values and sentiments, which constitute a pervasive religious cosmology that is dense, clearly defined and inflexible – a conscience collective. By contrast, modern societies

---

5   E. Durkheim, *The Division of Labour in Society*, New York: Free Press, 1984, pp. 31–126.

are integrated by organic solidarity: each person has an individual conscience that is differentiated and flexible, and he or she is individually morally responsible for his or her actions. When a member of a traditional community offends the collective, he or she (and his or her kin insofar as the individual is indistinguishable from the group) is repressively sanctioned. In a modern society, the deviant is required to make restitution; he or she is rehabilitated, reintegrated and the smooth functioning of social life is restored.

Collision culture

Durkheim's elaboration of 'traditional' and 'modern' enables the sociologist to speak meaningfully about the substantive differences between the regulated patterns of action that constitute the characteristic features of particular societies. For example Ireland, by comparison with other modern western societies, has been a racially and culturally homogenous, strongly religious, rural community, but it has been undergoing major social transformation, a process which accelerated in the 1990s due to the economic boom. This has produced a situation where vestiges of traditional community co-exist uneasily and often collide with the forms of modern society.

If one examines the rise in Irish suicide in terms of Durkheim's analysis, it can be argued that the suicide rate in Ireland is closely correlated to broad structural transformations. Foremost of these is the economic boom, where relative material affluence is manifest psychologically in a sense of boundlessness: the expansion of desires, the amplification of acquisitiveness and insatiability. Insatiability is always a sign of morbidity.[6] Coinciding and closely intertwined with a period of unparalleled economic expansion is an unprecedented crisis in the Catholic Church in

---

6   E. Durkheim, *Suicide*, New York: Free Press, 1951, pp. 246–7.

Ireland, which had for at least one hundred years enjoyed a moral monopoly.[7] The expansion of material horizons and the decline of the moral authority of the Catholic Church are the two primary sources of egoism and anomie in contemporary Ireland: banks offer extensive credit at low rates, promoting loans with such slogans as 'the sky's the limit' and 'whatever your heart desires'. At the same time, the Catholic Church, eclipsed by materialism and commodity fetishism and rocked by scandal, has its moral role reduced to apologising for its own excesses and abuses. Throughout the 1990s the Catholic Church in Ireland was repeatedly implicated in scandals, ranging from prominent individual clergymen fathering children, to a large number of high-profile prosecutions of individual clergy and religious communities for child sexual abuse and cruelty.

Such phenomena have a long history in religious institutions, and it is not merely coincidence that the Catholic Church in Ireland is the subject of such exposure and prosecution at this particular historical juncture. Rather it reflects a new institutional configuration in which the sacred authorities of community are eclipsed by the secular principles of society. Central to this is a democratic and legal rational discourse of rights – rights of the individual in general, and the child in particular; a discourse of sexual equality and associated measures to regulate the play of power, between men and women and between adults and children. These are influences linked to globalisation, mediated through the political culture of North America and the legal institutions of the EU. These global discourses coincide with a local economic boom in Ireland that, for the first time, provides a large number of people with alternatives to the Catholic Church as a provider for material, cultural and spiritual needs.

---

7   T. Inglis, *Moral Monopoly: The Rise and Fall of the Catholic Church in Modern Ireland*, Dublin: UCD Press, 1998.

Under these conditions of expansive individualism and the decline of a totalising and unifying religious worldview, we are 'unable to find any limitation, any check, any considerateness within the morality at our disposal'.[8] There are other important transformations taking place. Traditional gender roles and family forms collide with new alternatives. Young men, for instance, experience their traditional role privileges and securities as under threat or circumscribed by the influences of feminism and gender equality in employment. Young women experience the same changes positively, as an expansion of horizons (manifest in their lower suicide rates), but negatively as performance pressures. The stress to combine split roles intensifies: traditional homemaker, wife and mother, as well as modern, independent career woman (manifest in the increased rate of female suicide and attempted suicide). For both young men and women, the increase in the suicide and attempted suicide rate is most marked in country towns,[9] places that are neither villages where the fabric of community remains relatively intact, nor cities where conditions of anomie have themselves become normalised. Contemporary Irish country towns are in-between places: neither rural nor urban, but hybrid, liminal and characterised by uncertainty and anomie.

Suicidogenic tendencies in Irish society

The increase in the Irish suicide rate illustrates Durkheim's general thesis that the social form within which modern suicide rates can be interpreted and understood is anomie and egoism. Anomie points to the loss of a central, stable, normative framework; the proliferation of competing, confusing norms; an expansion of material and moral

---

8   F. Nietzsche, *Beyond Good and Evil*, New York: Vintage, 1989, pp. 211–12.
9   Department of Health and Children, *Report of the National Task Force on Suicide*, Dublin: Government Publications, 1998.

horizons; and an amplification of desires that in the contexts of limitlessness are insatiable. Egoism is related to the disintegration of traditional social bonds of family, kinship and community; the emergence of the unbounded subject; and the cult of the individual. But we are concerned here with suicide at the current conjuncture of Irish society. In order to see its particular content, what is unique and particular to egoistic and anomic suicide in Ireland, to understand and interpret the despairing, terrible action of suicide, we need to get close to the phenomenon. To grasp and understand what in the traumatic experience of living in contemporary Ireland is conducive to suicide we must focus more closely on the specific circumstances of Irish suicides.

In each of the cases examined here, we are trying to gain an understanding of 'the larger historical scene in terms of its meaning for the inner life and the external career of a variety of individuals'.[10] As Wright Mills says, 'neither the life [or the death] of an individual nor the history of a society can be understood without understanding both'.[11] Behind every suicide there is a realm of private trouble, an individual tragedy – a husband, wife, mother, father, son or daughter, a friend or neighbour – a life lost, other lives shattered. But a sociological imagination may help us to see and understand the ways in which biography and history are intertwined, so that private troubles are in fact symptoms of public issues. The tragic drama played out in the life-worlds of individuals constitutes a microcosm of the larger drama of collision culture in contemporary Ireland.

First case

A 26-year-old man, living with his parents in the west of Ireland, was found having shot himself at his parents'

---

10 C. Wright Mills, *The Sociological Imagination*, New York: Oxford University Press, 1959, p. 5.
11 Wright Mills, ibid., p. 3.

house. His mother discovered her son's body after she returned from a weekend abroad. She called her husband's office and then called a priest and the gardaí.

This young man, university educated and employed in the telecommunications industry, came from a wealthy, urban, professional family who had built a contemporary lifestyle based on country living in a rural retreat combined with frequent travel abroad. The incongruous element that reminds us that this is Ireland is that the young man was still living with his parents. Though employed and independent, he was not fully individuated and autonomous. In Irish traditional communities it would have been quite common and normal for adult children – if they had not emigrated – to be still part of the nuclear household, but in the 1990s, this domestic situation was no longer the norm. Successful young men are now expected to set up on their own and to assume the burdens of home ownership and autonomy. And there is a further incongruous and telling element: that, for this apparently very modern Irish family, it was the priest who was called upon immediately – not the doctor or ambulance, the helpers for a modern emergency, but the bearer of the authority and succour of a traditional community.

Second case

Another case is that of a 35-year-old woman employed in a managerial position and living in a village adjacent to a large urban area. She was married with children, but had in the past lived with her lover, who was also her employer, for several months. When the affair had begun her lover's wife began harassing her, and prior to death she had been taking medication for depression. On the night of her suicide she left home saying she would visit her mother. Her husband phoned his mother-in-law to say that she might call. She did not call to her mother. Her husband reported her missing later that night. He also phoned her employer (her lover), who said that he would help in the search and also that he would ask another employee to help. Her husband found her body.

In this case, the woman inhabited a bewildering space between two opposed forms of life. She lived in what was no longer a village, but also not part of the city: a 'rurban' area typical of contemporary Ireland.[12] On the one hand she was a modern woman: employed outside the home, making her own choices about her love life and kicking against the traces of conventional morality about the social roles of wife and mother. On the other hand she was still deeply immersed in traditional community: while she had a function in a modern, economic division of labour, this did not give her autonomy, as she was also married with children. Further, her boss was also her lover, re-inscribing the intimate sphere within the market relation that freed her from the constraints of the family. She had no anonymity: her husband knew of the affair, as did her lover's wife, as indeed did her own family and her in-laws, and all were in communication with one another. On the night of her death her husband called her mother and her lover to report her missing. Her lover/boss in turn called another employee, also familiar with the situation, to help. There was a dense network of social relations, a community to call upon for assistance.

The woman was sufficiently individuated to experience and acknowledge her own desires, and to act on them, and yet she was insufficiently free to act on them with autonomy, privacy and impunity. She lacked not only the anonymity of city life, but also its plurality – in a village within a large urban area, even in the Ireland of the 1990s, there were few women with whom she might share a common experience. Divorce, and life after divorce, for women in their thirties with children was not institutionalised as a social form, as

---

12 K. Bonner, *A Great Place to Raise Kids: Interpretation, Science and the Urban-Rural Debate*, Montreal: McGill-Queen's University Press, 1997, pp. 125–7.

it might be in a North American or European city. She was on her own: with no peer group, no support, and no model to follow. She was torn between desires and constraints belonging to two separate forms of life: her desire to be free and her obligation to herself to be autonomous and, equally, her desire to 'do the right thing', to fulfil her obligations as a good wife, mother and daughter. The challenge was to perform simultaneously two sets of roles belonging to the divergent moral orders of traditional community and modern society that co-exist in contemporary Ireland.

The tragic depths revealed in this story come through in the way in which the people involved were quite obviously trying to do their best to cope with the difficult situation. Her husband, her mother and her lover were in communication. They were motivated by their mutual care for her, but it is perhaps this very mutuality – no doubt charged with a potent mixture of love and anger, envy and desire – that formed the small, terrible world that became unbearable for her.

Third case

In our third case study, a suicide note reveals a painful and traumatic individual story of marital disharmony, unhappiness, recrimination, paranoia, fear, hatred, revenge and pain. The husband rages at his wife's alleged infidelity, and the shame and hurt that he says she has caused. He feels this acutely and intolerably. But to feel this shame implies that he considered himself to be a part of a community that shared a morality, a normative framework, a conscience collective. A community that 'knows what you have done', that watches and sees what its members are doing, that discusses these actions and judges them against normative standards and values that it holds dear, and that imposes repressive sanctions – of ostracism, humiliation and shame – on those who transgress these cherished values.

45

This man felt himself to be a part of such a social order. He could not go into the local pub, for fear that: 'people are talking about me, laughing at me behind my back'. He was furious at his wife, for 'messing around', messing up the ideal of the traditional family that he felt subject to, that he used to feel they were both committed to. His rage was directed against her for violating a collective agreement, shared by them both and by a wider community. He was vengeful and tried to punish her through his own death, hoping that by such a desperate shameful act (shameful within the traditional normative framework in which he lived, and in which, in his despair, he thought his wife also still lived) his wife would be shamed; she would be seen, and would see herself, as having 'done it'; she would be held responsible, and would hold herself responsible, to the community for his death. He invoked the collective moral authority of the traditional community to be a power that might torment and crush his estranged wife.

But he seemed to sense the horrible irony that might make his terrible act of vengeance impotent and absurd. Namely, that his wife is estranged, no longer a member of the traditional community that he felt himself so painfully to be a part of. He suspected a dreadful truth: that she could ignore them, and him; that she would 'put [her] head in the sand and hide from the shame and hurt'. He suspected that, unlike him, she enjoys much greater moral autonomy, and is not subject to the traditional repressive sanction of shame. It was this half-realised knowledge that he and his wife were living in different worlds, governed by different normative frameworks, which underpinned the extremes of desperation and cruelty in the timing of the act, at Christmas. Even if, as he suspected, she was no longer subject to the moral authority of the traditional community, she still belonged to a wider symbolic order in which Christmas continues to be an important event. So, he timed his act deliberately to corrupt Christmas and irreparably damage the symbolic order for his wife and family forever.

46

Fourth case

Another note, left by a young man in a midlands town, is again a symptom of ambiguity and ambivalence in the suicidogenic currents characteristic of the collisions between vestigial tradition and accelerated modernisation in contemporary Ireland. The note contains a clear articulation of the idea of the good life that this young man claimed to desire – 'a plain, simple life', understood in terms of the values of a traditional community: the nuclear family, the husband as breadwinner and provider for his wife and son; not an extravagant desire, but nonetheless a dream belonging to a worldview that was being eclipsed even as he rearticulated it. His worldview was in competition with other, often opposed, imperatives: to be independent and unencumbered, to have a successful career, not to be tied down to boring conventions.

This young man was halfway to having what he thought he desired: he had a loving relationship that 'gave him the best three years of his life'. Yet even when he had what he thought he wanted, it seemed to slip away from him, or, rather, he felt that, unwillingly, he pushed and drove it away by his 'self-centred personality'. He 'ruined what [he] had and what could have been'. On the one hand he understood his suicide as somehow altruistic: he felt obliged to kill himself for the good of his community, and he felt answerable to that community even in death. He did not want 'to ruin things for others' and thought that people did not deserve the trouble he gave them; he wanted people to be happy and was sorry for the trouble he felt he had caused and for the pain that his death would cause. On the other hand the note is symptomatic of the excessive egoism of modern culture: he felt himself to be responsible for the problems of his community: 'through my lies, my shows, my self-centred personality . . . I ruined . . . I don't want to ruin . . . I've hurt people . . . I'm sorry, I want people to be happy . . . I wish I could show you . . . I don't want to ruin every-thing . . . I've made my decision . . . I must walk my path'.

The centrality of the ego and the sense of individual conscience are striking here; they co-existed incongruously with his otherwise strong indications of social integration.

In the collision culture of contemporary Ireland, the person exists in an anomic and egoistic world where vestiges of the ideal forms of traditional community still haunt and hold sway over people, even as new forms, new ideas, new collective representations, not yet clearly formed, come into view; and a world which demands that action and choices be made and responsibilities be assumed by an individual ego, even as that ego is still integrated by the altruistic bonds of the community's conscience collective.

Fifth and sixth cases

This strange and profoundly ambivalent situation of the person subject to the collision culture of contemporary Ireland also emerges in the next two cases to be examined. The first example is that of a young man who left a brief note for his parents. It says, simply, that he is sorry for the hurt his death will cause, but that he hopes his insurance money will pay back some of what he owes them, and will pay for a nice holiday for them both. The second example is of a suicide, symptomatic of a small but significant category of deaths, in which a vehicle accident is used to disguise the suicide.

The case of the young man who left a note for his parents differs from the car crash suicide in the obvious way that it is not disguised. There is no explanation – nothing to be said, or too much to say – and yet the note is indicative of a certain troubled reality: the ambivalent influences of egoism and altruism. Although the young man did not feel obliged to account for his action, to explain himself, indicating his sense of individuation and moral autonomy, at the same time he felt himself to be part of a network of economic and financial relations that he was obliged to reciprocate. He had to 'pay back', and this was most conveniently done through the universal medium of modern social relations, money, made all the more impersonal as it was the insurance premium. And yet this is by no means a simple cash settlement for debts incurred in the material economy of the household budget; for it is also clearly a gift, from a loving son to his parents. Gift exchange is the fundamental social relation and here the gift, a token of reciprocal affection in the web of mutual obligations that constitute family life, demonstrates with excruciating poignancy how this man was enmeshed in that web, even as he fell or broke through it.

Suicide disguised as a car crash is obviously a very difficult case to prove in any particular instance, and of course this represents the crucial feature of this means of suicide: it is intended to disguise the deliberate action as accidental. One of Ireland's leading suicidologists notes the incidence, suggesting that 5 per cent of single-vehicle road deaths are suicides,[13] and this is supported by anecdotal evidence from gardaí and other researchers. This type of suicide is symptomatic of the same profound ambivalence underpinning the experience of living in Ireland today. The car is quintessentially the *sine qua non* of a young man's independence in the symbolic order and imaginative structure of modern society. And yet it is frequently the parents' car that is the vehicle in question. A road traffic accident disguises suicide, and thus avoids the stigma of suicide for family and community. The suicide is indi-viduated sufficiently (excessively) to make the act possible, and yet is simultaneously still sufficiently (excessively) integrated in communal life to feel obliged to save the family from shame and stigma. Not alone that, but as in the case above, there is the economic consideration of the insurance payoff, which again is both intended as a cash settlement and as a 'parting gift' in a fundamental, traditional, com-munitarian form in which gift-exchange is still formative, constitutive, reciprocal and obligatory.

---

13 Dr John Connolly, Mayo County Chief Psychiatrist, Secretary of the
    Irish Association of Suicidology, 1999.

Conclusion

Every case history of suicide has a personal story behind it, a story of depression, pressure and performance anxiety related to exams or career, marital disharmony, alcohol or drug abuse and so on. Medical and psychological discourses can identify the contributory factors that commonly recur, mapping an epidemiological pattern of typical cases. Such explanations of immanent factors in Irish suicide can be complemented and enhanced with an explanation of transcendent causal factors. A fuller explanation of the increase in the Irish suicide rate is possible if we situate suicides in a broader sociological framework that transcends the life-world of the individual. A sociological perspective enables us to see that private troubles are related to public issues; that the case history of a suicide victim is part of a broader, historical, social pathology. Sociology identifies the characteristic suicidogenic pathologies of modern society in general as egoism and anomie. These problems are exacerbated in Ireland in particular as they coincide and collide with vestigial traditional social forms. 'The old is dying and the new cannot yet be born. In this interregnum there are a great variety of morbid symptoms'.[14] Suicides are particularly acute symptoms of the prevalence of this social pathology in contemporary Irish society.

---

14 A. Gramsci, *Selections from the Prison Notebooks*, New York: International Publishers, 1971, p. 276.

CHAPTER 3

Sex in the City

KAREN SUGRUE

In 1996, the opening of the Utopia sex shop in Limerick was greeted with outrage by self-appointed guardians of morality. In 1999, Dublin was in uproar about the impending opening of the latest branch of the Ann Summers chain on O'Connell Street. The chief executive of the Dublin City Centre Traders' Association described the proposed shop as being 'totally inappropriate – on a street which is, after all, the capital's grandest thoroughfare'.[1] Thus Ann Summers opened its twenty-third shop (and its first shop in Ireland) amid outcry and debate. Women from all over the country rang the Gerry Ryan radio show clamouring about the inappropriateness of 'that type of shop' on O'Connell Street. *The Irish Times* ran articles calling it 'shocking', and wondering at the reaction of Padraig Pearse in 1916 had he been told that an Ann Summers shop would some day be located directly across the road from what was referred to as a 'sacred spot'.[2] The newspaper went as far as to speculate that Pearse, had he known, might not have bothered! However, the controversy quickly waned and Ann Summers soon became an accepted part of the Dublin scene. It has since been a huge commercial success.

---

1 'Sex On The Street', *The Irish Times*, 29 June 1999.
2 ibid.

51

Women's sexuality has long been an arena of contest and contradiction; therefore the task facing Ann Summers was particularly problematic given that the shop caters almost exclusively for women and their sexual pleasures and fantasies. This chapter explores the normalisation of erotica in modern Ireland.

Sociability and women's sexuality

Throughout history women have been portrayed as temptresses, but they have also been construed as guardians of morality and particularly of sexual morality. Moral rectitude has often been the responsibility of women. Inglis stresses how, from the middle of the nineteenth century, the discourse of sexuality in Ireland was nearly entirely shaped by the Catholic Church.[3] Fear and guilt were instilled in the minds of young Irish Catholics about anything associated with sexual drives. But by the 1970s this quasi-monopoly was already breaking down. In *Lessons in Irish Sexuality,* Inglis identifies five distinctive discourses about sexuality.[4] The traditional discourse continues to view sexuality as a potential threat to individual and collective wellbeing. But sexuality is more and more presented as a healthy and pleasurable activity in the media. It seems, then, that the multiplication of discourses about sexuality generates a fragmentation of sexual identities.

The public denial of all things sexual, even within the confines of married heterosexual sexuality, has in a very short span of time given way to an eager embracing of sexuality, particularly among the younger generations. But even today, grey areas of women's sexuality remain, to

---

3 Tom Inglis, 'Foucault, Bourdieu and the Field of Irish Sexuality', *Irish Journal of Sociology*, vol. 7, 1997, pp. 5–28; Tom Inglis, 'From Sexual Repression to Liberation', in Michel Peillon and Eamonn Slater (eds), *Encounters with Modern Ireland*, Dublin: IPA, 1998.

4 Tom Inglis, *Lessons in Irish Sexuality*, Dublin: University College Dublin Press, 1998.

which there are little or no references made – masturbation is a good example. Ann Summers caters in that sense for a practice that had been rendered unspeakable, but it never verbalises the nature of its goods and never presses its clientele into confronting the nature of their activity. It does not articulate a discourse about sexuality. A brief look at its catalogue or a visit to its Internet site clearly establishes this point. It does not profess any particular philosophy, other than one of hedonism and individual indulgence. Its catalogue is only that: a collection of items for sale, with indication of price and features. The text is absolutely minimal:

> Our Design Team have worked closely with our cus-
> tomers ensuring that all our products live up to Ann
> Summers promise – providing the perfect answer to all
> your desires.

> From flirtatiously feminine to exotically erotic, we
> really can promise you the perfect choice.

> Take a moment now to indulge yourself in the pages of
> our Spring and Summer collection, as you make your
> choice, remember . . . with Ann Summers the pleasure
> will be all yours![5]

A large part of the website is dedicated, interestingly enough, to Jacqueline Gold, who is chief executive of the firm and who introduces the site with a brief statement: 'My philosophy has always been to encourage women to feel good about themselves and their sexuality'. These two state-ments simply express a dedication to pleasure seeking for women. The website hardly provides a voice for Irish women's sexuality, nor does it confront the moral discourse about sexuality. Irish female sexuality remains voiceless

---

5 Ann Summers spring and summer collection 43D.

and, most importantly, unobtrusive. Ann Summers is no crusader for women's rights. Its success as a chain of sex shops has its roots elsewhere. It is tapping another way of constituting women's sexuality, one that relies on networks of sociability.

A high proportion of the sales are made through house parties rather than through the shop or catalogues. Ann Summers claims to have more than 7,500 house party organisers working for them and it is possible to book a house party on the Internet. The house party has always been the corner stone of the company's success. To have a house party, it is necessary to invite a number of female friends and an Ann Summers representative, who brings a selection of Ann Summers' products for the guests to examine. It is a requisite that wine be consumed. By the end of the night, it is usual for a large number of items to be purchased. By all accounts, the house parties are hilarious events with everyone present enjoying the night immensely. It is possible in this context to buy items and construct the purchase as a joke, for 'a bit of a laugh' or 'to show someone else'.

One may tentatively suggest that sexuality is partly constituted in this sociable way, through social relations. It is difficult to imagine that the widespread, but to a large extent silent, adoption of contraception by Irish women in the 1970s did not have a lot to do with participation in networks of sociability. The latter provide the context, quite removed from a public domain, where sexuality is in practice constituted: where what is normal is defined, what is acceptable is scrutinised and where expectations are formed.

The normalisation of sexuality

Ann Summers quietly opened its doors and waited for the furore to die down. It has since traded on the main street of Dublin, blatantly retailing sex. Sexuality has been effectively normalised, an acknowledgement that women have a sexuality to be commercially and openly exploited. Normalisation means, in this context, that the conventions that govern contemporary Irish society allow and possibly encourage this interest in, and expression of, sexuality. Norms relating to sexuality have not disappeared, but they have drastically altered in a way that grants far more space to this type of social relationship.

All the mannequins in the window model quite modest lingerie and the front of the shop is very much about selling run-of-the-mill lingerie. As one moves to the back of the shop, a semi-private area is signed overhead with a warning that only those over 18 years can enter the section, and that some people may find the merchandise offensive. But what so offended people that they were driven, in their droves, to ring every chat show in Ireland and to write letter after letter to the opinion columns of the Irish newspapers? It was not that Ann Summers sells a racy, lacy line in ladies' lingerie, or that it trades in erotica of all types and caters for most tastes. Time and time again, its opponents explained that they would not be so outraged if Ann Summers had chosen a back street from which to trade. A back-street location would have spoken of the inherent depravity of a shop retailing such wares.

I suspect that the public would have been happier if the shop owners had shown that they knew it was inappropriate. Critics were objecting to the expression of an open and public sexuality, with no attachment of guilt, fear or shame. To open such a place on O'Connell Street speaks of a lack of shame, a total disregard for the rules of propriety and, most grievous of all, a scandalous deficiency in guilt. The shop does the unthinkable – it sits in the public eye, unashamed, telling the passer-by that it is there because women not only have sex, not only enjoy sex, but might even like to try different types of sex. It flaunts sexuality without a word of apology, and the necessary apology for its own existence should of course have been to open in a back street. It opened on the brazen assumption that people would come in; and once in, would buy its products. The assumption was right! Ann Summers has been a huge commercial success in Ireland.

While the house parties and the catalogues have been in Ireland for some time, it was the opening of the shop that caused the outcry. The paradox is that the shop is utterly normal, even if the product is abnormal. That Ann Summers has been accepted in a way that other adult shops, such as the Utopia chain, have not, is largely accounted for by its position on O'Connell Street. This location lends it a credibility and a normalcy that back-street, neon-signed sex shops just cannot emulate. The shop is large, bright and open; whereas shops such as Utopia tend to be small and dingy, their doors locked and with small reflective mirror windows that allow no glimpse of the interior. In Ann Summers, shop assistants in austere black suits look cool and tasteful. Customers are invited to take a regular shopping basket from the stack inside the door. There is nothing grotty or smutty about Ann Summers; it sells its merchandise with a combination of humour and sophistication (two characteristics that are blatantly missing in our other sex shops). More essentially perhaps, a shop which is centrally located on the shopping circuit and which looks like any other shop or even like a better class (and rather expensive) retail outlet easily becomes part of a shopping routine. Ann Summers has successfully transformed itself into a 'normal' shop.

This conventionality and normalcy extends to the website, which also operates as an online shopping site. Like the catalogue, it presents a glossy image of the firm. A very sketchy company history is presented, in which the Dublin opening is put forward as an important landmark in the development of this multinational firm. Apart from the online catalogue, which represents of course an important element of the site, it would be difficult to guess the nature of its business. The focus is to a large extent set on Jacqueline Gold (who is not actually the founder of the firm) and mainly highlights her business achievements. She is also portrayed, in a series of glossy photographs, as an attractive and elegant woman posing in formal evening gowns in the aristocratic surroundings of her home. The normalisation of the firm is made absolute, and not a hint about the nature of the shop is allowed to mar this self-presentation. In that way, Gold becomes the prime example of the modern woman the firm targets: her utter respectability is not undermined by the playful pursuit and satisfaction of the private desires taken care of by the firm she manages.

This underlies the dual nature of normalisation. It does more than transform something that was considered strange and reprehensible into something that appears ordinary and natural. It does not merely remove norms, but instead applies different norms. Ann Summers produces a different kind of normal sexuality and in the process excludes all kinds of sexual interests, inclinations and relations. It upholds a very definite view of normal sex-uality, not in words but in the actual operation of its business. The very fact that it relies so heavily on house parties means that it reaches women who are well integrated into social networks of kin, friendship or neighbourhood. Women who do not belong to such networks, perhaps because of their exclusion or even self-exclusion on the basis of their sexual orientations or tastes, are also marginalised by such a normalising strategy. Could such social networks entertain, for instance, homosexual or sadomasochist gatherings? Most of the merchandise con-forms to male fantasies or provides the material for a successful hen night: diaphanous fabrics, fur-trimmed brassieres, plastic bodices. Nothing that pushes out the boundaries of 'tastefulness'. There is no doubt that Ann Summers has considerably widened the scope of what is considered normal sexual practice. It nonetheless promotes a sexuality that remains heterosexual and, in any case, practised by 'respectable' women. Ann Summers is very explicitly located in the safer end of the sex industry, where raunchiness is confined to the marital or perhaps premarital bed.

Sexuality has been normalised mainly through its transformation into a commodity. By placing erotica in the normal environment of a shop (there is even a coffee counter in Ann Summers) the message is that sex is a normal product. The monetary value of such objects has simply replaced moral assessment. By assuming the form of a commodity, such objects are emptied from any moral attachment; for example their purchase becomes as valid as that of any item of clothing, pair of shoes or book. Yet as we have already noted, the shop is not the main source of sales and consequently of profit for the firm. Ann Summers has turned to other forms of sales. It certainly generates massive consumption: it claims for instance that, by 1999, it had sold over one million vibrators. But this is mass consumption of a different kind, as the commodities are sold mainly through personalised networks of relatives, friends and neighbours. The shop has ceased to be the archetypal space of mass consumption.

Ambivalence and embarrassment

Sexuality has, in a very short span of time, lost its forbidden and unspeakable nature. It has become an acceptable interest and activity for many groups in Irish society. In the process, sexuality has been redefined and reconstructed in a particular way, with its own forms of exclusion. Yet sexuality is not experienced as totally normal. Attitudes and behaviours that relate to it often remain ambivalent. This ambivalence takes many forms, but it is expressed mainly through embarrassment. In an early essay, Goffman[6] suggests that embarrassment occurs when the individual has several selves invested in a social situation: 'Often important everyday occasions of embarrassment arise when the self projected is somehow confronted with another self

---

6 Erving Goffman, 'Embarrassment and social organization', in Erving Goffman, *Interaction Ritual*, Harmondsworth: Penguin, 1972, p. 108.

which, though valid in other contexts, cannot be here sustained in harmony with the first'.

Embarrassment continues to be experienced about sexuality and particularly about women's sexuality. This embarrassment has its roots in the various ways that sexual identities, or sexual selves, are constituted. The constitution of the sexual self through internalisation of a puritan discourse, and inculcation of practices that derive from it, no longer enjoys a monopoly. But, more crucially, a very different sexual identity is elaborated through networks of social relationship and sociability. Embarrassment is experienced when one sexual self is enacted out of context, that is to say when one sexual self is required to function in a social context where another sexual self usually holds sway.

Although it is socially generated, embarrassment is experienced privately and is not easily observed. The presence of mechanisms and procedures that emerge to avoid embarrassment provides the best indication of its reality. It is around the boundary of the public and the private domains that occasions for embarrassment are most likely to occur. For it is one thing to acquiesce privately with a liberal view of sexuality and even to construct one's sexuality on this basis, and another to enact it publicly in the wider world where another sexual self is invested.

Catalogue sales are of enormous importance to Ann Summers. This is also the case with Utopia. A staff member there who agreed to speak with me said that the majority of their sales are through their catalogue. He went on to explain that the embarrassment experienced by customers who come into the shop directly is eliminated in the catalogue transactions. The face-to-face element is removed and therefore the person does not have to confront the reality of this purchase and publicly declare this intent. The popularity of catalogue and of online sales says a lot about the preferences of many potential customers for an anonymous and private transaction, as opposed to facing the very public world of the shop. Even house parties act as a kind of semi-public occasion that can be laughed off. Sexual interest is acknowledged, but not in a serious manner. Embarrassment is negated through jokes and laughing around the topic of discomfort.

Yet shoppers do enter the shop, either to browse or to purchase wares. All kinds of rules and constraints are activated as soon as one enters a shop, and especially a shop selling erotica. In such a context, consumers of these products are not merely displaying their desire for the product itself, they are openly admitting to the intention of enjoying sexual pleasure. And that can hardly be a straightforward matter. In fact, men are rarely seen on their own in Ann Summers shops. Women on their own are more frequently observed, but not that often. The typical mode of shopping in Ann Summers seems to be either in mixed couples or women together. The declaration of a possibly playful quest for sexual pleasure seems easier to handle for a couple. Two or three women shopping together can always redefine the situation, if they have to, as a game, a joke, a dare or whatever deflects the seriousness of their intent.

The passage of the boundary that marks the private and public domains creates a clear opportunity for embarrassment. Another risky situation is opened when people have to interact with others. The work that has to be done in order to overcome embarrassment in the context of such face-to-face interaction is well illustrated by John, the shop assistant at Utopia in Limerick (a more or less standard sex shop, far less normalised than Ann Summers). The shop assistant's job is to normalise the experience, that is to neutralise possible embarrassment: 'it's just a normal shop, that's all it is'.

John endeavours to reduce the strangeness of the occasion by relying on the conventional language of shopping: 'what can I do for you?' he asked me when I first walked in. He is polite, friendly and helpful to his customers; he is not judging or moralising, he is merely selling. The transaction has to be assumed as shopping, rather than as an expression and sharing of private orientations with strong moral overtones. The social and cultural meanings attached to the transaction are neutralised when it is defined as consumption. His strategy is to reduce the admission of his customer's desire to the language of shopping: 'that'll be 5.90 please', 'do you want a bag for that?' and so forth. It matters that the assistant views the customers as merely shoppers and encourages them to view themselves as such. And this cannot be taken for granted, as the meaning of the objects has not yet been fully replaced by their monetary value, and old norms and mores regarding sexuality have not completely broken down.

Having insisted on the absolute normality of his job, he is asked: 'what about this job could you never get used to?'. And the response comes: 'it's not computerised enough for me, but that's just me, I'm big on computers'. The grounds of normality are obviously shifting. Embarrassment threatens too when shop assistant and customer happen to come across each other outside the confines of the shop. The reaction of John is to engage in what Goffman[7] calls tactful blindness: 'if I see a guy who has been in this shop, if I see him outside, if he salutes me, I salute him back, if he doesn't salute me, I carry on walking'.

Conclusion

Goffman emphasises that embarrassment does not arise from the breach of moral expectations: indignation rather than uneasiness is generated by moral lapses.[8] Embarrassment about the public admission of sexual interests is not rooted in feelings of guilt at having to admit of interests and engaging in types of activity that breach a moral code. It reveals, rather, the ambivalence of the moral code itself,

---

7 Erving Goffman, 'On face-work', in Erving Goffman, *Interaction Ritual*, Harmondsworth: Penguin, 1972, p. 18.

8 Erving Goffman, 'Embarrassment and social organization', in Erving Goffman, *Interaction Ritual*, Harmondsworth: Penguin, 1972, p. 105.

both in society and within the self. The view has been developed in this chapter that such an ambivalence, exacerbated of course by the multiplication of discourses about sexuality, is generated mainly by fundamentally different ways of constituting sexuality: the production of the sexual subject through a discourse and associated practices, and a constitution of sexuality through networks of social relations in which a socially embedded shaping of sexuality is worked out.

CHAPTER 4

Robbing the Revenue: Accounting for Deviant Behaviour

CIARAN McCULLAGH

I t is one of the paradoxes of the study of crime that most delinquents and criminals are in fact generally very law abiding. They subscribe to the same set of standards and conventions as the rest of us do in that they are in agreement with fundamental laws on murder, assault and property rights. Indeed Taylor has suggested, somewhat mischievously, that in Britain most criminals vote Tory, hardly the action of anarchic law-breakers.[1]

This raises the question posed by Matza: how do people who claim allegiance to social norms and values engage in deviant behaviour? The answer, he argues, lies in the subculture to which many criminals subscribe. This comprises a set of beliefs or techniques of neutralisation that 'function as the extenuating conditions under which delinquency is permissible'.[2] These beliefs enable delinquents to violate the norms and rules of society 'without surrendering allegiance to them'.[3] They enable them to be law-breaking conformists.

---

1 I. Taylor, *In the Underworld*, Oxford: Blackwell, 1984.
2 D. Matza, *Delinquency and Drift*, New York: John Wiley, 1964, p. 59.
3 Matza, ibid., p. 60.

In this chapter I intend to develop the notion of the accounts provided by criminals and deviants for their behaviour. As will become clear, this kind of analysis has only been applied to the study of juvenile delinquents. However the Dáil Public Accounts Committee's investigation into the manner in which the banks and financial institutions facilitated the evasion of tax provides an opportunity to see how respectable deviants account for behaviour that is legally and socially problematic.

Techniques of neutralisation

Sykes and Matza argue that five beliefs or techniques of neutralisation enable delinquents and criminals to evade the moral bind of the law and the constraints of the norms of conventional behaviour.[4] These beliefs allow deviants to argue that while the law is fundamental, there are certain circumstances in which it does not apply to them. The point about these beliefs is that they are generally available in the culture and are recognised as socially legitimate in certain circumstances. Where delinquent behaviour is concerned, they enable young men 'to commit crimes without too many pangs of conscience'. They operate as 'a sanitising prism . . . which softens criminal acts so that they assume the appearance of "not really" being against the law'.[5] This means that they have a double significance. They weaken the bonds of social control and so enable delinquents to engage in deviant behaviour, while at the same time they function after the act to provide defences and justifications for that behaviour.

One is the denial of responsibility. Here deviants may accept what they did but do not see themselves as

---

4 G. M. Sykes and D. Matza, 'Techniques of Neutralization: A Theory of Delinquency', *American Sociological Review*, vol. 22, 1957, pp. 664–70.

5 S. Box, *Power, Crime and Mystification*, London: Tavistock, 1983, p. 54.

responsible for this behaviour. Thus assault may be justified on the grounds that the individual was provoked by others, a common defence for street violence. A second technique is the denial of injury. This enables offenders to claim that, as no one was injured by their actions, no criminal offence was involved. Who, for example, is harmed by the vandalism of public property? Bus shelters do not cry when they are thrashed. This is somewhat similar to the third technique, which is the denial of the victim. This involves denying that one's criminal action had a victim either because the victim 'deserved' it or because the action was 'rightful retaliation'. The fourth technique is the condemnation of the condemners. This involves seeing those who condemn the delinquent as hypocrites, either because they are up to this kind of behaviour themselves or because they have some personal gains to be derived from such a condemnation. The final technique is the appeal to higher loyalties. Here offenders claim that their actions were justified in terms of loyalties and allegiances that are higher and more binding than those of the legal system. Thus friendship, family ties or gang loyalty may justify the use of violence in specific situations without condoning it as a general principle.

As things stand these kinds of concepts have been used to understand the behaviour of delinquents, categorised by Matza (1964) and Box (1983), as lower-class adolescent males. But the commission of crime is not limited to such people. An extensive literature shows that white-collar crime is, as both Sutherland and Braithwaite acknowledge, a frequent, widespread and routine feature of the business world.[6] Given that the kind of people who work in the business world see themselves as the epitome of law-abiding citizens, and indeed may be both the formulators and defenders of conventional morality, how then do they engage in behaviour that either is or can be construed as criminal?

---

6 E. Sutherland, *White Collar Crime*, New York: Holt, Rinehart and Winston, 1949; J. Braithwaite, 'White-Collar Crime', *Annual Review of Sociology*, vol. 11, 1985, pp. 1–25.

The capacity to construct justifying accounts is not limited to deviant or delinquent individuals. Organisations can also construct them. It is therefore of interest to see what kinds of accounts are provided by organisations to which deviant behaviour has been imputed.

Justifying accounts

An opportunity to explore this issue was presented by the parliamentary inquiry into deposit interest retention tax (DIRT) made by the Public Accounts Committee between August and October 1999.[7] At the heart of the hearings was the degree to which DIRT was evaded, the extent to which 'deposit-holders knowingly facilitated the practice' and the actions that financial institutions took to deal with the problem. The committee's report concluded that the evasion of DIRT was 'pervasive' in the banking sector and that 'the relevant authorities were very well aware of the problem'. Thus the inquiry represented an invitation to banks and financial institutions to account for problematic behaviour.

The actual evasion was not exactly rocket science. In 1986 the government introduced a new tax, deposit interest retention tax or, as it was more familiarly known, DIRT. It was a tax on interest earned on deposits in banks and financial institutions. It was the responsibility of these institutions to calculate the amount of DIRT for which their depositors were liable, pay it to the Revenue and deduct the relevant amount from depositors' accounts. However this tax did not apply to accounts held in Irish banks by people who were not resident in the state. To open a non-resident account it was merely necessary to fill in a form declaring

---

7 The accounts presented here are drawn from the Committee of Public Accounts, *Parliamentary Inquiry into DIRT. First Report*, Dublin: Government Publications, 1999. A fuller account would need to include the investigation by the Comptroller and Auditor General into DIRT evasion.

that one was indeed non-resident. The financial institutions either encouraged residents in the state to open such accounts or else did not check too rigorously whether all such account-holders were non-resident.

It was also possible to avoid tax by the practice of deposit splitting. Under existing tax law, financial institutions could pay interest of up to £70 (€88.88) on deposit accounts without the deduction of tax. As the evidence to the committee showed, the banks facilitated and encouraged depositors to spread their money over a number of different branches and accounts. This enabled depositors to keep their money in a series of different deposit accounts, none of which individually would be liable for tax. The purpose of this strategy was, like that of bogus non-resident accounts, simple and straightforward: it was for tax evasion.

So what justifications or accounts did banks and financial institutions come up with? It is important to establish a relevant context with such justifications, as the committee's report points out, non-compliance with the law on DIRT by depositors and deposit-takers is a revenue offence. As such it is also a criminal offence. This was established in a landmark judgment in 1945 (*State v. Fawsett*). Hence it does seem, to the outsider at least, to be the kind of behaviour that needs to be accounted for. What is interesting about the proceedings of the committee was the degree to which those coming before it did not feel the need to offer extensive justifications for the tax evasion that went on in their institutions. To the extent that such justifications were offered they were largely seen as technical matters and there was no real sense in the presentations that the banks and other financial institutions had done anything wrong.

One such justification was to see the problem as one of paperwork or to blame the complicated nature of the relevant form. To establish a non-resident account it was necessary for a depositor to fill in Form 37 declaring that he or she was non-resident. According to the bankers, it was either too complicated or else if it had been filled in by the depositor and there was little need or incentive to check it.

One banker told the committee that 'the feeling was that once the declarations were complete or once the declarations were there, and in some instances even if they weren't, that once the depositor said "I am a non-resident", then that was almost taken as good enough'. Another banker told the committee that the issue 'in so far as it existed at all, was merely documentary'.

The second justification was to blame someone else; in this case those lower down the organisational structure. Senior officials in the banks said that they relied on branch and regional managers to ensure legal compliance. The former chief executive officer of the Bank of Ireland told the committee that: 'I really find it very hard to understand how any member of our staff would have accommodated – knowingly accommodated – a bogus non-resident account. I find this very hard to understand'. Where another bank was concerned, in this case Ulster Bank, 'a scrupulous adherence to formal compliance seems to have been dictated from the top', but 'this was at variance with the practice discovered by Internal Audit in parts of the Branch network'. Another banker said that the failure of branches to comply with direct instructions on the issue and the fact that written assurances by branch managers were found to be materially untrue were the sources of the difficulty.

Others were less mystified by the problem. They cited the pressures of competition for deposits at local/branch level. One official told the committee that 'the imposition of withholding tax was going to have a negative effect on its business and it was seeking to investigate methodologies whereby that negative effect might be lessened'. The chairman of the committee replied that this was 'a very troubling sentence'. Another banker told the committee that a branch manager told his regional manager that his branch was losing deposits through not opening bogus non-resident accounts. The branch continued to open them even after an internal audit had insisted on a mass reclassification of bogus accounts. The problem for them was the loss of business. Their competitors were doing it, so if they did not behave in a similar fashion their customers would take their money elsewhere.

The final justification was that the board of directors either did not know or were not told. A number of statements to the committee indicated that the matter was never discussed at board level in the major banks. Beyond these, there is little evidence of any attempt or any need to attempt to offer justifications for the pervasive culture of non-compliance with tax laws in the banking sector. What is most striking about the accounts given by the banks is the limited extent to which they felt the need to defend themselves or to explain why, as the committee found, they encouraged and facilitated tax evasion.

Crime without guilt

This highlights an important difference between juvenile delinquents and white-collar deviants. The former use techniques of neutralisation to justify their behaviour when they are challenged about and have to explain it to pro-bation officers, policemen or the courts. The latter seldom have their deviance or criminality dramatised for them in this way and so operate in some security from the threat of apprehension and public explanation. This was clearly the case with the facilitation of the evasion of DIRT tax. The regulating authorities knew about it, but there was little indication of serious moves to deal with it. Pat Molloy of the Bank of Ireland, writing to his board of directors in 1986, concluded: 'it was not at all certain that the Revenue Commissioners have the will or the capacity to effectively police the DIRT regime'.

One auditor told the hearings that the tax regime was 'lightly policed' by the Revenue. The committee also found that boards of directors for banks and other financial institutions 'betrayed an overly relaxed attitude towards discharging their statutory and fiduciary duties in respect of the operation of DIRT'. In that sense the fact that the banks did not offer elaborate justifications for the behaviour of their institutions was simply because there was no established tradition of them having to do so. They existed in a situation where there was no need to justify their culture of non-compliance because there was no real desire by the relevant authorities to enforce the relevant legislation. This was despite the fact that the authorities were well aware of the problem. When one former senior Revenue official was asked what level of knowledge the Revenue Commissioners had of the situation regarding the abuse of non-resident accounts, he replied 'we all knew'. Similarly the Comptroller and Auditor General argued that 'the relevant authorities were very well aware of the problem'.

It is in this sense that consideration of the contexts of justification for white-collar deviants needs to move beyond the deviants and on to the policing agencies. White-collar deviants are seldom placed in public situations where they are required to defend their behaviour, so the focus must move to the justifications offered by policing agencies for their failure to act. The source of non-enforcement of tax legislation can be found in what Matza refers to as 'higher loyalties'. The matter was not treated within the confines of revenue law and its possibilities for criminal enforcement. It was considered within the confines of an economic theory. This was the theory of capital flight, which held that if the law on tax evasion was rigorously enforced it would lead depositors to take their money out of Irish banks and move it abroad. In the process, this would create a crisis in the banking system and undermine the value of the Irish currency on international financial markets. The committee indicated that 'all of the relevant agencies of state bought into this theory as being relevant. It became the official view'. The belief was that 'over-enthusiastic action by anyone could lead to a flight of funds'. As the committee pointed out, this proposition 'sits somewhat uncomfortably alongside the law as enacted' and was untested and probably incorrect.

The belief in capital flight appears to have effectively paralysed two major state agencies: the Office of the

Revenue Commissioners and the Central Bank. It provided the context in which decisions and policy choices were made. The evidence from former officials of the Central Bank indicated that they were well aware of the problem of tax evasion generally and of DIRT evasion in particular. They also discussed it with the Department of Finance. However they failed to use the powers available to them and indeed opposed attempts to introduce 'increased documentary evidence of non-residence', most notably in the form of a sworn affidavit of non-residency. The argument against this was that the 'expense and inconvenience' that this would impose on non-residents 'would cause over 50 per cent of non-resident deposits to move abroad'. Similarly, officials from the Department of Finance relied on the argument about the fear of capital flight to avoid tightening up the operation of DIRT. There was a loyalty higher than that to revenue law, a loyalty to the laws of capitalist economics.

Not sorry

For Matza the one characteristic that convinces him that delinquents are committed to conventional rather than delinquent or criminal values is the fact that when apprehended and confronted with their behaviour they initially express indignation but then proceed to 'either contriteness or defensive explanations'.[8] The failure of those involved in the DIRT inquiry to express either emotion indicates that, unlike juvenile delinquents, white-collar offenders may be committed to a subculture in which such reactions are appropriate. There is after all a final account that deviants can offer, Goffman calls it 'the apology', which involves explicitly confessing to one's errors and accepting that sanctions are expected and legitimate.[9]

---

8 D. Matza, *Delinquency and Drift*, New York: John Wiley, 1964, p. 41.
9 E. Goffman, *Relations in Public*, London: Penguin, 1971.

Speaking at the annual meeting of the shareholders of Allied Irish Banks in the aftermath of paying €38.7m to the state in overdue DIRT, interest and penalties, the bank's chairman, said that the whole DIRT business was an 'unhappy episode' and 'a regrettable episode'. It seems that in this context power and status are a bit like love: they mean never having to say you are sorry.

One thing is clear from the DIRT hearings: powerful financial institutions did not have to provide much in the way of explanation or justification to account for their facilitation of tax evasion. This was largely because nobody in authority really saw it as a serious problem. The institutions were allowed to see the issue of compliance with tax legislation as merely a technical matter to be sorted out between officials of like mind. This attitude was facilitated by the manner in which tax officials move from positions in the Revenue service and the Department of Finance to senior positions in the financial institutions and in the Central Bank. If this kind of rotation of personnel is combined with the existence of a shared community of assumptions between banks, the Revenue Commissioners and the Central Bank, then this group has the necessary qualifications for being identified as a power elite.

PART 2

MELANGES

CHAPTER 5

Trust Me! I'm Organic

PERRY SHARE

My first encounter with an organic vegetable was in an Australian co-operative wholefood shop in the early 1980s. The vegetable in question was a green pepper, or had been once. Rolling loose on a hessian-lined tray, it was small, gnarled, blotchy and remarkable in that it cost more than an ordinary pepper. Underwhelmed by the attraction, I did not buy on that occasion, nor when faced by a succession of other similarly unappealing fruit and vegetables.

Fast forward two decades: I am in a Sligo supermarket clutching a brace of peppers, one red, one yellow, positively bursting from their polystyrene tray. They too are 'organic' – it says so on the plastic wrapping. Shiny, plump, heavy and blemish-free; they could not be more distant from their earlier antipodean cousins. Most surprisingly, despite having journeyed from Spain, they are cheaper than their ordinary non-organic competitors. I am sceptical: the peppers are really just too shiny, too perfect, too unnatural. What is the point if you cannot tell an organic from a non-organic product? How can I know that these peppers are really organic? Perhaps a back-room employee is even now placing pesticide-soaked, fertiliser-stimulated 'ordinary' produce into packages marked organic, the better to reassure a nervous public, disturbed by news of BSE, e-coli and salmonella?

This is, at least partly, a story about trust – trust in the food we eat. The foot and mouth crisis of 2001 was a culmination of contemporary concerns about diet, food, the food industry and modern farming practice. Foot and mouth was added to the list of other familiar food-related pathogens and conditions that shape contemporary Irish and European discourses of eating. As with so many Irish institutions – from churches to politicians to blood trans-fusions – the populace may have become more nervous, sceptical and untrusting about food. Or rather, as I will be suggesting in this chapter focusing on organic food, the nature of trust in what we eat is being reshaped.

Organic food in Ireland

According to a recent survey of the Irish organic industry by Bord Bia, the Irish food promotion body, organic food has moved from the 'margins into the mainstream'.[1] To Irish consumers organic food means: chemical-free, natural and healthy, expensive, pure, better for you and good for the environment. It is now on the shopping lists of at least one-third of consumers, who spend an average of over €25 a month on organic food (€30m a year or 1 per cent of the total food market), primarily on vegetables, fruit, meat and dairy products. Significantly, over two-thirds of such purchases are in supermarkets, in line with broader European, and especially British, trends. Irish retailers, like their European and American counterparts, are keen to influence the organic food chain. Some have actively supported research and development in the industry, for example the Musgrave's Group (Centra, Supervalu) is a major sponsor of the Organic Centre in County Leitrim. Others, such as Superquinn, have developed close relationships with selected organic producers, especially in relation to meat supplies.

---

1 Bord Bia, *Prospects for Organic Food in Ireland,* Dublin: Bord Bia, 2000.

A barrier to further supermarket control of organic products is the lack of strong branding. Most organic sales are of unprocessed goods such as vegetables and many of these are sold under the producer's own label. Few strong Irish organic brands (such as Glenisk yoghurt or Noodle House pasta) have emerged. Meanwhile the global food industry asserts that people increasingly seek processed organic products such as juices, pizzas or snack foods. These are easier to brand and far more profitable for the food industry. Bord Bia concurs: 'development of a wider range of organic food products is expected to continue strongly over the next few years as retailers and suppliers alike try to grow the market by offering the maximum choice possible to consumers'. This provides a challenge for organic producers. Much of the food industry, especially in relation to convenience food, involves the recombination of inter-changeable and malleable starches, fats, sweeteners, flavours and stabilisers. Are long-life, 'organic' cook-in sauces or instant noodles likely to be a step too far for either organic producers or marketers?

Though the market is expected to grow by up to 30 per cent per annum, Ireland has one of the least developed organic sectors in Europe. Less than 1 per cent of our farmland, just 32,000 hectares, is dedicated to this form of production, compared with 6 per cent in Denmark and 9 per cent in Austria. In 2000 there were just over one thousand licensed Irish organic producers, concentrated in western and southern counties such as Cork, Clare, Kerry and Leitrim. Lack of production capacity means a shortfall of supply: about two-thirds of organic produce is imported, largely from Spain and Italy, but sometimes from as far afield as Zimbabwe and New Zealand.

After a period of scepticism and indeed some hostility from within the agricultural establishment, the Irish state has become more supportive of organic agriculture. It is also, at least implicitly, supported by the EU's blueprint for agriculture and rural society, *Agenda 2000*. Funds have been made available through the national development plan, mainly to be channelled through the rural environmental protection scheme (REPS) and a further €7.5m has been tagged to support distribution, processing and marketing initiatives. Teagasc, the farm advisory service, has established an organic research centre in Athenry, County Galway and the government has set up an organic development committee. Organic farming has moved closer to the Irish agricultural mainstream.

Why organic?

The shift towards organics is arguably the next major change in the world's food industries. Development and expansion of a global food industry, dominated by multinational food producers such as Nestlé, Cargill and Unilever, has been accompanied by a parallel and contradictory (or perhaps complementary) revolt towards local, 'authentic', less processed, natural, whole or even slow food.

Australian sociologist of food and nutrition, John Coveney, traces the wholefood movement back to the 1960s when it was linked to broader movements concerned with social change, in particular the environmental movement. It emphasised nature, ecology and humanism and was underpinned by a moral critique of the excess, artificiality and standardisation of modernity. The movement offered asceticism, authenticity and individual expression. It was not just about what you put onto your plate or into your body, wholefood represented a new food ethics. The ascetic strain was not new: it had infused the writings of the nineteenth-century wholefood pioneers John Harvey Kellogg (founder of the cornflakes dynasty) and Sylvester Graham (of American cracker fame). It reflected an 'anxiety about the moral consequences of gluttony and indolence, and a spiritual salvation through ascetics'.[2] Wholefood was

---

2   J. Coveney, *Food, Morals and Meaning,* London and New York: Routledge, 2000, p. 121.

always serious. Despite the folksiness of its treatises and recipe books, and later association in the public eye with illicit drugs and 'hippiedom', it could never be confused with the 'fun food' of the global food marketers. Its ascetic and 'scientific' nature also meant it echoed many of the concerns of mainstream nutritionists.

As the post-1960s wholefood movement developed, it coincided with a huge shift in interest towards matters of health and an aesthetics of the self. In an increasingly reflexive society, with an ever-greater focus on bodily identity, there has been concern about the effects and the safety of food. This was manifested in the mainstream food market with the introduction of low-fat and low-sugar products in the 1970s. Consumers then began to seek out products produced without the use of pesticides, hormones or artificial fertilisers. This trend intensified as people became more concerned with environmental issues, allergies and food scares. Along this trajectory a broadened interest in organic food was almost inevitable.

It also reflected the 'risk society'. The appearance of health is now no longer enough, as we may unwittingly harbour a myriad of environmental and genetic risk factors such as allergies or propensities to particular forms of cancer. Each may be triggered or negated by specific food products. Diet has moved beyond the modernist, industrial input–output model and has become more complex and holistic. For some it has become a matter of achieving some sort of balance; for others it may be about the search for almost magical super-nutrients such as phytonutrients, dietary zinc or antioxidants. The label 'organic' may have a similar talismanic quality.

The history of organic food has a specific social context: it is associated with an array of related social movements and a particular set of discourses about food and nutrition. Organics is not just a method of farming or a way to organise production, but a holistic approach to nature. And in as much as organic farming is not an output-maximising strategy, it is also a critique of mainstream capitalist agriculture. As Danish political scientist, Johannes Michelsen, suggests, organic farming may represent 'an important new type of interrelationship between agriculture and society'.[3]

Despite the increased influence and credibility of organic food, there is a real possibility that, with the mainstreaming of its consumption and distribution, it will be torn free of its original discursive setting. Similarly, the production methods of organic farming may increasingly be subsumed within mainstream industrial agriculture. What, then, will organic come to mean? Is it destined to join *lite, fresh* and *new!* as ultimately vacuous terms of product differentiation? Is organic farming likely to become just another way for cute farmers to extract money from Brussels, Dublin or Ballaghaderreen? The answer may lie in the types of social relationships that surround organic food production and marketing: not least that of trust.

Trust and regulation

For most of Ireland's history, trust in food derived from direct experience of production, gathering and harvesting, simple domestic processing and local distribution. While it is easy to romanticise the phenomenon of local food and local food systems (would we actually want to eat only cabbage, potatoes and wild garlic for the rest of our lives?), it remains true that it was only with the development of industrial and global food systems that the close connection between producer and most consumers was stretched and ultimately broken. The challenge for marketers and, increasingly, regulators, is to re-engender the relationship of trust; to rebuild, in the face of distance and complexity, a connection with the food we eat.

---

3 J. Michelsen, 'Recent Development and Political Acceptance of Organic Farming in Europe', *Sociologia Ruralis*, vol. 41, no. 1, 2000, p. 4.

When links between producer and consumer were close, embodied in kinship, community or propinquity, trust was based on interpersonal relationships. As food production industrialised, the personal touch was replaced by the impersonal mechanisms of the state (through food purity laws) and the market (through branding and advertising).[4] In recent times the integrity of these mechanisms has been challenged, and a return to the personal touch, or at least a simulacrum of it, can be discerned.

For organic food production, the trust mechanism has been central. In its early days producers tended to be personally known to consumers, and visible, for example on market stalls. Trust was based on the person of the producer, and in the ideologies of the networks within which they operated. In countries such as Holland and Germany, distribution of organic food still takes place largely through health food shops and a level of interpersonal and perhaps ideological trust is involved. In Ireland, where super-markets increasingly dominate, extension of markets in terms of volume and space means that original trust relationships have become attenuated. New relationships need to be created. The organic industry, and its allies in government, sought to do this through regulation and labelling.

Regulation of food is now central to the development of trusting relationships between producers and consumers. The essence of certification and regulation is labelling, without which there is no organic food and no organic production. For the consumer it is usually impossible to tell an organic product just by looking at, feeling, or even tasting, it. In a real sense, therefore, an organic product is no more than a product with an organic sticker or bag

---

4 E. M. Crawford, 'Food Retailing, Food and Nutrition in Ireland, 1839–1989: One Hundred and Fifty Years of Eating', in A. den Hartog (ed.), *Food Technology, Science and Marketing: European Diet in the Twentieth Century*, East Linton: Tuckwell, 1995.

attached – ironic when many of those who embrace organic food also oppose unnecessary food packaging. Bord Bia points out that: 'buyers expect that the organic character-istics for which they pay premium prices will be maintained as the product moves along the marketing chain and if this is not the case they will turn away from the product'. Organic producers are particularly vulnerable to dilution of their product. When numerous attributes can be attached to food, there is a danger that buyers will be attracted to less-than-organic products labelled 'environmentally friendly' or 'garden fresh'.

Organic food production in Ireland is ultimately governed by detailed EU regulations that cover the production, processing and marketing of organic foodstuffs, through the setting of standards in relation to inputs, inspection, practices and labelling. The regulatory process itself has been devolved to three organic industry bodies: IOFGA (the Irish Organic Farmers' and Growers' Association), the Organic Trust and the international biodynamic association, Demeter. These organisations employ inspectors who certify the integrity of the processes of growing, distributing and selling organic products.

As states, and bodies like the EU, the World Trade Organisation and the Food and Agriculture Organisation, have become more involved in certification, the issues have become increasingly contentious. An attempt by the US to introduce new organic criteria to permit the use of contam-inated sewage sludge, irradiation of food and genetically engineered organisms, provoked a storm of outrage within the organic community. The proposals were subsequently modified. Similarly, an Irish government decision to apply less stringent EU regulations in 2000 was met with strong criticism from the domestic organic bodies and one body, the Organic Trust, took the matter to the High Court.

It would be simplistic to see this as the story of a 'pure' organic movement reined in by the state. As Campbell and Liepins point out, in New Zealand (where the commercial possibilities of organic production have been embraced by food corporations) the discourses around organics are fluid and contentious.[5] As the industry is seen by some to become too mainstream, those in the organic movement may develop new ways to define and describe their products: for example by moving away from large-scale marketing and back to more local distribution. In New Zealand a second, parallel certification system is emerging that reflects the interests of small-scale local producers rather than the corporate food sector. A similar trend is discernible in Austria, one of the leading organic producer countries in the EU.

The Irish organic industry wants to make it easy for us to identify and choose its products. Yet it seems that there is very low recognition of organic labels in this country: according to Bord Bia, just 6 per cent of consumers recognise any of the three official organic symbols. It is not surprising then that one of the tasks of the government's organic development committee is to 'develop a national organic food label'. Yet Bord Bia also reports a high level of trust in organic food in Ireland. Consumers are happy to buy what they strongly believe to be organic food in increasing quantities. So what is going on? Are other trust-inducing mechanisms, rather than labelling, at play?

Trust in food

The concept of trust in food is a complex one. We know that the discourses operated by experts such as nutritionists and health promoters, and those of citizens/consumers, are variable, and may even be opposed. Whereas experts consider dietary habits, such as consumption of too much fat, to be the most risky; chemical contamination and food additives are the food risks that cause most concern among

---

5 H. Campbell and R. Liepins, 'Naming Organics: Understanding Organic Standards in New Zealand as a Discursive Field', *Sociologia Ruralis*, vol. 41, no. 1, 2000, pp. 21–39.

consumers.[6] As Wandel points out, concepts of healthy and risky food vary considerably across social groups, by age, class, location and other variables. A common thread, however, is the desirability of a diet balanced across binary oppositions such as natural/artificial, healthy food/junk food, home cooked/eaten out, raw/cooked and so on.

People, not surprisingly, do have strong opinions about food. A long tradition of sociological research shows that concepts such as a 'proper meal' and 'healthy food' are important. But few people in contemporary Europe feel generally insecure about the food they buy, nor, despite media hysteria, does there appear to be a real groundswell of concern about food safety issues. Crucially, people's responses on food issues tend to reflect the nuances of researchers' questions. For example when asked about health risks, people are more likely to focus on issues such as additives and pathogens; such questions are usually not to the fore when going out for a meal in a well-loved restaurant – though they may be more prominent when travelling abroad. Trust in food then, like public opinion, may be an artefact of our enquiries into it.

Trust in food has two important dimensions: trust in individual food products and trust in food control institutions. The latter assumes greater importance the further the consumer is distanced from the product: either in terms of the geographical location of its production or the complexity of its makeup. People have a strong degree of trust in state-run food safety authorities, but less faith in either the media, in its coverage of food safety issues, or food companies. Trust in the product is inevitably linked to trust in regulatory institutions. As Berg suggests:

---

6 M. Wandel, 'Safe and Healthy Food: What the Experts Know and What the Public Think', paper to an international workshop on 'Social Construction of Safe Food', Vikhammer, Norway, April 1997 [report no. 5/97, Trondheim: Centre for Rural Research].

Our direct trust in food depends on whether we, more or less consciously, have trust in a whole range of links in the food system. It is therefore not surprising when we find that 'direct trust' in food is linked to consumers' 'institutional trust', i.e. trust in the food market on the one hand and state control of the market on the other.[7]

How does the emerging literature on food trust help us to understand the almost blind faith that Irish consumers currently have in the integrity of organic food products? We can hypothesise that the level of trust is engendered by a combination of trust in the food products and in the workings of the production system. To date there have been no scares in relation to organic food. It has a universally benign image and there have been no high-profile cases in Ireland of either adverse health effects or of sharp practice in relation to the presentation of food as organic (though apocryphal stories exist of dealers smearing battery eggs with chicken manure and selling them as free range). Furthermore the organic movement has a positive public profile. Its regulatory bodies have not been subjected to scandal of any sort or engaged in public infighting. They even enjoy some mainstream political support.

Trust in organic food and farming in Ireland seems almost to exist by default. Organic food is able to bask in a warm glow of generalised public enthusiasm for nature, rurality and authenticity, backed up by promotion from certain retail groups and endorsement by celebrity chefs and food critics such as Darina Allen, John McKenna and Gerry Galvin. Whether, in the absence of strong branding, it would survive a threat such as a high-profile case of food poisoning or illicit substitution is debatable. Similarly, it remains open to organised attack from other elements of the food industry, as has occurred in the US and Britain.

---

7   L. Berg, 'Trust in Food in the Age of Mad Cow's Disease', SIFO Report
    5 (Norwegian National Institute for Consumer Research), 2000.

The future of organics

Organic food has become serious business for both the state and the corporations that market, distribute and produce it. From its almost literal status as a cottage industry, organic food now finds its place in mega-supermarkets and in the regional and economic development plans of the Irish state. It has been institutionalised.[8] The question then, is whether organic farming is destined to be 'swallowed up' by the globalised food industry, or is it able to survive in the interstices of that industry?

In those countries farthest along the trajectory foreseen by the Irish state, institutionalisation and corporatisation of the sector are well advanced. In New Zealand, Campbell and Liepins see a transition from organic growers being part of a social movement to organic export growers being 'technically compliant producers of a specific type of product'.[9] Producers have entered into the contract farming – farming to order, under strict corporate control – that typifies industrial agriculture. In the US the small operators are being squeezed out, while in Britain the major players in the organic food sector are now giant retailers like Sainsburys, Tesco and Iceland.

Organic farming in Ireland is in its infancy. There is evidence that the state would like to see the Irish organic industry develop in a similar way to that in New Zealand: both countries feature a family-farm-based, export-oriented agriculture that buys heavily into a bucolic 'clean and green' image. Such a development would have ramifications for existing Irish producers and consumers of organic food. Already the state is pressuring the organic bodies to adopt streamlined procedures more compatible with industrial

8 H. Tovey, 'Messers, Visionaries and Organobureaucrats: Dilemmas of Institutionalisation in the Irish Organic Farming Movement', *Irish Journal of Sociology,* vol. 9, 1999, pp. 31–59.

9 H. Campbell and R. Liepins, 'Naming Organics: Understanding Organic Standards in New Zealand as a Discursive Field', *Sociologia Ruralis,* vol. 41, no. 1, 2000, p. 34.

agriculture. This has led to tensions within the movement and, if the New Zealand pattern asserts itself here, we may well see the emergence of a dualistic organic sector, where a small-scale, local market based on highly perishable products (for example salad leaves and herbs) exists alongside a corporatised export sector based on more durable products (for example meat and processed foods).

There may also be implications for existing trust relationships. It is likely that as organic food is integrated into the mainstream food system, trust relationships will depend increasingly on trust in products (where promotion and branding will replace personal relationships) and in systems (the perceived integrity or otherwise of the major supermarket chains). If this happens the trust that people have in organic food will become no more than a subset of their broader relationships with the mainstream food industry: we will trust Heinz organic soup because it is Heinz, not because we know anything about the grower of the tomatoes. Just as a belief in evangelical Protestantism is no longer required to enjoy the benefits of Kellogg's cornflakes, it will no longer be necessary to buy into the ideological package of organic food to choose to consume organic food products.

CHAPTER 6

The House that Jack Built

STEPHEN QUILLEY

As is the case for many people fresh off the boat at Dún Laoghaire, Ireland is not what I expected. I had convinced myself that Dublin would be a more upbeat and metropolitan version of Liverpool or Manchester: a capital city, but a northern, Celtic capital, informal, laid back and 'liveable'. How hard could it be to find a small garden flat for one, relatively well-paid, man and his dog? Almost impossible, as it turned out. Kipping on a friend's floor in an unheated house in Clontarf, and facing stifling bouts of road rage each morning in my efforts to drive to work on the other side of the city, I experienced a rising tide of anxiety. Had Dublin been such a good move after all? Luckily, I was not alone. Wherever I went, the conversation focused on traffic and housing, the two being indivisible facets of Ireland's 'urban problem'. Even relatively well-paid professionals find it difficult to afford a mortgage unless they bring a substantial slice of equity to the deal. The rest are forced to rely on a venal and entirely unregulated private rented sector that allows landlords to extract exorbitant rents.

The consequences are entirely predictable. At the bottom of the income ladder, students routinely share bedrooms in order to cushion the impact of high rents. Young professional dinkies,[1] struggling to get into the run-away housing market, are faced with a choice of either a small but massively overpriced apartment within a cycle ride of their workplace, or a new semi-detached townhouse or bungalow on one of the vast tracts of low-density developments that are swallowing up agricultural land along all of the main approaches to the capital. For those who opt for the garden and perhaps a scenic view of the Dublin mountains, the price is paid in time and stress: hours each day, in slow or stationary traffic, on roads that have simply no hope of coping with the ever-rising volume of traffic. Of course they pay in financial terms as well. In Ireland, a car is an absolute necessity. The annual record-breaking totals of new car registrations are not only an index of conspicuous consumption in an atmosphere of unprecedented economic growth, they also reflect the catch-22 of the car economy: the more dispersed and decentred the pattern of urbanisation, the more congested the roads, the less viable public transport becomes and the more people become dependent on their cars.

Dormitory town blues

Having struggled for two months to find a landlord willing to countenance a man with a dog (thank God I wasn't pregnant!), I decided that enough was enough, and proceeded to buy a small bungalow on a hilltop overlooking Wicklow town. On the positive side, number 76 Rose Hill had a garden and was within walking distance of a wonderful local amenity, an often-deserted coastal estuary. However, the reality of commuting from Wicklow to Dublin was brutal. Even at six thirty in the morning, I would have to join a queue just to get out of town. The subsequent journey along the N11 was tetchy and usually took an hour and a half, and the return leg could not be contemplated

---

1   Double income, no kids.

anytime before seven o'clock. As a result I was permanently tired, had no social life and felt like I had swapped the healthy, metropolitan, cycling sociability of south Manchester for a kind of Stepford Wives' somnambulism in Dublin's ever-expanding commuter belt. This situation might have been mitigated if I could have oriented myself more around Wicklow town. However, whatever autonomous charms this small Georgian town, with its picturesque harbour and main street, may have once had, they have been increasingly sapped by its function as a dormitory for Dublin's booming tertiary sector. Spending hours in stationary traffic, I had plenty of time to reflect on my personal situation. But I was also drawn to a series of wider questions about the nature of urbanisation and urban policy in Dublin.

My bungalow was one of thousands of identical little boxes that were creeping up the pastured hillsides among which the old harbour town used to nestle. Like everyone else on the estate, my connection with the town was superficial. I never bought anything on the high street, preferring to sleepwalk my way around the Tesco supermarket that I passed everyday on the main approach road. Once a week, I ventured with my next-door neighbour, a similarly exiled colleague, for a few pints in the over-25's section of one of the local pubs. And that was that. Sixty miles a day, a weekly trip to the supermarket, four pints of Guinness and a walk down the estuary at the weekend. For all its recent growth, Wicklow remains badly served in terms of shops and services. The nature of that growth ensures that most of the disposable income of its relatively wealthy new residents is spent in Dublin. The result is evident in the town's retail amenities: a string of barely viable high street shops, which frequently change hands, and a dearth of good restaurants and food outlets.

Why is it that this manifestly irrational situation seems to be accepted as a matter of course by both the general public and local planners? A situation including:

- thousands of would-be Dubliners biding their time and riding the housing wave whilst camping out in Wicklow

- dispersed patterns of urban development underwriting the kind of 'Edge City' that even a Californian might be proud of[2]

- a seeming inability on the part of local authorities to question a design and planning idiom that assumes that everyone, regardless of age, occupation or family circumstances, must ultimately desire exactly the same thing, namely a three-bedroom house on its own plot of land

- a reluctance on the part of public authority to intervene and mould market processes for the public good.

Imagine a different kind of development in Wicklow: a mixture of family housing, and high-density, high-quality, architect-designed apartment blocks; cobbled and pedestrianised streets, framed by arresting and aesthetically pleasing street furniture; café bars, newsagents, restaurants; a super-modern, super-fast electric tram connection to Dublin, with room for bicycles at no extra charge.

Imagine a different kind of wake up call: the alarm goes at a quarter to eight; I get ready whilst looking out of my balcony window across the harbour; I walk my bike down the street and stop for a coffee and a newspaper before cycling down to the station; there I board the tram, put my bike in the rack, and settle down in the clean and spacious carriage for the 45-minute ride to Dublin; I cycle into UCD for nine thirty. Later, I leave work to meet up with some friends. We go to the theatre. After catching last orders, I cycle to pick up the last tram at midnight. At the weekend, some friends from Dublin come down to visit me in Wicklow – time for a walk with the dog and a meal in the old town,

---

2   J. Gareau, *Edge City: Life on the New Frontier*, New York: Doubleday, 1991.

before catching the last ride back. Increasingly, as a combination of transport links and information technology make central Dublin locations more dispensable, and the architectural and cultural ambience of Wicklow makes the town more attractive in its own right, companies and institutions begin to relocate some of their activities there. In time, some of my neighbours actually walk to work.

To re-think a place like Wicklow, and its relationship to Dublin, in these terms you have to love cities and urban living. However you also need to appreciate the countryside through urban eyes and priorities. This involves an aesthetic commitment to the distinction between city and countryside, with the latter understood more in terms of natural landscapes available for consumption in various ways. But for such a sensibility to frame the planning regime, it is necessary to have a political culture that can generate forms of decision making that rise above the needs and perceptions of individuals and which are informed by a more collective vision of the common good.

Clearly, any planning or design project will express very particular social interests. In this chapter, my aim is to pose a series of questions about the sociological and historical reasons for the apparent failure of Ireland's planning system and the absence of a coherent urban policy. I take as my point of departure the long-running controversy over the role of bungalows in the Irish countryside.

The bungalow as a metaphor for modernisation

Bungalows have become symbolic of a much wider debate around housing, transport and the despoliation of the Irish countryside, one that has been raging since the 1960s. For much of this time the two most prominent protagonists in the conflict have been Jack Fitzsimons, the author of *Bungalow Bliss,* and Frank McDonald, environment correspondent for *The Irish Times.* Their long-running altercation is indicative of a much deeper fissure in twentieth-century Irish culture. Since it was first published in 1971,

Bungalow Bliss has been through many editions and sold nearly 200,000 copies. The book was not particularly original; in America and the UK, compilations of standard plans and off-the-peg designs for bungalows, have been in circulation since the late nineteenth century.[3] However Fitzsimons' book, with its alliterative title and eighty standard plans pre-approved for housing grants by the then Department of Local Government, captured the public imagination. It also provided a service precisely tailored to Irish conditions – and specifically the Local Government (Planning and Development) Act, 1963, which established for the first time a unitary regulatory framework for planning and development control. The book provided would-be homebuilders with everything they needed to know to take the project from inception, planning and technical regulations, right through to kitchen design, lighting and home furnishings. *Bungalow Bliss* spoke to a deeply embedded culture of land ownership and proprietorial individualism that meshed with the populist and ruralist nature of national politics. In his introduction to the fifth edition, James Tully TD, then Minister for Local Government, proclaimed that Jack Fitzsimons was providing a popular and much-needed service. Such high-level endorsement underlined the fact that any reservations expressed by professional architects and other members of the Dublin-based literati were extremely marginal and at odds with popular sentiment.

The Irish state has, for decades, consistently emphasised the importance of home ownership regardless of the incumbent party. With this in mind, a variety of state grants have been available to subsidise the construction of private housing, with a particular emphasis given to rural applicants earning part of their living from agriculture and to the rural poor. In the mid-1970s for instance, the

---

3   For example R. A. Briggs, *Bungalows and Country Cottages*, London: 1891 (later editions: 1894, 1895, 1897, 1901).

subsidies could amount to over 10 per cent of the cost of construction, and up to 20 per cent in Gaeltacht areas. Although there was never any explicit articulation of a policy of dispersed development based on detached, individual, family homes on separate plots of land, the structure of the grant system always leaned heavily in this direction by emphasising rurality, a connection to agriculture and the alleviation of overcrowding. Consequently, the economic-demographic shift away from agriculture was not translated into a process of urbanisation. In the context of rapidly increasing car ownership, the unconstrained dispersal of private housing across the rural landscape has resulted in what might be described as a post-urban landscape or the suburbanisation of the countryside: that is to say, urban social and economic relations (increasingly nuclear families, organised around consumption and the non-agrarian economy) without an urban core.

The modernisation of economic and social relations, which is associated with this kind of post-urbanism, was identified repeatedly by Fitzsimons as a core component of the bungalow project: 'bright, modern' bungalows were synonymous with the escape from rural poverty and domestic drudgery. He celebrates the consumer durables and technological conveniences of the modern kitchen.[4] Given that, in many cases, the alleviation of overcrowding, an explicit policy objective, involved the positive institution of the nuclear family, it is perhaps not surprising that Fitzsimons also anticipated the needs of the (modern) housewife. But there was also a subtle recognition of rising female participation in the labour market and the emerging non-agrarian, rural economy. For instance he refers to the oven-timer as a 'wonderful idea for working wives . . . who want to . . . feel certain that the family are well cared for with a hot meal at midday'.[5]

---

4   J. Fitzsimons, *Bungalow Bliss*, Kells: Kells Publishing, 1975, 5th edition, pp. 319–20.
5   Fitzsimons, ibid., p. 321.

Fitzsimons' own account provided a ringing endorsement of the modernisation of social relations that had taken place since the 1950s. He linked bungalows quite explicitly to the visceral desire of ordinary, working people to escape from the deep-seated pattern of impoverished rural life. For Fitzsimons, *Bungalow Bliss* represented the revolt against traditional, Catholic, male sensibilities and a celebration of the youthful, secular revolution unleashed in the 1960s: 'Mini-skirted females were . . . giving male chauvinism a knee in the groin'.[6]

Fitzsimons was presenting a populist manifesto in which everyone had the right to a stake in a modernising society. There was an impatience for progress; and questioning the right of ordinary people to build bungalows was tantamount to the denial of social and economic development per se. Developing this theme, he quotes Tony Lynch, a retired housing inspector from the Department of Environment:

> [Tourists and environmentalists may lament the disappearance of thatched cottages, but they don't have to live in them]. Man must progress . . . [Traditional cottages are picturesque, but] my heart really leaps up when I behold a cluster or string of bright modern bungalows, near a modern school, served by a tarred road, with the majestic curve of the pylon-borne power lines sweeping along the mountains and through the brown bogs. And the glitter of the television aerials in the evening light. And the modern fish-factory or other industrial buildings outlined fearlessly against the rolling sea. And the poetry of the flushing of a W.C. and the music of a hot bath filling. Surely the tourists wouldn't begrudge us that – if they do, well let them just try to live in Disney Land and they'll soon discover the vast difference between the illusion and the reality.[7]

---

6   Fitzsimons, ibid., pp. 2–3.

7   J. Fitzsimons, *Bungalow Bashing*, Kells: Kells Publishing, 1991, p. 23.

This kind of language struck a chord with ordinary people. *Bungalow Bliss* can be seen as a plebeian and rural, but nevertheless, modernist project. And in its own terms, the project can be seen as progressive. In a country scarred by over a century of economic stagnation, rural depopulation and emigration, this bricks-and-mortar populism represented a watershed in national self-perception. As Fintan O'Toole has pointed out, the bungalow aesthetic derived in part from America.[8] Along with country and western music, white picket fences and Mexican verandas, it bears witness to the steady flow of iconically modern domestic imagery from American emigrants to their relatives in rural Ireland.

Starting in the 1960s and accelerating from the 1980s, the proliferation of bungalows across the Irish landscape was an index of real economic growth. And, in perception, it was synonymous with a specifically Irish modernity, which however retrogressive in planning, environmental or aesthetic terms, was part of a much broader process of social, cultural and technological modernisation. This process included, amongst other things, the loosening grip of the Catholic Church on rural society, an economic shift away from agriculture, rising female participation in the labour market and the changing pattern of family formation. However the distinctive feature of Irish modernisation is that such transformations were not associated with a wholesale demographic shift to the city (at least not Irish cities). This is to say that since the 1960s, the modernisation project and the transformation of social and economic relations associated with *Bungalow Bliss* was synonymous with the suburbanisation of the countryside rather than the growth of cities.[9]

---

8   F. O'Toole, *Sunday Tribune*, 22 April 1984, quoted in Fitzsimons, *Bungalow Bashing*, Kells: Kells Publishing, 1991, p. 16.

9   Suburbanisation is clearly an inadequate term. The classical suburb is demographically far denser than the one-bungalow-per-acre plots that stretch out as far as the eye can see over much of Ireland, and still implies a division between town and a relatively sparsely

Despite the self-evident hegemony of bungaloid growth and ribbon development, and the unwillingness to regulate on the part of both national and local political elites, Fitzsimons saw himself as taking on 'paternalist bureaucrats' in the establishment – a metropolitan elite who wielded undue influence on the planning process and were thwarting the legitimate aspirations of ordinary people. However, the media weight of the critics was certainly out of proportion either to their popular support, or their political influence. This is evident from development control statistics for the 1980s and 1990s, which show that even in environmentally sensitive areas such as Galway, the vast majority of planning applications are granted. At the same time, less than one per cent of applications were declined on the grounds of ribbon development.

Whilst there had long been a degree of anxiety about unregulated development in the countryside on the part of those charged with preserving Ireland's rural landscape, the debate came to a head in 1987 with Frank McDonald's series of articles in *The Irish Times*. The title, 'Bungalow Blitz', was an obvious reference to Fitzsimons' manual of plans, and McDonald's comprehensive critique linked problems of aesthetics and the poverty of house design with planning and transport problems related to ribbon development. Downplaying the obviously class-laden aesthetic agenda, and quoting gloomy reports by both Bord Fáilte and the Irish Tourism Industry Confederation (ITIC), the series emphasised the negative impact that the degradation of the rural environment would have on tourism.[10] Bungaloid

---

9   *(contd).*
    populated countryside. However, for a country with such a low overall population density, rural Ireland frequently feels crowded and even claustrophobic. The impression is of a landscape that has been parcelled-up and fenced-off down to the last square foot. Rarely is there any sense of the open and empty space associated with Scotland or the English moors.

10 See, for example, *The Irish Times*, 15 September 1987.

growth and ribbon development was cast as a pathogenic infection of the unspoilt landscape, a 'spreading fungus'.

For McDonald, bungalow blight was a tragically Irish phenomenon stemming from the 'rabid individualism' that was intrinsic to the post-colonial psyche. He railed against the 'screw you' style of architecture, which equated a rejection of the historical, rural poverty with a pervasive vulgarity. Instances of architectural vulgarity included mock Georgian facades, the inappropriate use of red brick, the split-level Mediterranean style, Mexican verandas and the 'Southfork-style' ranch. Given the strong association between this history of poverty and British/Anglo-Irish domination organised from Dublin, it is perhaps not surprising that detractors of the bungalow, and critics of the clientelist politics associated with Section IV planning permissions,[11] have often been constructed as metropolitan elitists and cultural imperialists ('West Brits').

Bungalow bliss: politics or culture?

Writing a decade after the original 'Bungalow Blitz' series, McDonald asked whether the process of rural suburbanisa-tion and ribbon development was now irreversible. Was it time, he asked, to write off the Irish countryside? With the pace of house building showing little sign of slowing down, and strong government regulation as unlikely as ever, it is tempting to answer in the affirmative. However the failure of rural planning is intimately linked to a failure to develop a coherent urban policy. In fact, both sides of the argument rely too much on supposedly immovable characteristics of Irish culture or the Irish psyche. For instance, there is the

---

11 Section IV of the City and County Management Act, 1995 allows councillors to override the advice of planners and officials, in the 'interests of their constituents'. This effectively undermines local planning regimes and opens the door to forms of patronage and clientelism in local politics.

truism that the Irish are not natural urbanites, repeated by McDonald. He argues that Fitzsimons tapped into the cult of individualism which is still part of Ireland's post-colonial psyche and that: 'by choosing to live in a bungalow in the countryside it is as if the bungalow builders have consciously reverted to the dispersed pattern of Celtic settlement'.[12]

It is almost churlish to point to the role and numbers of Irish people involved in the construction of Manchester, Liverpool and New York. In fact from a historical perspective, one could argue that the Irish diaspora was at the forefront of capitalist urbanisation in the nineteenth and early twentieth centuries. The phenomena of suburbanisation, ex-urbanisation and the growth of the 'Edge City' relate to market and technological dynamics, albeit unfolding in locally specific ways, and certainly not to any cultural predisposition. There is no reason to suspect that bungalows and dispersed patterns of urbanisation are any different in Ireland.

In fact, social constructions of nature, landscape and the appropriate form for both dwelling and community are precisely that – social constructions. They develop in very specific historical circumstances and, equally, they change. Given the speed and depth of the social and economic transformation associated with the 'Celtic tiger', there are good reasons to expect that the cultural frameworks which have channelled and actively constructed both urban and rural landscapes over the last thirty years will themselves begin to change.

The Irish bungalow has its roots in utilitarian and practical vernacular concerns that mark the aesthetic predispositions of peasant and small farming communities everywhere. Typically, a farming family would take advantage of building grants to build a modern dwelling alongside

---

12 *The Irish Times*, 26 June 1997.

their decrepit cottage that would be abandoned, perhaps later to be rescued as a weekend/lifestyle project by a more aesthetically 'sensitive' urbanite. Irish rural development has never been village-based and the siting of houses in the middle of large, private plots made sense when householders were responsible for providing all of their own services. Since the 1960s, as in the UK, the provision of community-based services, such as electricity, water and rubbish collection, shifted the pattern in favour of ribbon development along roads which facilitate access to these services. However the dispersed pattern of development around individual plots continued and became culturally embedded in terms of the habitual design inclinations of developers and the social-cultural expectations of potential house builders. It also became embedded in the clientelist structures of patronage that dominate local politics.

The housing encroachment became, from a planning perspective, more problematic, as it was combined with the sectoral shift away from agriculture and the increasing geographical distance between work and home. The situation in the west of Ireland was greatly exacerbated by the proliferation of second homes and developments relating to the tourist industry. In both cases, developments followed the now well-worn path that has resulted in dispersed, ribbon development and plot-by-plot construction of individual bungalows to standardised designs.

Aesthetic objections aside, the real problem with the Irish bungalow is not the architectural form, but the planning regime that goes with it. Culturalist arguments, which focus on a putative Celtic mindset in relation to settlement patterns, greatly underplay the complexity of intertwining and re-enforcing political, economic and social factors that contribute to the planning and market configuration, which is undoubtedly heavily weighted towards dispersed bungaloid growth. The question facing policy makers in the twenty-first century is how this planning–market matrix might be re-configured.

Conclusion: Towards a new social construction of the Irish urban landscape

On the back of the rapid economic growth of the 1990s, the suburbanisation of Ireland's rural landscape has become synonymous with escalating crises in relation to housing and transportation. Spiralling house prices, crippling private sector rents and traffic gridlock are fast becoming stifling impediments to future economic growth. Whilst the sectoral shift away from agriculture continues unabated, an essentially rural form of proprietorial individualism, rooted in farming, continues to frame both the structure of consumer demand in the housing market, and also the planning and development regime through which this demand is expressed. However there is nothing preordained about this 'blood and soil' attachment to the land, nor the apparent impotency of the regulatory capacities of the Irish state and political system. Both can rather be seen as symptoms of the speed of economic transformation.

The historical underdevelopment of an industrial urbanism in Ireland has a corollary in the weakness of any urban, class-based politics built on the collectivist premise of regulatory interventions to secure environmental common goods such as clean air, public transport and public housing. But, paradoxically and for the same reason, absent also are the kind of cosmopolitan, urban constructions of nature and countryside as landscape (an aesthetic category) which, through organisations such as the Council for the Protection of Rural England, played such a crucial role in limiting suburban sprawl and framing the highly interventionist town and country planning regime in the UK.

This would suggest the need for debates around an urbanism appropriate for the needs of twenty-first-century Ireland to be connected to debates around the significance of Irish landscape and nature, both in terms of cultural heritage and identity, but also as an economic resource, not least for the tourist industry. Visions of high-density, sustainable and liveable urban landscapes, served by imaginative public transport systems, need to be linked to an understanding of the countryside as more than an aggregation of small farms. In practical terms, those lobbying for sustainable towns and cities need to co-opt a wider set of organisations into their agenda, for example the tourist industry, wildlife protection and conservation bodies and agencies concerned with heritage.

Engendering the political will and the institutional capacity to seriously curtail ribbon development demands the development of a coherent vision for both the sprawling urban centres and the rural landscape. The obstacles impeding the re-configuration of popular Irish constructions of urbanity and rurality might be less entrenched than culturalist explanations imply. The experience of ordinary Irish men and women struggling with escalating traffic and housing problems is a daily reminder that the existing configuration is not working. How long that sense of frustration takes to find expression in the political system is a different question. However it is certainly not pre-determined by any hard-wired Celtic culture of proprietorial individualism.

CHAPTER 7

Celebrity
Case Studies in the
Localisation of the Global

CARMEN KUHLING AND KIERAN KEOHANE

O n a visit to Galway, our daughter wanted to go to McDonalds, which in fact was Supermacs, an import-substitute, 'Irish owned family restaurant', indistinguishable from McDonalds in every substantial respect. The confusion of McDonalds and Supermacs, even to the keen eyes of a child, epitomises a broad historical process of homogenisation of Irish culture and identity wherein the local is transformed so that it resembles the global: the localisation of the global.

Later the same day she recognised a Claddagh ring as 'the ring Angel gave to Buffy' [the Vampire Slayer]. The Claddagh ring, an artefact with a genealogy particular to Galway, has now become a floating signifier of traditional local culture, appropriated by the global culture industry to give connotations of anchorage in community and a sense of historical continuity to brooding, transcendentally homeless Los Angeleans (for LA is the setting of the *Buffy* spin-off *Angel*). Irish social structures, institutions, culture and identity are being transformed by processes of globalisation: technologies and markets of production, distribution and consumption generated by transnational corporations; and administrative systems, governmental strategies and legal-rational principles developed by transnational institutions. At the same time, our social structures and institutions are shaped by the re-localisation of the global: local institutions, communitarian norms and principles of action translate and re-work external processes of globalisation, attuning them and making them consonant with local institutions. Irish culture and identity is characterised by the ambiguous and paradoxical ways in which the globalisation of the local and the re-localisation of the global are played out, sometimes in concert, sometimes colliding, in a social field crosscut with antagonism.

The local and the global, community and society, tradition and modernity, are not forms of life that supersede one another in linear historical progress. They exist contemporaneously and interpenetrate, collide and collude with one another, in the time and space of contemporary Ireland. Borders and boundaries between local and global, community and society, tradition and modernity are permeable. We have a foot in many camps and, in contemporary Ireland, we live in an in-between world, in between cultures and identities. The experience of modernisation and modernity in Ireland is ongoing, uneven, and fed by many sources, and hence perhaps best understood in terms of Bauman's notion of 'liquid modernity'.[1] 'Liquescence' expresses the idea that there is no such thing as modernity, the modern world, or a singular linear process of modernisation which brought it into being; instead there are modernities, multiple modernities. There are also multiple traditions, for 'traditional' and 'tradition' are modern ideas, the world as defined retrospectively by modernity as the pre-modern. Thus, this chapter explores some aspects of the melange of modernities and traditions, the co-existence and collision of which animate the identities and cultures of contemporary Ireland.

---

1 Zygmunt Bauman, *Liquid Modernity*, London: Polity Press, 2000.

In this chapter, we examine celebrity in Irish popular culture and, in particular, the representation of celebrity in the *RTÉ Guide* as an example of what we call collision culture. Collision is the central unifying metaphor which expresses changes in Irish society today: collisions between the traditional and the modern, between the local and the global, between community and society, and between the values of collectivist and individualist worldviews. We hope to show that traditional communalism and more modern forms of individualism have each positive and negative dimensions, and are impacting upon one another in interesting and diverse ways in Irish culture as a result of the forces of globalisation.

The celebrity as an expression of the 'cult of the individual'

One of the most marked effects of globalisation has been to promote the values of individualism against those of community. According to Durkheim, the division of labour – occupational specialisation – means that people become valued not for their resemblance to the group (their belonging to family and kin, parishes and villages; their sharing the same beliefs and values as others) but for directly opposite reasons.[2] Increasingly, individuals are valued as individuals, for their uniqueness and peculiarity, for their distinctiveness and irreplacability. The primary arena in which this can be seen is in the labour market, where one's value, as measured by salary and status, is determined by the unique skills and abilities that one brings to the marketplace. Traditional bases of occupational stratification and life chances – for example to whom one is related ('pull' in our Irish idiom) or one's gender – matter increasingly less. In the contemporary Irish labour market, the essential criteria of entry and advancement are technical and professional qualification and expertise. This

---

2   Emile Durkheim, *The Division of Labour in Society*, New York: Free Press, 1984.

systematic erasure of the vestiges of traditionalism, the prejudices of nepotism and patriarchy, what Durkheim calls forms of forced division of labour, is one of the primary tendencies pushing towards the equalisation of social relations in Ireland today.

However this individuation of Irish society has had both positive and negative effects. Along with this formal equalisation through educational qualification and similar progressive developments, Durkheim sees some ominous tendencies, most notably the 'cult of the individual'.[3] As one's unique and individual qualities become the source of value in the occupational arena, individuality in all aspects of life becomes valued and celebrated. This has ambiguous and paradoxical consequences. On the one hand it is the basis of the newfound freedoms of contemporary Ireland: freedom of thought and expression, and of consciousness. It is simultaneously the source of egoism and anomie – discussed earlier in this volume in terms of suicide in Ireland – the characteristic pathological tendencies of modern society. The cult of the individual is expressed throughout contemporary Irish culture and identity, by the replacement of the hero by the celebrity. But as with all of the phenomena of Ireland's collision culture, the new forms are not clearcut breaks with the past, but hybrid fusions in which vestiges of earlier social forms live on and are reproduced in what at first appear to be new institutions of Irish culture and identity.

Durkheim claims that each and every society constructs an ideal-type member, who embodies and represents its values.[4] The ideal member is the model that others aspire to emulate and is the cornerstone of the entire social order. In traditional society the hero is worshipped because he fights on our behalf. Irish culture, up until quite recently, has been brimming with heroes – usually martyred, who fought for

---

3   Emile Durkheim, *Sociology and Philosophy*, New York: Free Press, 1975.
4   Durkheim, ibid.

Ireland. Celebrities are worshipped because they 'fight' for themselves, and in modern society the cult of the individual is manifest in the social form of the celebrity, the highest mark of individual success. But consider the contrast, and the continuity, between Irish traditional heroes and heroines, those champions who from Daniel O'Connell to Michael Collins, from Countess Markiewicz to Nell McCafferty, fought on our behalf, and contemporary celebrities who span a wide spectrum from Tony O'Reilly to Ronan Keating. We continue to lionise these celebrities as though they were heroes whose exploits somehow elevate us all. Similarly, there is continuity between 'the Boys', which refers to the collective, generic name for heroic Irish insurrectionaries (who remain nameless, non-individualised – the boys of Wexford, the boys of Kilmichael) and Boyzone and members of 'boy bands'. The faces and names of celebrity bands are prominent, and their 'personalities' are extravagantly exteriorised in biographies, 'frank' interviews and 'intimate' photo-sessions, but as undifferentiated collectives, and even families – Boyzone, Westlife, The Corrs. They are not merely celebrities, but Irish celebrities, heroic for their victories on the global battlefields of the UK charts and the MTV awards.

The popularity of Irish talk radio is in part due to its dual function of celebrating modern individualism and simultaneously reconstituting traditional community; in articulating a unified sense of the common good despite the fragmenting, individualising effects of modernity and the plurality of worldviews recent social transformations have engendered. The celebrity personality, typified by the likes of Gay Byrne, Marian Finucane and Pat Kenny, embodies the ideal of fully actualised individualism in modern society. But in Ireland, these people are simultaneously household names, embodiments of the idea of community. Furthermore, Irish talk radio individuates, elicits and celebrates the diverse views of individual listeners, related to Gerry or Marian always on an intimate, personal, first-name basis. Simultaneously, the heroic work of the Irish talk show host as a good listener is to re-collect the audience as a community of individual people who, despite their often diverse views, share common values: we, the modern Irish public, are all neighbours and friends concerned with an issue/problem that affects us all. Thus Irish talk radio is a strong representation of the localisation of the global: it is a forum which both articulates and reflects on the recent changes in Irish society, and which upholds a sense of the collective onto the increasingly differentiated and globalised voice(s) of the people. Gay Byrne's *Late Late Show*, frequently celebrated as a cornerstone in the liberalisation of Irish society, equally addressed traditional community. A characteristic feature of this television show was the quintessential primordial form of community binding, namely gift exchange. In every show, in exchange for 'your being so good to come all the way to Dublin' (the audience's gift is their presence, attention and applause), Byrne always had a gift of 'something for everyone in the audience'.

The celebrity as an object of collective gaze

Despite the fact that it is a manifestation of the cult of the individual, the celebrity enables us to articulate a unified sense of the common good in the context of the fragmenting, individualising effects of modernity. Celebrities sometimes function as 'lightning rods', whose stardom amplifies or makes visible particular negative aspects of their societies. For instance, Marilyn Monroe and Elvis Presley are still objects of public fascination by a nostalgic global public: small-town innocents who succumbed to overdoses of drugs, food or alcohol in the context of the loneliness and anomie of stardom, they function in the collective imaginary as symbols of the decline of American society, as archetypal sacrificial victims of its hyper individuation, egoism, mass consumption and excess. The intense outpouring of grief at the death of Princess Diana can also be seen as a public identification with her as the victim of an archaic and rigid royal family, and thus as a symptom (which is manifesting

108

itself at many levels of the social hierarchy) of the decline of British civilisation. However, locating these celebrities within their particular national, social and cultural context is not to say that either these celebrities' fans, or the particular nature of their traumas, are limited to their countries or cultures of origin. Diana is also perceived as a victim of globalisation insofar as she was hounded by the celebrity-seeking media, and was quite literally the victim of a collision of worlds where royalty meets celebrity in a high-speed car chase through Paris in order to evade the paparazzi. In this sense, celebrity itself is paradoxical: the celebrity is conceived and shaped by both local and global desires, audiences, traumas and representations.

As the inquiries in the wake of Diana's death have illustrated, the media approach to celebrities is often invasive, voyeuristic and cruel. The stock and trade of mass magazines such as *Hello, OK, Now* and numerous others is the elevation and denigration of celebrities. Movie stars, media personalities, public figures and the vestiges of royalty are simultaneously lionised and brought down to earth by alternately publishing representations of an ideal (such as the blissful perfection of the royal or celebrity wedding) and candid snapshots of celebrities caught un-awares in unflattering poses (such as Princess Diana on an exercise machine or Jerry Hall revealing her cellulite in a bikini).

Mass audiences of popular culture are familiar with this ambivalent representation of celebrity, as news and as entertaining spectacle. We may know very well that these representations are fabulous constructions of dream machines and spin doctors, but still we need the ideals that they represent: ideals of perpetual youth and beauty, individuality, fame, success, wealth, power and influence, which are central to modern living. And yet, as these ideals are more often than not far beyond the reach of ordinary people's everyday lives, just as we need the celebrity to represent them for us, we need to deflate the ideal, cut it down to size, so that we are not in thrall to it. The shortcut to profaning the secular equivalent of the sacred realm – the realm of the 'stars' – is to knock the celebrities off their pedestals. Thus the relation to celebrity in modern society is ambivalent, and it is simultaneously elevated and debased through its representation in popular culture.

In contrast to the dominance of American and British celebrity coverage in international magazines such as *Hello, OK* and *Now,* and perhaps to the invasive approach of some members of the international paparazzi, Irish magazines have tried to maximise coverage of Irish celebrities and thus to corner the Irish market through a variety of different formulas. For instance, *VIP* has retained the *Hello* formula of depicting celebrities on their estates, in glamorous clothes and at elite events (and thus has replicated its association of celebrity with wealth and beauty, if not youth), but focuses on the entertainment and entrepreneurial elites of Ireland rather than Hollywood stars and European royalty.

The *RTÉ Guide*, Ireland's biggest-selling magazine, has adopted a more original formula of depicting Irish celebrities in terms of their commitment to family, work and community rather than on the basis of more superficial qualities of youth and beauty, which is perhaps a factor maintaining its readership in the face of stiff external competition with regards to celebrity coverage. In the *RTÉ Guide*, what is celebrated is Irish celebrities' heroic ability to maintain qualities of unpretentiousness and ordinariness in spite of their fame and the forces of the global culture industry.

Ambivalence towards celebrity in the RTÉ Guide

The *RTÉ Guide* has successfully developed a niche market wherein the globalisation of the local and the re-localisation of the global are articulated. The ambivalence between modern individualism and traditional community are reconciled in the hybrid form of the Irish celebrity, who is represented simultaneously as a unique individual and as 'one of our own'. Irish stars are invariably represented by the *RTÉ Guide* as principled, hardworking, modest and tenacious, and are perceived as being in control of their media image. Marian Finucane is applauded for being exactly the same on air as in real life.[5] The closing summary of an article on the band Westlife claims: 'It is obviously gonna take more than a couple of tornadoes to blow this group away'.[6] As well, several cover stories feature an Irish star, Gaybo, Pat Kenny, or someone in one of the home-grown soaps, Miley or Biddy, or some new addition to the cast of *Fair City*, who, in the course of an interview framed as an intimate chat amongst friends, assures us that the cast of *Glenroe*, or RTÉ as a whole, is a nice happy family, a microcosm of the community of Irish life, with values and vices that we all share and love. And another obligatory feature: the profile of the Irish Hollywood star, Pierce Brosnan, or Liam Neeson 'your man' from *Michael Collins*, which reassures us that although they live among the stars (and so, vicariously, we all share their elevation), their hearts belong to Ireland. The profile reveals them to be 'grand ordinary lads'.

More explicitly, this celebration of the local is usually achieved through a devaluation of the global, or life outside Ireland. In an interview with RTÉ's foreign affairs correspondent, Mark Little, the barrenness of his successful life as a Washington correspondent is clearly juxtaposed to the fulfilment of life in Ireland. His life in America is summarised by one particular anecdote where he felt lonely and disconnected while stuck in an airport hotel lounge, in contrast to his new, 'more normal life in Dublin'. Similarly, his critique of the 'venom' of public debate in Ireland is attributed not to local political culture, but to invidious global influences: 'US-type apathy is creeping in here'.[7] In a similar vein, many articles eschew individual achievement in favour of everyday values of community and family. Sonia

---

5   *RTÉ Guide*, 10 November 2000, p. 4.
6   *RTÉ Guide*, 17 June 2000, p. 4.
7   *RTÉ Guide*, 13 January 2001, p. 5.

O'Sullivan's hard work and success is equated with the traditional role of an Irish woman: 'Her mothering skills are obviously as effortless and as natural as her running ability'.[8] The paradox of Irish celebrity is that the notion of the star, and the cult of individualism on which it is based, are fundamentally antithetical to some of the principles underpinning Radio Telefís Éireann – radio and television for the Irish community, public service broadcasting committed to endorsing the values and the ethos of Ireland. RTÉ is torn between the objectives of reinscribing the symbolic boundaries of Irish community, and doing this through a medium that prioritises the individual over the collective, the transnational over the national. Paradoxically, Irish stars themselves are used to reinscribe the symbolic boundaries of the Irish community. Celebrity is acknowledged as the dominant social form, and is ritualistically paid homage to, but at times with criticism; even as it is torn down, there is an attempt to usurp and appropriate this form, to incorporate it into the collective body.

This ambivalence is expressed in a content analysis of the *RTÉ Guide* for the years 1999 and 2000, which reveals that the guide simultaneously tries to reassert the priority of the collective over the individual, while at the same time championing Irish celebrities at the expense of non-Irish celebrities, who are frequently depicted as morally or intellectually vacuous. The coverage of Irish celebrities in the guide represents an important process of self-assertion, which recognises the achievements of Irish actors, musicians and radio personalities in the context of the cultural emergence of Ireland on the global stage. However, as we illustrate below, the guide at times devalues non-Irish celebrities on fairly spurious grounds, and frequently for excessive individuation, or tries to domesticate the non-Irish celebrity by casting them as individuals who, though rich and famous, truly desire what we Irish see ourselves as

---

8   *RTÉ Guide*, 26 August 1999, p. 4.

112

having: a form of life morally anchored by values of family and community.

Whereas non-Irish magazines such as *Hello, OK* and *Now* uniformly and voyeuristically seek to reveal flaws (such as marital squabbles or physical imperfections) of all stars regardless of nationality, the *RTÉ Guide* criticises non-Irish or particularly American stars, and specifically for expressing sexuality or individuality. An examination of the *RTÉ Guide* reveals the following standard features: RTÉ reporter flies out to meet Hollywood star in a hotel or studio in Los Angeles, New York or London, to conduct an interview in which the star is shown by the reporter to be deficient in some way. For instance, Catherine Zeta Jones-Douglas's hope that her new family can live with some privacy prompted the response: 'She's just going to have to stop trading in that star status then, isn't she?'.[9] Gossipy snippets concerning affairs, drug or alcohol problems are the fare here; for example, the innuendo is made that Matthew Perry has fallen off the anti-prescription drugs wagon.

There is also an implicit censorship of celebrities in terms of a traditionalist discourse of sexuality, and for women, a sexual double standard. For example, an article on David Bowie, an icon of both individualism and subversive sexuality, and the model Iman, his Somalian wife, ends with: 'Goodness me, if that's what they are like, then a small stack of disposable nappies in the hot press and the 3 a.m. feed will do them the world of good'.[10] Their transgression in the preceding interview was to claim that they still have sexual passion for each other. In one column of 'Who's On', it is implied that Sharon Stone's on-screen sexuality, and specifically her below-the-waist nudity in *Basic Instinct,* means it is impossible that she be, as it is claimed, a Mensa member with a high IQ.[11] Stars, such as George Clooney

---

9 *RTÉ Guide*, 20 January 2000, p. 5.
10 *RTÉ Guide*, 1 March 2000, p. 69.
11 *RTÉ Guide*, 20 January 2001, p. 68.

and John Cusack, who avoid the limelight, are treated more kindly and perceived as 'down-to earth'.

What is unique, peculiar and idiosyncratic in the Irish representation of non-Irish stars in the *RTÉ Guide* is that it is not conducted in terms of the collective representation (the idea) of the star with perpetual youth and beauty, but in terms of normative standards of Irish society. Thus, while *OK* might focus on a star's appearance or weight gain, the *RTÉ Guide* focuses instead on her unfulfilled dreams of motherhood or her loneliness and lack of friends; motherhood and community are more familiar ideals to an Irish readership than perpetual youth. If non-Irish stars are depicted in a neutral or even positive light, it is because they share perceived Irish values of family and community or because they state a longing for what we perceive we have. Jennifer Anniston may be rich and famous, but the article focuses entirely on her recent rift with her mother: 'So, as Jennifer relaxes in her mansion in the Hollywood Hills, the rest of us can muse that no matter how many satellite links, e-mails, faxes, pagers, voice-mails and answering services we acquire, communication between human beings can stand a lot of improvement'.[12] Jennifer Lopez may be gorgeous, and may have her posterior insured for a reputed $300m, but what she really wants is a baby. Michelle Pfeiffer may have starred in many blockbusters, but the headline for her interview reads: 'Being a Mom is my toughest role'.[13]

This is not to say that there is a one-to-one correspondence between the content of the *RTÉ Guide* or the dominant attitude of its readership, for individuals who read the guide are a very diverse group, many of whom undoubtedly read ironically, critically, playfully and instrumentally (some may only read it to get TV listings!). Nor is it to contest the extent to which such representation is an implicit critique of the

---

12 *RTE Guide*, 11 March 2000, p. 6.
13 *RTÉ Guide*, 8 April 2000, p. 25.

ideology of meritocracy in America. There, successful entertainers in America are clearly accorded a dispro-portionate degree of monetary reward, power and privilege: a symptom more generally of the polarisation between rich and poor and of the prioritisation of entertainment over social improvement. Rather, our analysis is intended to bring to light some questions about the way in which lines between 'us' and 'them' are being drawn in our understandings of the relationship between individuality and community.

'Kian's Diary': the (ironic) ideal ego of the 'Celtic tiger'

In a classic work of media content analysis, Adorno examined astrological columns in the *New York Times* in order to illustrate how astrology serves a variety of ideological functions in American society.[14] Adorno's critique of astrology focused on how it operates as wish fulfilment, exploiting ego weaknesses, narcissistic defences and other vulnerabilities of its readers in order to reproduce the dependence of individuals on its advice. Specifically, astrological advice is positioned midway between the actual social position of the reader and how they ideally imagine themselves. The point of Adorno's analysis is to demonstrate how astrology, like the American culture industry as a whole, is complicit in reproducing the ideological illusion that individuality can be achieved through consumption: that authoritarian personalities are made dependent by being wedded to an ethic of consumerism. Although his analysis of the culture industry has been critiqued for posing consumers of culture as uncritical, passive 'cultural dupes' in contrast to our current understanding of readers/ viewers as active and critical agents in the consumption of culture, his notion of culture as wish fulfilment and his use of psychoanalysis in formulating the collective unconscious

---

14 Theodor W. Adorno, *The Stars Down to Earth, and Other Essays on the Irrational in Culture*, London: Routledge, 1994.

of American consumerism provide an interesting angle on our understanding of contemporary Irish culture.

Using Adorno's analytic model, we argue that Irish ambivalence to individualism is manifest in the ideological representation of the superiority of the local over the global in Kian's weekly column in the *RTÉ Guide*. Although most readers probably read this column ironically or with tongue in cheek, aware that the portrayal of Kian (a member of the band Westlife) in this column is a fantasy construction concocted in combination with his publicist and an *RTÉ Guide* writer, this particular construction of Kian operates as the ego-ideal of how we should negotiate the excesses of globalisation that the 'Celtic tiger' has brought: he is at home in the global, yet espousing the values of the local. Despite its over-the-top quality, this column is appealing in that we are allowed to flesh out our self-perception, our collective fantasy of our imagined, new cosmopolitan selves through vicariously experiencing the fame, glamour and travel of Westlife.

Thus Kian and similar new Irish celebrities become 'ideal types of the new dependent average'.[15] In this column, Kian is portrayed as a hardworking, self-denying lad from Sligo. He does not get carried away with the glitz, glamour and excess of the international jet set. Kian is portrayed as a 'good boy' who 'misses his mammy'. For instance, most columns start or end with a statement of how little sleep he has had: 'I got up at 6 a.m. to write this', to represent him as hardworking and committed to the folks back home. Kian writes home every week, no matter how tired, thus portraying the new Irish global elite as self-sacrificing ambassadors for Ireland and continuing the tradition of the loyal emigrant. He jet sets at parties with the likes of Lionel Ritchie, George Michael or Mariah Carey, yet implies that his presence at these parties is for the good of Ireland, to

---

15 Theodor W. Adorno and Max Horkheimer, 'The Culture Industry: Enlightenment as Mass Deception', in *Dialectic of Enlightenment*, London: Verso, 1992, p. 145.

illustrate the basic decency of Irish people on the global stage.

The portrayal of Kian is intended to illustrate the superiority of Irish values over more international ones: he re-localises the global by describing these parties as 'a good laugh', 'a great buzz' or 'good craic', yet a pale substitute for 'watching the *Late Late Show*, going to the pub with my friends', and when on tour he says that he misses Irish sausages, claiming the food on tour is different and thus inferior. Thus the phantasmic depiction of Kian as familiar with the global but more fond of the local, as friend with the stars but a good Irish lad at heart, is designed to reconcile the contradictions between local and global by pretending that the global can be negotiated through the adherence to the values of the local – through the values of family, work, community, friendship and so on.

Similarly, in a separate article in the *RTÉ Guide*, Nicky from Westlife, one of the two lads in the band from Dublin, tells us how he writes to his girlfriend (incidentally Taoiseach, Bertie Ahern's daughter), 'who's always been there for [him], through thick and thin', reiterating and reconstituting the traditional Irish form of the faithful couple. The subtlety of this ideological fantasy woven around Kian and Nicky is a credit to the ingenuity of Irish boy-band impresario extraordinaire, Louis Walsh. Walsh is a master at negotiating the delicate and fragile liminal spaces between the symbolic orders of community and society, the rural and the urban, the local and the global, tradition and modernity. He is a successful Irish 'star-maker' because he can negotiate both the idioms of traditional community and modern society through which Ireland's collision culture is constituted: a 'culchie' from Mayo moved to the city, he is a combination of 'cute hoor' and 'global player'.

Though readers probably read 'Kian's Diary' as a deliberate and self-conscious fantasy construction, this representation of Kian resonates with and expresses the desires of the contemporary affluent Irish: to be able to speak

117

within the vernacular of the local and espouse cherished values of community, friendship, family and hard work, yet be equally at home in the global and an object of desire on the international stage.

Conclusion

The profile of Irish celebrity constitutes an index within which we can see the tensions between individual and community, tradition and modernity, and global and local. These tensions are not reconciled into one or other side of these analytic dichotomies. Rather, they produce hybrid fusions of contrasting forms, reflecting Ireland's collision culture. The notion of the Irish celebrity captures interesting tensions between the tendency towards individuation and community, and between the local and the global. This contradiction between the global and local gets prematurely reconciled in popular culture and becomes subsumed by the imperative of commercial success. In the context of the popular celebration of the success of Ireland's 'going global', the *RTÉ Guide*, and more generally the ambivalent discourse on celebrity in Ireland, keeps alive the idea that success in contemporary Irish culture should not be measured solely by mass commercial standards and by the universal global standard of cash value.

CHAPTER 8

The Cultural Economy of Dublin

ELLEN HAZELKORN AND COLM MURPHY

W riting in the 1940s, the Frankfurt School's Theodor Adorno and Max Horkheimer raised the spectre of the commodification of culture when they identified a growing link between business and art.[1] The culture industry, they wrote, administered a phoney, barbarised and anti-democratic mass culture; technology aided both its spread and influence. While contemporary theorists have offered a more nuanced understanding, suggesting that audiences are more inquisitive, selective and discerning than otherwise perceived, the cultural industries today are witness to the growing interpenetration between commerce and cultural goods and services. Their significance extends far beyond the pleasurable qualities of the visual and performing arts or the city-marketing strategies of cultural tourism built around museums, theatres and theme parks.

Across the globe, there has been a growing realisation that cultural products and services are important, not because people are spending more on leisure products and services, but because of the profound link between culture and new information and communication technologies

---

1 Theodor W. Adorno and Max Horkheimer, 'The Culture Industry: Enlightenment as Mass Deception', in *Dialectic of Enlightenment*, trans. John Cumming, New York: The Seabury Press, 1972.

(ICTs). Digital technology has provided the mechanism by which the productive base of an economy can arguably be expanded by transforming traditional arts (for example visual art, crafts, theatre, music, museums) into commodities of a cultural/media industry (for example broadcasting, film, recording, online publishing and new media products such as games). Cultural products and services have been drawn into the heart of the entrepreneurial initiative on the basis of their productive value rather than their aesthetic pleasure.[2]

Cultural commodification and its economic significance

The 1990s saw Ireland achieve an economic about-turn, a key element of which was new technology. Irish policy makers focused increasingly on a growth strategy led by the ICTs, which they saw as a means to leapfrog the historic and geographic limitations of the earlier industrial revolution and jump-start Irish economic growth. Taking advantage of rapid changes in social structure, relatively high public investment in and endorsement of education and advanced skills, and a natural reservoir of creativity, the strategy sought to market Ireland as an 'information gateway', an English-speaking beachhead between the US and Europe, with an emphasis on information distribution and products with a high cultural content. The government's commitment to carving out a niche for Ireland in the digital world as a provider/creator of cultural content is exemplified by the following extract from the report of the National Software Directorate:

> In many ways, Ireland is ideally situated to benefit greatly from the opportunities being offered by the Digital Age and the Internet. Ireland has a Diaspora of some 70 million in every corner of the world and the

---

2   David Morley and Kevin Robins, *Spaces of Identity. Global Media, Electronic Landscapes and Cultural Boundaries*, London: Routledge, 1997, p. 37.

Internet is a perfect technology with which to tap that huge potential market. For example, culture will be a primary product in the new millennium and Ireland has this in abundance.

Ireland has a plentiful supply of music, literature and a growing reputation for film/video production, not to mention excellent skills in the vital software area. These are the 'raw materials' of multimedia. However, these raw materials, unless they are properly exploited and turned into finished product, will be of little real benefit, in the sense that multimedia is about the synergy of these skills.[3]

That the arts and culture are at the centre of this debate about Irish economic development is not really new – state patronage of and involvement with the arts has a long history. What is new, however, is the level and attention that has been given to the role of the arts and cultural activity as a mechanism in urban regeneration since the 1980s. In this respect, the arts are seen as having an economic spillover effect in terms of labour intensity, tourism or as a vehicle for attracting business to a particular area.[4] Thus, planners have deliberately courted cultural/design innovators and brought them together in small clusters as part of urban renewal projects. The emergence of an arts-led strategy has concentrated on a crossover between the media and visual arts, drama, dance, music, design/craft and fashion, and their respective consumptive and productive elements, located around small managed workspaces and studios.[5] Dublin has followed the path of Glasgow, Barcelona and other cultural capitals of Europe and North America.

---

3   National Software Directorate, *Ireland: The Digital Age, the Internet*, Dublin: Enterprise Ireland, 1997.

4   John W. O'Hagan, *The State and the Arts. An Analysis of Key Economic Policy Issues in Europe and the United States*, Cheltenham: Edward Elgar, 1998, p. 31.

5   Derek Wynne, 'Cultural Industries', in Derek Wynne (ed.), *The Culture Industry*, Aldershot: Avebury, 1992, pp. 5, 15.

Zukin's statement that: 'culture is more and more the business of cities – the basis of their tourist attractions and their unique, competitive edge' is today an acknowledged truism.[6]

Dublin's Temple Bar initiative, announced in 1991, was aimed at the regeneration of a previously derelict and neglected urban space critically juxtaposed between two main commercial districts. The scheme sought to overlay a burgeoning but commercially ineffectual cluster of counter cultural bohemianism with 'commercially safe chic' using a combination of image industries (film, music, art, design, drama, multimedia and photography) as the engine of visual attractiveness on which to drive urban and economic revival. Despite the deliberate marketing of the area as the cultural quarter of Dublin, with an array of state/city-sponsored cultural and educational centres, shops, restaurants and public and private housing, it did not become a localised cultural–industrial district. The over-determining force behind such urban renewal/regeneration projects has, however, been driven by the consumer not production. Thus, while these areas are and remain popular with tourists and day-trippers, there are significant doubts as to their ability to generate real wealth.

As global competition heats up, national and supra-national (for example the EU) economies have sought to identify new sectors ripe for take-off. Cultural activity was once associated only with traditional visual and performing arts and entertainment activity, although it did include museums and exhibitions; beginning in the 1980s, it took on a greater importance as a vehicle or focal point of urban regeneration. This chapter looks at the way in which cultural and creative activity has become increasingly identified as a potential mechanism of national economic regeneration, drawing upon the growing intersection between software, content and cultural products.

---

6   Sharon Zukin, *The Culture of Cities,* Malden and Oxford: Blackwell, 1995, p. 2.

Ireland's multimedia industry and Dublin's digital media district

In 1996 the government was being strongly urged to establish a digital media/multimedia industry as the centrepiece of a new economic strategy. Multimedia sits at the intersection between advanced (digital) technology and cultural products and services. It integrates and blends a wide range of creative skills, such as graphics, moving and still image, text and sound, with a computer software platform, to produce new, interactive, 'content'. This is in contrast to television, film, radio or print, which require only a passive and limited engagement with the material being viewed or listened to. Accordingly, there is a distinction between lean-back and lean-forward technology; the former are more traditional audio-visual formats that can lead to 'couch-potato syndrome', while the latter are new-media formats that require the user to become actively engaged. The design, development and, arguably, the work practices associated with multimedia are also distinctive, combining software programming and creative skills as part of an integrated team or, increasingly, within the same multi-skilled individual.

Ireland had been one of Europe's pioneers in multimedia, effectively stumbling into it through an involvement in software research, a key strategic mission of various government agencies since the 1980s. However by the mid-1990s, both its reputation and state interest had waned due to the (mis)belief that multimedia was not a viable proposition. The sector revived after 1997, this time without state involvement. Instead, it was propelled by technological convergence that accompanied the move from analogue to digital and the diffusion of open standard Internet technology. Dublin emerged as the preferred location for 87 per cent of the Republic's software companies by 1998; its large customer base, international airport and skill base facilitated multimedia's growth, the latter benefiting from the former's technical skill base.

Table 1: *Dublin's multimedia sector, 2000*

	Number of companies	Number employed
Home-based one-person operations	79	79
Micro-enterprises	144	360
Indigenous businesses (25+ staff)	12	970
Foreign-owned businesses (25+ staff)	7	680
Total	242	2,089

Source: *Dublin Institute of Technology Survey.*

The rate of growth has been significant, expanding from 57 multimedia companies in Dublin in 1997 to 242 by March 2001, directly generating an estimated 2,089 jobs.[7] The sector can be divided into four distinct tiers: small 'kitchen-table' operations, micro-enterprises, internationally competitive Irish companies and foreign-owned companies (see Table 1). The majority, 59 per cent, are micro-enterprises with few staff, usually producing websites or engaging in maintenance and training on a contract basis for local companies. These are generally located within a one-mile radius of Dublin city centre, with the only significant cluster to emerge located around Baggot Street, in the south city centre. The bottom tier includes home-based, one-person operations, generally concentrated in the north and south Dublin suburbs and working on small-scale Internet development to service local businesses: they account for 3.7

---

7   Figures calculated from industry directories, companies' registration office filings and information from individual companies; cf. Farrell Grant Sparks, *The Irish Multimedia Industry. A Current Profile and Future Development Strategy,* Dublin, 1995.

per cent of employment in the sector in Dublin and 33 per cent of companies. The larger multinational companies, like world leaders AOL and Microsoft, localise in Dublin their primarily North American multimedia content for international audiences and provide customer service for the European market.

Only twelve indigenous multimedia companies have made the transition to internationally competitive operations, having originated as text-based computer trainers in the mid-1980s. Of Dublin's six largest such companies, half of them, SmartForce, Riverdeep and Intuition Publishing, all global leaders in their online training niches, trace their lineage to CBT Systems, a text-based trainer set-up by former salesman, Pat McDonagh, in 1985. These six companies had annual sales in 2000 of €189m and were valued at €2.3bn. They accounted for more than 40 per cent of employment in the multimedia sector in Dublin. More significantly they have produced a number of spin-offs, helping to create a self-sustaining multimedia milieu in Dublin.

The indigenous Irish multimedia companies are primarily focused on professional training and e-learning products for global niche markets. Originally concentrated in information technology and financial services, these products have expanded into the American school curriculum, telecommunications, healthcare, customer service and general management. Sub-contract website-development work and localising multinational publishers' multimedia titles for non-North American markets are also important. In the future, the sector could build upon this expertise, using new broadband capacity to deliver interactive content in different languages to international markets in a variety of digital formats.

The Irish government has had a sporadic relationship with multimedia until recently. Its determination to catapult Ireland into the twenty-first century's global digital economy, coupled with these companies' successes (see Table 2), led to the announcement in 2000 of the development of

Table 2: *Multimedia companies' contribution to Dublin's economy, 2000*

Rank by sales	Name	Total employees globally	Total sales	Description	Valuation
1	SmartForce	1,200	€145m	Global leader in online IT training	€1,661m
2	WBT Systems	66	€18m	Global leader in online training infrastructure	€40m*
3	Digital Channel Partners	150	€9.4m	Online site construction	€35m*
4	Riverdeep	410	€7.7m	Global leader in online high school learn-ing aids	€605m
5	Intuition Publishing	60	€5.4m	Global leader in online financial services training	€15m*
6	Interactive Services	110	€3.7m	Online training for telecoms	€12m*
Total			€189m		€2,368m

Note: * *Estimates based on private investments made in companies.*
Sources: *Nasdaq; Companies Registration Office, Dublin; individual companies; Davy Stockbrokers; Goodbody Stockbrokers.*

two digital hubs, one in the Liberties area of Dublin and the other at Citywest, a new industrial park on Dublin's western outskirts. Under the auspices of Enterprise Ireland, these hubs form a key part of an industrial development strategy incorporating the multimedia sector. The Tele-communications Advisory Committee, the Content Advisory Group of the Information Society Commission and, more recently, the Irish Council for Science, Technology and Innovation (ICSTI) recommended the creation of designated districts to galvanise this dispersed sector into an innovative digital media cluster. ICSTI argued that it would bring Ireland to a higher level in the global ICT market, an achievement unattainable without such intervention. In this way, the final element of the government's triangular strategy was borne: provision of technological infra-structure; alterations to the financial and regulatory/legislative environment, including fiscal policy, security and intellectual property rights; and provision of content innovation and development.[8]

This consensus meant that when the Massachusetts Institute of Technology's (MIT) Media Laboratory, one of the world's leading digital media research centres, approached Taoiseach, Bertie Ahern TD, seeking a European base, it was effectively a done deal. As one senior civil servant described the process: 'We don't have a bureaucratic system like the French and Germans. We are just opportunistic future grabbers'.[9] Media Lab Europe (MLE) opened in Thomas Street, Dublin, in July 2000, after the state agreed to provide €36m for MIT management, intellectual property rights and running costs for the first five years. In return, MLE proposes to become fully self-financing by 2010.

Earlier, Forfás, the industrial policy development agency, had been asked by the government to identify possible

---

8   See Ellen Hazelkorn, 'The Dynamics of Cultural Production in Ireland: Economic Strategy, Digital Technology and Public Policy Making', in K. Ernst, M. Halbertsma, S. Janssen and T. Ijdens (eds), *Trends and Strategies in the Arts and Cultural Industries,* Rotterdam: Barjesteh and Company, 2001.
9   Background briefing to one of the authors in May 2001 by a senior civil servant who advises the Irish government on economic policy making.

locations for clusters of digital media industries where a node for a new broadband pipeline, capable of carrying data at fifteen times its speed and at a fraction of current costs, could also be placed. Forfás identified the Thomas Street/ Coombe area of south city Dublin, around the Guinness brewery, in 1999. The availability of cheap land in close proximity to the city centre, already a hub for arts/cultural activity via Temple Bar, was a further attraction. Forfás argued that creative individuals would be unwilling to work in the more sterile National Digital Park at Citywest, where the second node for technical e-commerce was to be located. Significantly, Dublin Corporation had also designated the Thomas Street/Liberties/Coombe area for regeneration; after decades of industrial decline and the gradual with-drawal/restructuring of Guinness, the area was blighted by social and physical dereliction.

The south city location brings together several significant elements: a digital media industrial strategy, international research and urban regeneration. MLE is viewed as the crucial 'anchor tenant', around which research and develop-ment facilities, small business incubators and support services will grow. While Silicon Valley (San Jose, Cali-fornia) and Silicon Alley (New York City) grew 'naturally', the Irish government, like other national and city govern-ments around the world, is seeking to recreate these 'regional systems of creativity and innovation' via 'the right mixture of entrepreneurial know-how, creative energy and public policy'.[10] Accordingly, projects like Dublin's digital media district have become an important ingredient in city/regional (economic) (re)development strategy.

A political economy of cultural production

The emergence and growth of a digital media/multimedia sector in Ireland and elsewhere has been associated with

10 Allen J. Scott, *The Cultural Economy of Cities,* London: Sage, 2000, pp. 17, 209.

significant changes in working practices and company structures. These changes have undoubtedly been influenced by the very radical shift from analogue to digital technology, which has significantly simplified and democratised the process of production, as well as reducing the costs of production, enabling almost anyone with access to computers and creative talent to produce content.

Face-to-face interviews with multimedia workers reveal several common features.[11] Irish multimedia companies, like their staff, are predominately young, with a handful of employees. The workforce needs to be flexible with respect to working conditions and time. Perhaps unusually, educational pathways are diverse, encompassing all levels and types of educational qualifications, but nevertheless focused on some core skills: visual arts, computer/technical and business/managerial. There is a significant level of fluidity or criss-crossing between firms, with many of those interviewed having only recently arrived at their present job. Pay levels vary accordingly, with sophisticated programming and/or good experience highly rewarded. Most work is conducted via small project teams, built around a group of multi-skilled individuals, although there is a significant element of sub-contracting amongst each other. Comments include:

> Basically, my job changes all the time and that suits me fine . . . I like to be doing a mixture of programming and graphics . . . It's trying to balance skills really . . . So it's really a big benefit if you can cross over those two areas.

> You really have to be a self-starter . . . you just presume it's up to you to get the job done, if you don't do it right then its on your head.

---

11 Interviews were conducted during winter/spring 2000 among employees of a small but representative sample of Irish multimedia companies.

Conclusion

By choosing to focus on the opportunities arising from the ICTs, and particularly the links between arts/culture, commerce and ICTs, the Irish state is seeking to play to its internationally acknowledged strengths. Perhaps most importantly, by welding a broad industrial economic strategy to an urban regeneration project, the city/state strategy seeks to emulate some major global success stories. These 'commodified cultural production systems' have thrived by virtue of their size, density and heterogeneity, and the 'right mix of know-how, creative energy and public policy'.[13] Some claim that the 'Digital Media District will provide a platform from which to leverage and stimulate the opportunities within the media environment . . . [which] is vital if knowledge exchange and integration of creativity and technology can occur'.[14] In addition, the Dublin Chamber of Commerce has been lobbying to establish an air link between the Silicon Valley and the Silicon Island.

Will the strategy work? After explosive growth between 1997 and 2000, the multimedia industry has recently gone into an equally sharp decline with several showpiece indigenous multimedia companies, like Nua and Ebeon, disappearing overnight. With the focus on cost containment among the remaining indigenous multimedia companies, getting the Digital Media District off the ground may prove just as challenging for the state as the Temple Bar and International Financial Services Centre urban renewal projects.

---

13 Allen J. Scott, *The Cultural Economy of Cities,* London: Sage, 2000, p. 209.
14 Enterprise Ireland, *ITS 2007*, Dublin: Enterprise Ireland, 2000.

CHAPTER 9

A Century of Change

J. PADDY O'CARROLL

If the twentieth century in the Republic of Ireland has to be encapsulated briefly it may be possible to see it as having been devoted to two main aims: the legitimation of the state and the development of the economy. The first section of this chapter deals with the origins of the society and the legitimation of the state in the aftermath of independence. This was achieved by the promotion of an intensely centred, monolithic culture, which, despite globalisation, still retains much influence. The second section examines the largely state-led pursuit of prosperity in the latter half of the century. Despite recent successes, it is still a prosperity distributed on the basis of a distinct hierarchy of entitlements, underwritten by the dominant political culture.

Finally, no description of the politics of the last quarter of the twentieth century can omit the efforts of various social movements to challenge the corporate state to expand its vision of democracy by including a social and cultural project. A key thesis of this analysis is that, though the dominant political culture with its focus on consensus has contributed significantly to both political integration and state-led economic development, it has stymied develop-ment of the public sphere as a forum in which communities can articulate their differences and thus develop a sense of agency and skills in self-organisation. The establishment of a more participative political institutional structure is seen to be vital in addressing contemporary issues such as immigration and equitable redistribution of wealth.

The epoch of identity formation, 1922 to 1948

The beginning of the twentieth century saw the culmination of a number of processes that had been underway for almost a century. Throughout most of Europe the power of the landed elites had been under threat by the rise of industrial society. In Ireland the outcome of this struggle was the various land acts, culminating in the Wyndham Land Act of 1907. Most of the land of the country passed into the hands of the tenant. Ownership of the land in a predominantly rural economy not only conferred enormous economic power on this class, but also enabled it and its commercial cohorts to shape the history of Irish society throughout most of the twentieth century.

As its economic situation improved, the tenant class became more concerned with its lack of prestige and political power. The response was the many cultural and political movements of the last quarter of the nineteenth century, many of which are still very influential today, such as the Gaelic Athletic Association (GAA), the Co-operative Movement, the expansion in education and in the activities of the Catholic Church and The Gaelic League. These movements followed quickly on the growth of prosperity and did much to raise the status of these classes.

In the political sphere various nationalist movements, most notably Sinn Féin, sought power commensurate with their economic position and ultimately achieved independence. The response of the different classes to the outbreak of World War I indicated a parting of the ways: the former landed classes and the poor joined the British forces and the middle group remained at home to pursue its burgeoning political interests.

The Wyndham Act, therefore, should probably be regarded as a key foundation event of Irish society. Indeed, it could be argued that, as a symbol of the society which evolved in the twentieth century, it is more important than 1916 and the achievement of independence. Certainly the latter would have been very unlikely in its absence. The land acts are also symbolic in that they formed the basis of the major social cleavage in Irish society – that between owners and non-owners. They also presaged a salient characteristic of Irish society that has persisted to this day – a clear notion that within the national community there should be a strict hierarchy of entitlements – because, from its inception, the benefits of land reform were to accrue only to the sectors of the community already in possession of the land.

In modern Ireland, capital still appears to get preferential treatment from the state, and educational policies do little to ensure that all citizens are provided with cultural capital commensurate with their abilities. Ireland has not yet become a meritocracy; with the result that society is denied the benefits of the potential achievements of many.

The formation of identity is a continuous process in every society, but in certain circumstances societies are forced to focus their energies almost completely on this objective. It will be argued that so effective was the 'revolutionary' generation's pursuit of hegemony in this period that it not only ensured the legitimation of the state, but also produced a political culture that was so intensely centred that its effects are hindering the development of a democracy appropriate to the evolving concerns of today's society.

Despite the rhetoric of a new beginning, most existing laws continued in force and, to this day, their continuation is provided for under Article 50 of the Constitution; an unwritten British constitution of Ireland as it were.[1] The new elite was, to a large extent, happy to adopt the socio-political and socio-moral views reflected in the laws of its

---

1   J. O'Connor, 'Article 50 of Bunreacht na h-Éireann and the Unwritten English Constitution of Ireland', in J. P. O'Carroll and J. A. Murphy (eds), *De Valera and his Times*, Cork: Cork University Press, 1983.

predecessor. Identity changed slowly. Fifty years later, it is difficult to credit that in 1952 the front page of the *Irish Independent* was published with a wide black surround to mark the death of King George VI and that in Dublin many middle-class girls still vied with each other in collecting cuttings of 'the princesses, Elizabeth and Margaret Rose'.

Cumann na nGaedheal's political style was aloof and largely unresponsive to the particular popular expectations of a polity in the early stages of independence. Tending to confuse government with politics, it depoliticised most decision making.[2] As a result, the regime crucially failed to incorporate into a political community the two-thirds of the electorate, mostly from the poorer sectors of society, who had recently been given the vote. The benefits of economic development accrued mainly to the better-off sectors. Cumann na nGaedheal's inability to create an inclusive political community left the way open for the new Fianna Fáil party to adopt a more symbolic approach.

De Valera's pursuit of a more complete independence and self-sufficiency placed national pride before national product. Of even greater symbolic import was the decision to withhold the payment of land annuities to Britain, repayments due for loans extended for the purchase of land from previous owners. This, along with the emphasis on the revival of the Irish language and the campaign to end partition, struck a chord with all the popular symbolic codes of the community: the primordial (land), the mundane (rural way of life) and the cultural (nation).

De Valera's choice of the foreign affairs portfolio reflected his re-introduction of political tensions into a relationship his predecessors had left to professional diplomats. In 1937 he produced a new constitution, which, though largely reflecting his own views, stopped short of declaring a republic. His mission of political integration and identity

---

2   R. Fanning, *The Irish Department of Finance 1922–1958,* Dublin: IPA, 1978.

formation was greatly assisted by his avid support of the popular demand for neutrality and by his reply to Churchill's victory speech snub in 1945. In summary, de Valera's main contribution was to prioritise the building of a political community, a task largely neglected by the previous regime. The method was the construction of a Catholic, nationalist narrative of Irish identity based on opposition to Britain, nativism and a version of history emphasising shared heroic victimhood. The image of the small community was central. Such communities were, in reality, largely the property-owning rump of a society riven by emigration. Ownership formed the basis of the greatest cleavage in society and also in the family, as surplus family members were generally faced with loss of status.

Idealisation of the family concealed the potential for considerable sexual suppression. Ownership, which came largely with age, not only demanded extreme deference, but also validated knowledge which, given the limited opportunities for formal education, could be acquired largely only by experience. Church, state and community thus created an extremely centred culture in which authority was supreme. John B. Keane's assertion that 'authority was God' characterised exactly the penetration of all domains of traditional life by the sacred. Power depended on all of this remaining largely unspoken, and it took the changes of the impious 1960s to reveal its latent foundations.

The moral monopoly implied by Fianna Fáil's claim to be more a national movement than a party thus contributed powerfully to the marginalisation of the diversity of identities that reflected the wide range of Irish historical experiences involving conquest, colonisation and integration into an empire. Urban culture was a major victim. This narrative privileged farmers, business and associated professional classes, placing them close to the centre of society and thus underpinning the communal hierarchy of entitlements. The consequence of the continual emphasis on common experience was the denial of the alternative narratives and interests of Protestants, labour, women and all other minorities. The importance of interdependence and of the creation of a fully participative democracy was concealed.

Both regimes also shared a vision of a largely rural society and a distinctly 'Irish' Ireland. Widespread censorship became the order of the day. Furthermore, the nationalist elite and the Catholic Church shared an idealistic conceptualisation of Irish identity, which incorporated a strong element of anti-modernism. The dominant class had arrived and were full of confidence and satisfied with life. The seminaries and novitiates were the growth industries of the times and the volunteers for the foreign missions reached unimaginable proportions. Instead of considering measures to reverse the processes that marginalised large sections of society, the establishment struggled incessantly to ward off the forces of change.

Typical of this course of action was the campaign to combat the evils of jazz. One rural parish priest, for example, organised a monster ceilidh band which he conducted in his soutane with a blackthorn stick. He would 'poke you in the guts' if you were not keeping up with the music. Simultaneously, however, former traditional musicians in the same parish were entertaining their dance hall audiences with *Yes, we have no bananas* long before it was ever heard on radio or gramophone. The sheet music had come from Bridie X, one of the marginalised, a former parishioner in Chicago.

Pax Americana, *Europe, economic development and social change*

Both governments, Cumann na nGaedheal (1922–32) and Fianna Fáil (1932–48), had been confronted with the need to solve the problem of extreme urban and rural poverty. Civil war, a world depression, an economic war with Britain that lasted until 1938, and World War II, all stymied the course of development. The state's vision did not stretch to a policy of industrialisation that might have provided employment and stemmed emigration. There was considerable export of capital. Like his predecessor, de Valera attempted a gradual modernisation, but this was based on self-sufficiency rather than free trade.

Ireland entered the post-war era undamaged by war, with a huge labour pool, considerable external reserves and a small contribution from the Marshall Fund.[3] Yet, while other countries enjoyed unprecedented prosperity under the new *pax Americana,* Irish development reached crisis point with the lowest productivity in Europe and a level of emigration that seemed to threaten the state's very survival. Many communities lost a complete younger generation. It might be asked why all of our European neighbours, who were burdened with debt and had seen much of their property demolished and young men maimed and killed, had responded much more effectively to the rising post-war tide.

The immediate answer lay in the continued dependence on agriculture and the British market with its policy of cheap food. The failure to industrialise and enjoy the benefits of the post-war boom can be related to the narrowness of vision of the industrial class and their total lack of professional training. On a broader front, the role of emigration was crucial. Denmark's poor, for example, did not allow themselves to be marginalised into emigration, but organised politically and forced a compromise that brought about institutional change.[4] In Ireland, emigration, which relieved political pressure to take action, must be recognised as the main cause of continuing institutional stasis throughout much of the twentieth century.

The outcome of the crisis was a greatly increased involvement by the hitherto reluctant state in economic

---

3   K. Kennedy, T. Giblin and D. McHugh, *The Economic Development of Ireland in the Twentieth Century,* London: Routledge, 1988.

4   L. Mjøset, *The Irish Economy in International Institutional Perspective,* Dublin: National Economic and Social Council, 1992.

affairs. The move to industrialisation had begun. Henceforth, the scale of the state's involvement in promoting economic development dwarfed that of indigenous business. Much of the material infrastructure and many of the institutions that still guide the economy in areas such as manufacturing, services, agriculture, tourism and fisheries, were founded in the 1950s. In 1958, the year the Treaty of Rome was signed and as de Valera was about to retire from active politics, serious economic planning commenced; a process that gave rise to a powerful cadre who did much to shape modern Ireland. Gradually, both agriculture and industry began to be put on a competitive footing.

Exports of industrial goods increased, at first indigenous entrepreneurs were very slow to enter export markets, but the pace quickened as foreign businesses responded to incentives such as very generous export tax relief. By the late 1960s industrial exports equalled those from agriculture, tourism was booming and the economy was moving away from complete dependency on the British market towards free trade under the aegis of the European Community, which Ireland joined in 1973.

In the process the Republic of Ireland had become an industrialised society. For the first time more than half the population were living in settlements of more than 1,500 inhabitants, universal second-level education was on offer and unemployment and emigration had decreased to levels never before experienced. These economic changes were soon to run into difficulties, but the more lasting effect of this opening up to the outside was the initiation of a radical and far-reaching change in popular culture.

The response of farmers to the Common Agricultural Policy quickly gave the lie to the 'traditional' label that had been foisted on them. Production grew enormously as those who could moved to a high-cost, high-output regime that exported most of the output. The face of the countryside was changed by investment in both home and business. Co-operatives grew enormously and were very quickly de-mutualised to create huge agribusinesses with a worldwide reach. This sector in time provided most of the significant home-grown transnational corporations.[5]

The move to global capitalism was soon signalled by the soaring cost of inputs, the cyclical collapses of commodity prices, the threat to health and tourism from widespread environmental pollution and the escalation of competition that soon marginalised two-thirds of farmers as costs of relentless technological innovation increased. Finally, the ordeal that is change was fully comprehended when taxation became a central concern for the successful, while those who could not claim their birthright faced loss of status as they joined the ranks of the rural non-farming sector.

The same globalisation created the context that gave rise to the 'Celtic tiger'. The state's membership of the EU, favourable taxation policies, and a tractable English-speaking workforce fulfilled the American transnational corporations' need of the moment for a foothold in the EU markets. Ireland is now best understood as a link between Boston and Berlin. Three-quarters of industrial exports originate in a very small number of transnational companies in the pharmaceutical, soft drinks and micro-electronic sectors and US companies employ 30 per cent of the workforce.[6] The intrinsic weakness of such an economy lies in the predominance of this mobile sector and the failure of most indigenous corporations to integrate into the global economy.[7]

It is obvious, therefore, that the capacity of the state to control events and create prosperity is much more limited than is claimed by the cheerleaders for recent techniques of

---

5   H. Tovey and P. Share, *A Sociology of Ireland,* Dublin: Gill and Macmillan, 2000.

6   D. O'Hearn, 'The Celtic Tiger: The Role of Multinationals', in J. McLoughlin and E. Crowley (eds), *Under the Belly of the Tiger,* Dublin: Irish Reporter Publications, 1997.

7   J. P. O'Carroll, 'Cork: The Political Context', in B. Brunt and K. Hourihan (eds), *Perspectives on Cork*, Cork: Geographical Society of Ireland, 1998.

governance such as the ubiquitous partnership arrangements. Such success as has been achieved is due to a fortuitous, and possibly ephemeral, correspondence between the Irish situation and the need of the moment of international capital over which the Irish state has no control. This has not lessened the hegemony of the powerful state apparatus.

The limits of the capacity of the state had been obvious from the beginning. It is remarkable, for example, that, despite the euphoria of independence, the level of public sector expenditure fell far below that of other European states at the time. This was in no small way due to resistance to the taxation of property, one of the most remarkable and persistent features of the taxation system. Furthermore, while poverty and emigration increased, Ireland continued to be an exporter of capital. When the state turned its attention to industrial development, capital was provided from borrowings and ultimately paid for out of taxation, a burden that still falls disproportionately on the poorer sections of society. Widespread tax evasion, which persisted despite numerous tax amnesties, has been revealed by a number of tribunals. At the height of rural prosperity, the income tax contribution from farming was miniscule. Among the developed economies, Ireland has the second most inequitable distribution of wealth and has been congratulated by a Texan think tank as the third 'freest' economy in the world.

Social, cultural and political change

The changes and upheavals of the 1960s provided an initial vantage point from which the scope and depth of the 'taken-for-granteds' of the previous generation could be seen. The Catholic, nationalist narrative was incapable of accommodating the conflict in Northern Ireland, participation in the European Community and the gradual Americanisation of culture and the economy. These experiences, and exposure through television and travel to other global

cultural changes, undermined the hegemony of establishment culture. It rendered visible the full diversity of
identities and allowed them social space in which to thrive.
From the point of view of politics and governance, the most
significant development was the decentring of what had
been a very centred culture.

As a result of the expansion of industrial employment in
the 1960s, the whole nature of community life was changed
by the presence, for the first time in living memory, of many
young people, female as well as male, with money to spend.
The contrast between these and their siblings kept waiting,
often in drudgery, penury and celibacy, to inherit family
businesses and farms did much to highlight the morphology
of the culture and to provide the impetus to question the
taken-for-granted aspects of patriarchal peasant life
idealised by church and state. The many private tensions
and challenges arising from these changes foreshadowed the
political and cultural strife of the remainder of the century.

The growth of industrial employment and a rural non-
farming culture diminished the social and political pre-
eminence of the urban-commercial and farming classes.
Industrial employment offered a five-day week, undreamt of
remuneration and the possibility of convivial weekends.
Young women were now able to find work locally but
rejected liaisons with impecunious young farmers, giving
rise to the rural bachelor phenomenon. Patriarchal power
and authority was weakened by the new generation and in
some instances surrendered completely on the grounds that
'they are earning more in a week than I ever earned in a
month'. Prosperity gave rise to a baby boom.

However, deference was still the order of the day at the
national level. Lemass upbraided Radio Telefis Éireann
(RTÉ) for running an Irish Farmers Association response
immediately after an interview that he had given concerning a dispute between the government and farmers.
Bishops, unused to being asked to defend their views in
public, felt aggrieved by the confrontational style of television. The introduction of television, the explosion of youth

culture and the expansion of education from the 1960s onwards greatly undermined these claims to deference and led to the questioning of authority.

The next three decades witnessed extraordinary cultural changes that challenged most of the central tenets of the official culture. The 1970s commenced with the rise of identity politics in Northern Ireland and the resulting outbreak of conflict soon gave rise to a revision of the nationalist narrative. The recognition of the autonomy of the northern state weakened the particular understanding of the guiding aspiration to national unity. A second identity movement, for women's liberation, soon challenged the official attitude to family and sexuality. Finally, after the triumphal first visit of a Pope to Ireland, it was soon revealed that the apparently monolithic institutions of Irish Catholicism were in disarray, a development welcomed by some, but a source of apprehension to those aware of the dearth of any secular replacement for its moral monopoly and community services.

The sight of a Taoiseach entering the lobbies in opposition to his party's liberalisation of controls on contraception symbolised the extent to which the duties of faith continued to supersede those of citizenship. These departures quickly gave rise to a politics of cultural defence around issues such as contraception, divorce, abortion and homosexuality. The debate around the divorce referendum, for example, stirred emotions emanating from elements deep within the culture: property, family, religion and nation. The intense reaction to these proposals ignored many changes in family and sexuality that had, in fact, already occurred, treating them instead as a threat to identity.

Political change followed quickly on economic development and cultural change. A second layer of political parties arose based on a left–right cleavage more characteristic of an industrial society. Labour appeared to be emerging at last from the shadows to which nationalism had relegated it and reached its highest degree of popularity. The identity of

Fianna Fáil, so long the dominant party in the political system, was shaken by having to enter coalition. Probably the greatest political conversion of the century was the fervent adoption of the market principle by parties that owed their legitimacy to their success in depicting the state as a subsidy-oriented community.

However, the expansion in education and in access to information through the Internet, increase in numbers of women employed outside the home, and exposure to global cultural change soon added a third, largely extra-parliamentary, layer to political life. This was composed of movements such as the Green Party and the women's movement, with the latter being effective in the election of President Mary Robinson. They challenged the reduction of politics to the narrow pursuit of affluence and the mono-polisation of legitimacy and attempted to usher in a concept-ualisation of democracy as a social and cultural project.

In the last two decades of the century many older cultures emerged from the shadows, and new cultures evolved in response to growing affluence, creating a diversity that would have been anathema to the guardians of earlier monolithic orthodoxies. The celebration of anniversaries such as the founding of the GAA, the famine and the 1798 rebellion showed both a growing official sophistication in bending the past to current advantage and an increasing willingness on the part of many diverse groups to challenge official interpretations. The GAA felt that RTÉ's commemorative programme failed to conform to orthodoxy and was able to insist on a remake. Commemora-tion of the famine opened the state to severe criticism for neglect of emigrants both prior to and after emigrating and the official harnessing of the celebration of 1798 to the peace process evoked mild dissent from Sinn Féin and howls of protest from some Wexford communities who felt their role had not been properly acknowledged.[8]

---

8   See P. O'Carroll, 'Re-membering 1798', in E. Slater and M. Peillon (eds), *Memories of the Present*, Dublin: IPA, 2000, pp. 15–23.

145

community and partnership for a long time served the purposes of the state, its inner circle of supporters and its mandarin class, by covertly bolstering political integration, loyalty and partisanship among a relatively homogenous population. However, despite its success, this ideology questions the validity of dissent, renders independent voluntary activity suspect and encourages cronyism and clientelism. Control and marginalisation is the aim. Corporatism limits agendas and curtails agency, particularly among the poor, who are usually unorganised. Most alarming, the *Report of the Constitution Review Group* seems to suggest that no change is needed and has little to say about the future development of democratic structures.[10]

The current ideology, banal though it may be, conflates society with nation and economy, and fails to identify and discriminate between the nature and appropriate functions of community, public sphere and the state.[11] Society itself has been largely neglected. There is thus a failure to recognise the importance of the public sphere, a key component of modern democracy in which communities articulate their differences, attempt persuasion and ensure enforcement of legal entitlements. The weakness of the public sphere is reflected, for example, in the fact that inequities and malfeasances that all were aware of could remain so long uncurbed. As long as this culture lag exists, as long as the state prioritises its own legitimacy to the detriment of elements of the polity, it will deprive its citizens of the opportunity to develop their own culture and identity.

---

10 Constitution Review Group (CRG), *Report of the Constitution Review Group,* Dublin: Government Publications, 1996.

11 J. P. O'Carroll, 'Culture Lag and Democratic Deficit in Ireland: "Dat's outside de terms of d'agreement"', *Community Development Journal*, vol. 37, no. 1, 2002, pp. 10–19.

PART 3

UNEASY INTERFACES

CHAPTER 10

The Business of Culture:
New Media Industries in Ireland

APHRA KERR

W
e live in a changing media environment that has
significant consequences for our everyday lives.
There is an increasing number of cinema screens,
there are more television and radio channels, as well as a
proliferation of personal computers providing multiple information and entertainment platforms. Early information
society writers believed that these new technologies would
lead to more decentralised media companies, two-way
interactive communication between users and producers,
and radically new forms of authorship. In the new
information society, there would be a flowering of new forms
of community and culture alongside increased access to, and
appreciation of, older forms of culture.[1] At the same time,
the spread of global corporations, global media systems and
global travel has lead others to fear that new media
technologies may promote global homogenisation and the
elimination of cultural differences.

While it is easy to quantify the increasing numbers of
media channels, it is somewhat more difficult to assess the
scope, quality and diversity of communications content, and
its impact on local cultures. Has there been any increase in

---

1   S. Jones (ed.), *Doing Internet Research: Critical Issues and Methods
for Examining the Net*, Berkeley, CA: Sage, 1999.

cultural expression and participation as a result of the introduction of new media during the 1990s? Have users become more or less involved in the content production process because of new technologies? As corporate bodies move to establish their presence on the Internet, will minority or dissenting voices be heard? Rarely do we get a chance to look behind the scenes and ask who controls the cultural production process and what factors shape the messages that inform our daily lives. New media industries are not subject to a regulatory regime in the same way as traditional broadcast services. Therefore, the key values that inform public service broadcasting, such as quality, accessibility and diversity, are lacking. In the purely commercial environment of the multimedia industry, what are the key factors that determine the creation of symbolic content and spaces of communication?

The purpose of this chapter is to examine the increasingly complex relationship between local, national and global culture as mediated through new media technologies. Drawing on case studies from the multimedia sector in Ireland, I will examine how public policy, cultural factors and techno-economic issues shape multimedia content production.[2] This story highlights the complex relationship between end users and particular local cultures on the one hand, and global corporate strategies on the other. It also points to the continuing, if changing, role of the nation-state in the global politics of industrial location, regulation and promotion.

Toward a definition of multimedia

Multimedia technologies are an evolving cluster of digital technologies which include the Internet, CD-ROMs, DVDs,

---

2   This chapter is based on research I conducted for a PhD thesis entitled 'Ireland in the Global Information Economy. Innovation and Multimedia "Content" Industries', Dublin: Dublin City University, 1999.

satellite and cable technologies. Online multimedia technologies are distinguished by their ability to overcome space and time. We can easily email family on the other side of the world or play online games against strangers in the next town. Multimedia technologies also enable people to locate themselves beyond physical spaces in what has been called a 'space of flows.[3] Certainly, as more people spend more time in non-physical online and offline space, there are implications for their experience of physical place, community and culture. But we must be careful not to completely separate this space from physical space and real life. People bring to their media experiences a wealth of experience and knowledge and these can be actively reshaped in both real and virtual spaces. Culture, whether local, national or other, is not a fixed entity but is continually in the process of being remade through everyday practices.

What distinguishes multimedia content producers is not that they use digital technologies, but that they produce content for dissemination on/by these digital technologies. As such, these industries are involved in the production of various forms of information that are used by companies and citizens to create both knowledge and culture, broadly defined. A critical mass of multimedia companies developed during the 1990s in Ireland.[4] These combined a range of different skills including computer programming, print, graphic design and audio-visual techniques.

The multimedia sector in the early 1990s produced commercial Internet and CD-ROM products and EU-funded, interactive installations for heritage centres and museums. A feature of the wider Irish context of new media development throughout the 1990s was the move from multiple definitions of multimedia, to one stable definition

---

3   M. Castells, *The Rise of the Network Society,* Oxford: Blackwell, 1996.
4   This includes hardware, software and content companies. The use of the term multimedia in Ireland is explored in the next section.

that reflected the vested interests of particular groups in society. Commercial rather than cultural imperatives formed the basis of the emerging policy context.

Interviews with important actors in the multimedia field in Ireland in 1995 reveal a considerable degree of 'interpretative flexibility' in the way multimedia was defined.[5] People within education and the performance arts defined multimedia as multiple media or multi-media, with a hyphen to signal that it meant the combination of different media in a communication act. Most agreed that the term multimedia referred to the use of a variety of media simultaneously. Over time, however, multimedia became synonymous with the use of many different media within one digital channel, that is, the personal computer.

This privileging of the digital and the technological was neither inevitable, nor self-evident, when the term multimedia was first used. The term was appropriated by the advertising and marketing divisions of large computer producers, driven by the need to describe the evolution of the computer from a single mode information calculator to a multi-mode entertainment and communication device. By the mid to late 1990s, public policy makers in Ireland had adopted the personal computer as the basis for a definition of multimedia, aligning themselves with the major computer hardware and software companies, and framing the discourse about multimedia in technological content terms. Private and public sector discourses, therefore, valued the transmission capabilities of multimedia and its interactivity, to the virtual exclusion of its cultural content or wider social role. It is as if one were discussing cinema without any reference to film.

This social construction, however, fails to recognise the forms and types of products developed by multimedia companies. Multimedia companies fall into three categories:

---

5   W. Bijker, T. Hughes and T. Pinch (eds), *The Social Construction of Technological Systems,* Cambridge, MA: MIT Press, 1987.

those that produce hardware, those that produce software tools, and those that produce content goods and services.[6] This chapter is particularly concerned with the latter. These goods and services may be produced for other businesses (producer services) or for final consumers (personal services). One can also distinguish between the production of instrumental information goods, for example car sales information, and the production of cultural content. Cultural content products, in particular, are shaped by very specific cultural and geographic market boundaries and can play an important role in the construction and reconstruction of culture.

The production processes and artefacts produced by companies involved in multimedia content production, closely mirror traditional (old) media processes and artefacts. The particular production and consumption characteristics of cultural content products have been comprehensively analysed by political economists of the media like Nicholas Garnham, whose work is concerned with how the capitalist mode of industrial production determines content production in old media and the impact this has on the diversity and quality of content.[7] He has found that the high costs of content production and the relatively low costs of content reproduction have lead to concentration in old media corporations and in turn this has placed limits on the diversity of content available. Given the role that cultural content products can play in relation to the regeneration of culture, and the potential role that cultural products distributed by new media can play, an analysis of how the public policy content and corporate production structures are influencing the diversity and

---

6   Macromedia Dreamweaver and Microsoft Office are examples of multimedia software tools. The Virtual Museum of Colm Cille on CD-ROM or the Ireland.com website are examples of multimedia content.

7   N. Garnham, *Capitalism and Communication. Global Culture and the Economics of Information*, London: Sage, 1990.

quality of content production in the multimedia industry in Ireland is especially pertinent.

The public policy context in Ireland

The social construction of multimedia industries as a technology/software industry in Ireland meant that this sector fell within the remit of the Department of Enterprise, Trade and Employment, the Industrial Development Authority (IDA) and Forbairt/Enterprise Ireland. Consequently, multimedia industries were aligned with manufacturing industries and internationally traded service industries. The programmes and policies developed by these bodies reflected the socially agreed definition of the sector, and focused on its ability to transmit large quantities of undifferentiated information and transactional services. Foreign multinationals were invited to use Ireland as a centre for the localisation of multimedia products developed elsewhere, while indigenous companies were encouraged to develop e-commerce initiatives.

At the same time, these industries were marked as different from culture industries, such as music, broadcasting or film, which come within the remit of the Arts Council and the Department of Arts, Heritage, Gaeltacht and the Islands. Arts and cultural policies in Ireland pay great attention to the cultural content of the products being produced. Where there is not a sufficient market to sustain local content production, cultural policies tend to subsidise it. The commitment on the part of government to the core values of national culture, creativity and heritage ensures support for, and subsidisation of, the cultural industries and the arts in Ireland. At the same time, the government prioritises wealth creation and the generation of employment through its economic and industrial development policies. In the Irish context, multimedia industries are viewed as producers of undifferentiated information for global dissemination, rather than as producers of spaces for cultural expression and communication.

The multimedia sector falls under the aegis of industrial rather than cultural policy, as a perusal of the Information Society Commission's report demonstrates.[8] The five key pillars of Ireland's information society – awareness, infrastructure, learning, enterprise and government – prioritise and support commerce, rather than citizenship or culture. The broadly defined 'content industries' are discussed in relation to their ability to generate wealth. No mention is made of their potential role as a channel for cultural creativity and innovation. The report highlights the content industries as a sector with considerable growth potential, it fails to offer any recommendations aimed at developing an indigenous production sector. Again the focus is on foreign direct investment and localisation, policies with a long history in Irish industrial development history. Ironically around the same time as the publication of this report, the National Software Directorate began withdrawing from promoting the multimedia industry, having realised that multimedia content production was quite different from other forms of software production. The Multimedia Technologies Ltd/Into White research laboratory in Limerick was closed for similar reasons. The social construction of multimedia as a computer/software industry leads to very real policy and institutional problems.

To illustrate these problems, the experiences of four companies in the multimedia sector in the late 1990s will be examined. The four cases include: a multinational company, a traditional media corporation, a local arts organisation and a new multimedia start-up, all of which were developing online and offline multimedia content services. Government and industrial agencies played a very small role in facilitating developments in these four companies. From the perspective of three of the four case studies examined, the public policy context was problematic. In the case of the

---

8   Information Society Commission, *Information Society Ireland: Strategy for Action*, Dublin: Forfás, 1996.

foreign-owned company, Compuflex, little direct support was needed.[9] The latter's decision to move into multimedia was made at their headquarters outside Ireland and funded by profits within the company. Given the generous tax incentives provided by the Irish government and the availability of a skilled labour force with the relevant experience, the localisation function was assigned to Ireland. Clearly there is a correspondence between the corporate priorities of Compuflex, and those embedded in Irish industrial development policies. Crucially, the company has been in a prime position to influence national policy development, given its involvement on the steering committee for the development of a strategy aimed at realising the potential of Ireland's information society[10] and its representation on committees involved in the Technology Foresight exercise conducted by Forfás in 1999.

The situation was somewhat more difficult for the three indigenous companies. Without the massive financial capital and distribution networks of a multinational firm, these companies needed seed capital, training and capital resources for their cultural content projects. The new multimedia start-up, Nua, received some state assistance for general market research but had to cross-subsidise its online cultural service using funds earned from more commercial developments. The local arts organisation, the Nerve Centre, received EU funding after protracted negotiations and numerous rejections from local and national industrial development agencies. In the final case, the national broadcaster, RTÉ, moved into multimedia content production as an experimental measure prompted by a desire to reach Irish audiences abroad and this was cross-subsidised from other activities.

---

9 For reasons of confidentiality, Compuflex is an alias name.
10 Information Society Commission, *Information Society Ireland: Strategy for Action,* Dublin: Forfás, 1996.

All four companies tried to develop cultural content products despite the lack of state support in Ireland for such
work, although it is noteworthy that the multinational
received indirect state support through tax incentives. In
the case of Nua and the Nerve Centre particularly, their
search for public funding was hampered by confusion over
what multimedia content really was, who their market for
cultural content might be, and to which funding category
they belonged. The social construction of multimedia
companies as similar to manufacturing and internationally
traded services had serious implications for the firms
involved. They had to develop five-year business plans with
projected export earnings and growth figures in order to
qualify for funding. Most failed to qualify because they could
not adequately quantify the market opportunity in terms of
national economic development priorities, namely future
export and employment potential. Cultural content products
and services aimed at an Irish audience at home and abroad
were perceived as high risk and too culturally specific to
generate large export earnings.

On closer analysis it would seem that there were
weaknesses on both sides. Clearly the main funding options
available for these companies were informed by the administrative culture of enterprise, exports and employment.
There were no alternative national funding sources available that would value the wider cultural impact of the
products. At the same time the applicants were small to
medium-sized enterprises, with little business or marketing
experience of the area into which they were moving. Clearly
these cases point to key structural and conceptual gaps in
relation to state support for new indigenous media industries and their wider role in relation to local, national or
global culture. They also point to the role that major social
groups, like government agencies and multinational
corporations, play in shaping the discourse and conditions
which in turn shape the types of content available on new
media systems.

159

Localisation and its discontents

The special nature of cultural content goods, as compared to other goods and services, and the continuing salience of cultural and geographical barriers between markets in an era of increasing globalisation are highlighted in the case of the multinational, Compuflex, to which we now turn. This case challenges the bipolar views often adopted in relation to the impact of new media technologies. On the one hand, it is argued that new technologies will provide greater access to, and appreciation of, other cultures, while on the other hand, globalisation of production and distribution is seen as leading to standardisation of content and by implication to the homogenisation of cultures. This case study demonstrates that the reality is considerable more nuanced than either of these positions allows for. In fact, there is an ongoing negotiation between the corporate drive to maximise global audiences at least cost, and the end user's preference for technologically and culturally accessible content. While the case points to channels where end users can intervene in the production process, both directly and indirectly, it is a long way from the notion of the user as a co-producer of content, except in strictly limited spaces like bulletin boards. Instead it highlights how the corporate culture of production, in this case a commercial enterprise in the US, can encode technological, aesthetic and cultural assumptions into a content service that may ultimately prove unsuitable for other cultures.

Compuflex is one of the largest producers of software tools in the world with 25,000 employees worldwide and 1,000 in Ireland.[11] Compuflex moved into producing multimedia content in 1995 when they launched an interactive online service the Compuflex Network (CFN). Initially this service provided specialist content aimed at computer users. However, with the growth of the Internet worldwide and the success of competitors such as America Online, Compuflex

---

11 Company and interviewees' names have been changed.

was re-launched as an Internet-based, entertainment-driven service aimed at final users in the home. Media reports at the time speculated that Compuflex was about to become the first company to span computer, telecommunications and content sectors – a product of digital convergence. As it turned out, although the company had an acknowledged expertise of software production and localisation, it faced many challenges in attempting to move into the area of cultural production, an area that requires different competencies and knowledge.

The company's organisational strategy for CFN was to establish teams of content producers in the US whose work would then be distributed and localised using existing channels developed for their software tools business, including a branch plant in Ireland. The Irish branch was in charge of European localisation. The content strategy was to develop television-like 'web-shows' for the service aimed at general audiences, for example environmental and news shows, and specially tailored shows aimed at women and children. This content was seen as the main attraction of the service, supplemented by information and communication services. The service included the latest technologies making use of a range of techniques including graphics and video, chat rooms and fora. In order to have access to 'premier content', end users had to pay a monthly subscription fee. By 1998, however, this highly centralised technology and subscription-driven content strategy had been abandoned. Instead, the company refocused its resources on software tools production and the provision of a free infrastructure for transactional and communication services, combined with content produced locally in each market. Within the space of two years, CFN changed from a highly centralised, vertically integrated service to a more horizontally integrated, publishing and communications service. Compuflex, in effect, moved from being a content producer to being an infrastructure service provider.

Interviews with the localisation team in Dublin help to explain this change in strategy. The turnabout was in part

161

attributed to indirect signals from their various markets, including lower than expected subscription levels, especially outside the US. Adverse media coverage and the success of competitors in the sector were also partly responsible for the change in strategy. Direct feedback from users via focus groups, surveys and email pointed to the technological, cultural and aesthetic barriers encountered. Market share and negative feedback, however, were much less significant than the cost of production and localisation in determining the strategy change. Unlike software tools, which are released to the market every couple of years, the online service required constant innovation and up-to-date content. With estimated annual production costs of $400m, the service was losing $200m a year, after two years. The high cost of content production is a feature of the culture industries, but in the case of CFN, this was supplemented by the overall business strategy for the service, which aimed to deliver content using the latest technologies:

> Compuflex started six months ago to [be] the best content provider on the Internet . . . and they basically tried to walk over competitors with technology and quality and tried to create the wow! factor.

> (Harry, engineer).

The focus on technology, as opposed to content, meant that the company embarked on a number of costly acquisitions in order to gain greater access. The availability of these technologies tended to shape the development of content. While technologically the service was very innovative, end users found it extremely memory hungry and slow. This was especially annoying for end users in markets outside the US, where online use is charged by the minute. In addition, the set-up CDs required to install the service took a long time to load and contained serious bugs that tended to crash users' machines. This generated considerable negative media publicity for the service.

The high cost of content production meant that Compuflex was forced to recoup its costs by maximising users. However their localisation strategy for the service showed a failure to appreciate the different cultural tastes of different markets. Interviewees believed that the organisation's entrenchment in procedures and concepts from software tools production were responsible for substantial delays and subsequent loss of revenue. They noted that the automatic translation, re-engineering and repackaging procedures in place for software tools needed to be significantly adjusted for the online service. The online shows developed in the US required that translation and extensive revision be done in conjunction with the Irish team and other local teams, before they could be launched in target markets. Politically this was a very sensitive issue and required a shift of editorial power away from the main production centre in the US to centres nearer the local markets. The US teams were reluctant to allow this:

> We had a lot of problems with editing material because [Compuflex] had never used editors before and the French and German producers were turning down the localised shows . . . saying the language was unsuitable . . . so [this entailed] setting up a slightly different production process to what we would do for a regular CD-ROM . . . my role is to evaluate the program and give my opinion of it. A lot of the time the Americans and French won't even talk to each other.

(Ann, content editor).

Much of this case study deals with the micro-politics of localisation and cultural hegemony. By failing to take into account the differences between tools production and content production, and failing to take account of the cultural and political differences between markets, CFN learnt a costly lesson. Repeatedly, subscription levels for CFN failed to live up to expectations in markets outside the

US. The process was made even more difficult by the spatial and temporal gaps between production, localisation and in-market teams. The Irish team played a key role in negotiating between the market-driven concerns of the US producers and the cultural concerns of the in-market local teams.

> We'll take some of the stuff we like. Some of the other content we won't – there's no point. It's not relevant to the market and would cost too much to localise it. It would be much cheaper to pay someone in the UK to develop unique UK content rather than localise.

> (John, engineer).

When the strategy for CFN was reformulated in 1998, the service became a portal site providing generic communications and transaction services. While these were produced in the US, they were combined with local content produced by specialist media companies in each of the company's target markets. Clearly, the company had learnt about the specificity of cultural content, and had decided to focus instead on its strengths – the production of software tools:

> [CFN is] an interactive online service that provides easy and inexpensive access for users . . . [CFN] offers a business model and platform for independent content providers as well as powerful development tools. The online service provides access to the Internet, e-mail, bulletin boards and myriad additional services.

> (Company website, March 1998).

Conclusion

The social construction of multimedia as a software industry by major actors in the Irish industrial context has lead to the industry being dominated by companies producing transactional services and localising products developed outside Ireland and destined for worldwide markets. Any consideration of multimedia as a potential new cultural form has consequently been sidelined. Even for global companies, localising entertainment and information services for different cultural markets has proved problematic. For those companies that have tried to produce content for the Irish markets – RTÉ, the Nerve Centre, Nua – little state institutional support has been forthcoming. They have been forced to search for European funding or to cross-subsidise from other commercial activities. At the time of writing, one of these cases, Nua, has gone into liquidation.

The evidence from both the indigenous multimedia sector and that of Compuflex is, therefore, not encouraging. In a purely commercial environment, it would appear that neither multinational organisations nor the indigenous multimedia companies will develop multimedia content for Irish markets, given the small size of the market and the lack of state support. And despite the technological potential for any individual or community group to publish their own website, the costs of producing and maintaining a substantial website in terms of knowledge acquisition, infrastructure and time, remain beyond the means of most. While cultural products may provide spaces of resistance, this resistance is clearly only marginally effective when faced with the marketing and financial might of global multinationals.

Industrial policy in Ireland is driven by the mantra of exports, profits and employment. By contrast, national cultural policy is still focused on those cultural institutions most bound up with the national project and high culture. What of popular culture? The film and audio-visual industries had to wait until the 1990s before funding and other support was made available for indigenous productions. Cultural innovators have had to fight against both the profit and efficiency gatekeepers, as well as the high cultural elite. New media industries must now take on that

165

challenge. What is needed is not protectionism against the flood of foreign-produced content, but rather support for the production of multimedia goods and services of minority and national interest for which the market clearly fails to provide. While the major gatekeepers in the Irish context are some way from offering blanket support to the new media industries, the development of two digital media hubs in Dublin (dealt with earlier in this volume) is suggestive of a policy re-orientation. Furthermore, a recent decision by the Council of the European Union to develop programmes aimed at stimulating the development and use of European digital content and linguistic diversity provides some grounds for hope in a multimedia future.

CHAPTER 11

Rethinking Urbanisation: Struggles around Rural Autonomy and Fragmentation

HILARY TOVEY

A n intriguing feature of contemporary Irish social comment is the way in which urbanisation, as an account of social change, appears to have lost its attraction. In the 1980s, many sociological texts used the term to refer to large-scale or macro-societal transformation – the movement of Irish society as a whole 'into modernity'.[1] Urbanisation nearly always came in tandem with industrialisation, and often also accompanied modernisation. For example one introduction represents Ireland as: 'undergoing a transition from a predominantly agricultural society to an urban, and in some respects at least, advanced industrial structure'.[2]

In the 1990s, sociological texts were still talking about industrialisation, but they had become much more wary and self-interrogatory about the idea of modernisation, and talk

---

1   See M. Peillon, *Contemporary Irish Society: An Introduction*, Dublin: Gill and Macmillan, 1982; C. Curtin, M. Kelly and L. O'Dowd (eds), *Culture and Ideology in Ireland*, Galway: Galway University Press, 1984; P. Clancy, S. Drudy, K. Lynch and L. O'Dowd (eds), *Ireland: A Sociological Profile*, Dublin: IPA, 1986.
2   P. Clancy et al., ibid., p. 15.

of urbanisation had virtually disappeared. In its place we start to see a discourse of 'urban processes'.[3] This appears not to express a thesis about historical, societal transformation, but rather indicates a growing sociological interest in the economic, aesthetic, cultural, infrastructural and social production and organisation of cities. The trajectory of these concepts in Irish sociology is not so different from that found elsewhere. In English-language sociology in general, use of urbanisation to refer to the transformation of a whole society is now virtually confined to discussions of the 'developing world', and even there, attention is shifting to the study of 'third-world cities' and their specific forms of growth. Paralleling that, is the consolidation of urban sociology as a specific but central ingredient in the sociology of 'developed societies'.

There were, of course, good critical reasons why we should abandon the older view of societal transformation or modernisation as urbanisation. These were exhaustively presented by founders of the new sociology of urban process, such as Castells. However, one of the problems Castells did not emphasise was the implication that in a modernised world rural society ceases to exist: that modernity means replacement of rural by urban; or at best, that rural worlds exist only in residual and uninteresting ways. In many of its manifestations, the new urban sociology strikingly reproduces the same idea in an even more taken-for-granted way. Initially it represents itself as the study of one dimension or one phenomenon of modern life, but then quickly identifies this with 'the social' in general.[4] Thus, the distinctive

---

3   See C. Curtin, H. Donnan and T. M. Wilson (eds), *Irish Urban Cultures*, Belfast: Institute for Irish Studies, 1993; P. Clancy, S. Drudy, K. Lynch and L. O'Dowd (eds), *Irish Society: Sociological Perspectives*, Dublin: IPA, 1996.

4   See P. Dickens, *Urban Sociology: Society, Locality and Human Nature,* London: Harvester Wheatsheaf, 1990; A. Giddens, *Sociology*, Cambridge: Polity Press, 2001, 4th edition.

concern of urban sociology is a 'focus on how social systems and people combine in locales and localities'.[5] Apparently only urban locales and localities carry any sociological significance! Much urban sociology is indistinguishable from a general sociology of consumption. Urban sociology also often understands itself as the sociology of civil society, making the urban the location of citizenship, the public sphere, democratic political processes, new social movements and cosmopolitan outlooks. The result of such unacknowledged imperialism is that modernity becomes urban, and the rural is assimilated into nature; the developed world simply *is* an urban world. The first volume of this series invited us to 'uncover the structure of modernity in Ireland' by taking on the role of the *flâneur* or urban walker, described as 'an icon of modernity'.[6] The stroller in the countryside, it seems, will not observe anything of relevance to an understanding of modern Ireland.

In Ireland today, as (since 1996) in the world as a whole, more people live in urban than in rural settlements. It is also the case that this is a remarkably recent phenomenon (urban first outnumbered rural residents in the 1971 census of population) and that the urban majority is still pretty small (probably not above 60 per cent) and mostly concentrated in just one urban agglomeration, Dublin. Outside its towns and cities, Ireland is not empty space. More importantly, counting up where people live may not tell us much about how they define and understand their society. The older concept of urbanisation could be defended on the grounds that it did try, in a clumsy and preconceived way, to capture something of how broad transformations in culture and identity are connected to the changing social uses of space driven by economic growth. Contemporary studies of

---

5   Dickens, ibid., p. 180.
6   M. Peillon and E. Slater (eds), *Encounters with Modern Ireland: A Sociological Chronicle 1995–1996,* Dublin. IPA, 1998.

169

urban process can only do this insofar as they assume that the important transformations in society are those taking place within the urban.

The rise of globalisation theory further marginalises a rural–urban framework for understanding contemporary society. Globalisation theory conceptualises change in a different way from earlier theories of urbanisation: it may have started out describing change as a movement *from* the local *to* the global, but it moved fairly quickly to focusing on interactions *between* local and global and to an emphasis on the influence which each has, however unequally, in shaping the other. This can lead to thinking of localities as disarticulated from each other and articulated individually into the global whole, whether that means global capitalism, transnational politics or patterns of cultural consumption practices. Spatio-social settings larger than localities, such as nation-states (Ireland) or larger regions (Europe), are problematised in globalisation theories and the trans-formations that take place at this level are made difficult to address.

Dublin is in many respects a globalised city and understanding that fact is essential to our understanding of contemporary Irish society, but it is not sufficient for it. Dublin and other Irish cities are also located within a larger space, which is not urban and cannot be understood simply through a study of urban process. Can the older concept of urbanisation help us, after all, to grasp some of the trans-formations occurring in this broader social setting? Clearly, it would need substantial re-working. First, it needs to be detached from a value-commitment to change as progress or modernisation. Second, by analogy with globalisation theorising, we should replace the assumption that change is from rural to urban by a recognition that it involves both rural and urban and interactions between them. Third, it needs to be given some dynamic content, which would allow us to grasp not just change but also resistance to change, and the construction of new cultural meanings for old actors and practices.

Reconceptualising the rural as a field (with apologies to John B. Keane)

The concept of urbanisation takes as a given that rural and urban are different – even if one eventually turns into the other. How is it that we are able to talk about 'rural Ireland' as if it is some sort of coherent entity, which has emerged from a roughly uniform past and is following a uniform direction of development towards a specifiable future? The question is particularly pressing since most objective analyses suggest that such a notion of a coherent and bounded rurality should be extremely precarious. They indicate that the key process of change in rural Ireland over recent decades has been growing differentiation between rural households and between rural areas.

Farm families are becoming increasingly diverse in terms of how much of their household income comes from farming, how much of family labour time is devoted to farming, how much they even define themselves as farmers or understand themselves as seriously engaged in the occupation of farming. It has become quite difficult to establish how many farmers or farm households exist. Some stop defining themselves as 'in farming', even while they still own a few cattle or sheep; others stop being officially regarded as such, whatever their own self-definition. The numbers of rural households that have no connection with farming – and the numbers which have never had any, being newcomers into rural areas – are increasing steadily. Few localities remain where the majority of households are in farming. Farming itself is becoming geographically concentrated in the south, midlands and east, while the rest of the countryside becomes a space to be used in increasingly varied ways from the construction of high-tech or low-tech industrial estates, to diverse forms of mass and niche tourism, to the creation of a culture economy based around music, film, television and the Irish language.

We can also note a growing acceptance on the part of politicians, state development agents, farmers' leaders and

171

other elites that this differentiation between rural and urban is inevitable and right. Rural Ireland today may not, in fact, be any more diverse than it was in the middle of the nineteenth century, before land reform policies and the co-operative movement began to make their impact. But it follows on a period when the specifically 'modern' agrarian ideal of a relatively homogeneous, agriculturally dominated society, based around moderate-sized family farms and incorporating the 'disadvantaged' as well as the 'developed' regions in the state, had become the established orthodoxy in social thinking about the countryside. If under these conditions belief in a distinctive and coherent rural Ireland survives, it seems an interesting puzzle for Irish sociology to address. With regard to contemporary Irish society, for whom do such beliefs continue to make sense, and for what purposes are they mobilised? For whom do they make no sense, and how has that happened? What social processes operate to reconstruct notions of rurality, and what processes work in the opposite direction to encourage their deconstruction? And how are they linked to the expansion of the urban in Irish society?

Bourdieu's concept of 'field', which offers a way into rethinking urbanisation, might help us to develop these puzzles.[7] Bourdieu thinks of society as a struggle between actors who seek to reproduce the status quo and those who seek in various ways to challenge, resist or change it. Thinking in terms of fields is a way for him to explore how social reality is diverse: fractured into a plurality of social spaces, each with its own more or less distinctive logic of practice and with varying degrees of autonomy from the relations of power and hegemony that dominate in society as a whole. Fields are networks of social positions in relations

---

7   See P. Bourdieu, *The Field of Cultural Production*, Cambridge: Polity Press, 1993; P. Bourdieu and L. J. D. Wacquant, *An Invitation to Reflexive Sociology,* Chicago: University of Chicago Press, 1992; L. J. D. Wacquant, 'Pierre Bourdieu', in R. Stone (ed.), *Key Sociological Thinkers*, London: Macmillan Press, 1998.

with each other, structured around a particular pattern of distribution and exchange of capital, which may be cultural and symbolic as well as material in form. Fields define the value of capital for their particular arena. But fields are also phenomenal categories within society. They exist because their participants believe in their distinctive logic and in its worth: a field is defined through commitment to the field or 'belief in the game'. This makes the capacity to define what the game is, which Bourdieu calls 'symbolic capital', of great value to its possessors. Class processes played out within a field thus involve both objective changes in the structure of relationships and changes in the subjectivity of actors.

As fields are both social constructions and objective structures, the structuring of the world into organised fields confirms and is confirmed by the organisation of personal identity. The 'facticity' of a rural–urban division in society depends upon people's personal identities being shaped around these distinctions; Bourdieu and Wacquant speak of an 'ontological complicity' between persons and the social world in which they live. The specificity of a field comes from pre-reflexive assumptions about what behaviour is appropriate in terms of the particular game being played – what sort of cultural style, knowledge, sensibilities one needs to display to be accepted as a 'fit' player in this field. Conflicts may bring these assumptions into consciousness and ignite a struggle to redefine the orthodox understandings of the field. Social struggles characteristically involve 'heretical' attempts to challenge the taken-for-granted orthodoxies, which in turn generate attempts by the dominant agents to restore common assent. As Wacquant puts it, every field is 'the site of an ongoing clash between those who defend autonomous principles of judgement proper to that field and those who seek to introduce heteronomous standards because they need the support of external forces to improve their dominated position in it'.[8]

---

8 Wacquant, ibid., p. 222.

Arenas usually cited as examples of fields are art, science, religion, the economy, politics, the law, even sociology – in other words, 'fields of cultural production'. Arguably, 'the rural' is less a field in itself than the site of a number of overlapping fields. But Bourdieu leaves the issue of field boundaries vague; he intends us to take the concept as a heuristic device rather than a description of reality. As a heuristic device, its power comes from the way it allows us to look at social life as structured by two sorts of social struggle. There are struggles between actors within fields, which try to change the distribution of capital or to generate better returns on exchanges of particular forms of capital; and struggles to change fields themselves, to turn them into a different game or to dissolve their boundaries. This allows us to reconceptualise urbanisation as societal struggles to convert the rural into an urban game – struggles in which the heterodox may be slowly overcoming the orthodox, but with results which neither, perhaps, can predict in advance. The countryside is then one of many battlefields in society where changing power relations among social agents play out their 'structuring' consequences. Some key social agents exercise power because of their 'rootedness' in or control over rural resources, material or symbolic; others get power from their capacity to mobilise resources from outside the rural field. Material, spatial, social, institutional, cultural and ideological/symbolic processes are all involved; changes in ownership of authority and knowledge about the countryside seem potentially as important as changes in material ownership.

Developing these ideas could lead to a huge agenda for 're-doing' both urban and rural sociology in Ireland. Out of many possible processes of rural transformation to which we might apply Bourdieu's approach, I will sketch out three.

Heretical farmers

My first sketch is of a particular group of farmers – successful farmers, attractive to and tightly incorporated into the food industry, and regarded by the state as fit beneficiaries of developmental and other supports. They are mostly dairy farmers, who have succeeded much better than other Irish farmers in developing a form of full-time, family farming which, although moderate in scale, is nevertheless productive and profitable. They are the group we might most expect to articulate the orthodoxies of the rural social field – to represent themselves as the principal creators and carriers of the rural as a social, economic and cultural space and their participation as vital to any process of countryside revitalisation or rural renewal. But, for much of the last fifty years, such farmers have been progressively detaching themselves from that role – redefining themselves first as professionals, later as technicians for agro-industry, and most recently as entrepreneurs or small businessmen. Their subjective understanding of their own class position no longer encourages them to identify with other farmers as a collective agrarian actor.

Professionalisation was embraced as part of a modernist project that saw agrarian progress as the adoption of new and more universal standards of practice in farming. It detached farmers from others in rural society and encouraged them to act and to organise on a sectoral basis, collectivising them as an occupational group and providing a role model of the vanguard farmer to which all farmers could aspire. Over time, however, professional standards became increasingly identified, among leading farmers and perhaps particularly in dairying, with the adoption of 'scientised' practices. These farmers began to think of themselves less as agrarian producers and more as technical workers within a larger industrialised production system: 'I see myself as a producer of milk solids, not milk; all my milk goes into cheese. The reality is that I am selling kilograms of fat and protein, so it is logical to breed for solids'.[9] Commodity divisions within farming, and organisations of

---

9   Comments of one large-scale, Munster milk producer to the *Irish Farmers Journal*, December 1997.

and networks among producers in specific commodity lines and stages, began to replace their professional representative organisation in engaging the interest and time of such farmers.

Scientised conceptions of 'quality farming' and the transfer of technological practices and self-images into farming are supported by powerful, external institutions – the food industry, banks, universities, state development organisations and agricultural advisory agents – which provide a range of external reference groups to support their heretical understanding of their role. Increasingly, good farming is identified with entrepreneurial farming: the best farmer is not the farmer who produces most but the farmer who produces most profitably; farming is about financial or business management as much as technical practices, and farmers are addressed as people who run a business. For the *Irish Farmers Journal*, a good farm business today must be able to achieve high profits and grow in net worth, just as in any other business sector: 'Many farmers are so engrossed in the daily technical tasks that they fail, to their detriment, to focus on the broader picture of business development and wealth creation . . .'.[10]

The rise of this business discourse is part of a new process of class transformation, in which successful farmers are detached from other rural people, from other farmers and from an agrarian base, and encouraged to identify themselves with a class of small-business entrepreneurs in society as a whole. In terms of their practices and standards of evaluation, they see themselves as having more in common with other business groups than with other farmers. They no longer believe in the rural game, including the rules about appropriate farm-family relationships. The meaning of land, for example, as a form of material capital deployed within a rural field, is beginning to change as farm

---

10 Editorial comment, *Irish Farmers Journal,* 22 November 1997, p. 31.

family and farm enterprise become detached from each other. Dairy farming may be undertaken as a strategy for generational class mobility out of farming or as merely one, revisable, element in a wider range of family business interests. Among the most successful farmers, the class reproduction or even upward mobility of the family no longer closely depends on reproduction of the farm enterprise. Dairying may be seen as a source of profits to be invested in whatever enterprise might best secure the continuing wealth and status of the family.

Heterodox 'knowledges'

The second set of processes sketched here involves the rise of new knowledge classes in European society, this phenomenon has changed the value of cultural capital within the rural field. New knowledge classes redistribute symbolic capital, in the sense of the capacity to define what the rural game is and, therefore, what values any particular form of capital, including cultural capital, may realise within the field.

The collapse of the status of farmers, and of the agrarian world generally, in Europe is linked to the agricultural deskilling that follows the 'scientisation' and 'technologisation' of farming. Deskilling most affects the less 'developed' farmer. Entrepreneurial farmers have gained many new skills even if these have no distinctively rural character. Marginalised farmers lose confidence in the artisanal skills that were autonomous to and definitive of a bounded rural universe. In the broad sense implied by the term cultural capital, agricultural deskilling includes both loss of knowledge and loss of confidence in the value of that knowledge. Productionist agricultural policies and the expansion of Fordist forms of food industry have transferred the technological production packages developed within industrial laboratories onto the farm. Changes in consumer orientations towards food are also significant, if less often discussed. 'McDonaldisation' – the rationalisation and

177

'instrumentalisation' of food associated with the rise of convenience food industries – helped to detach food, as an available consumable item, from any knowledge by consumers as to how it is produced. Agricultural deskilling goes hand in hand with deskilling food consumers. Thus autonomous rural skills, standards and knowledges command little value, among farmers themselves or among outsiders to the field.

Coinciding with this, a different set of skills and knowledges in regard to nature has arisen: land-use planning, environmental management, landscape and heritage conservation including both ecological systems and archaeological artefacts. These are urban-based and acquired, and 'credentialised' through participation in formal education; they are highly transferable across space and time and are assumed to have a universal application, in other words to be scientific. Knowledges generated within the rural field were generally localised and dependent on personal reputation: acquired through experience and the practice of doing and imitating, rather than through processes of formal learning. They were known only to specialised circles of neighbours or enthusiasts, lacked 'credentialisation' and had to be constantly re-exhibited at fairs and competitions. Farmers, particularly landowners, still have low levels of formal education compared to other social groups, which increasingly exposes them to the charge of ignorance. Scientific or formal educational skills have much greater social power than such localised, relativised and experiential skills and knowledges.

Authority to regulate and control the countryside is increasingly claimed by elites who possess the capital of a formal, scientised knowledge of nature. Rural Ireland is incorporated into a broader struggle, led by new knowledge groups, over power and social prestige and challenges to authority based on ownership of material capital. Their success is apparent in the development and implementation of agro-environmental schemes, and in the forms of 'quality control' increasingly exercised over food, which again are determined through science rather than the sort of experiential, life-world understanding of food quality shared by chefs, gourmets and some food producers. The decline in society's valuation of rural skills facilitates a transfer of authority and control over the rural environment and its uses from agrarian to urban authorities, which further intensifies the loss of status and credibility of those skills. Non-urban versions of, or visions of, the countryside become less easy to articulate in the public domain. Rural orientations to nature become culturally decentralised: the rural is reorganised as a spatial extension of urban activities and interests, an opportunity to construct parks and recreational spaces and routes linking urban centres to each other.

Hybrid identities

The third set of processes connects with what have been called new geographies of distinction: struggles around the meaning of space and of its uses. They are gender and generation (or more broadly, lifestyle) processes, as much as class ones.

Spatial transformations have a prominent position in discussions of what is happening to contemporary rural areas: new patterns of rural out- and in-migration, movements of populations from rural hinterlands into local centres, the re-drawing of local and regional transactional boundaries following new forms of economic or social development. Thinking of the rural as a field suggests however that such socio-spatial changes – for example changes in the physical use of space associated with increasing tourism, rural industrialisation or the decline of agriculture as a livelihood – may be less important than changes in ideas about the use of space, in particular understandings of what are the legitimate, appropriate or prestigious ways to use and to relate to space, its social meanings and links to social capital and to personal identity. The reorganisation and 'stretching' across time and space of people's social lives and relationships, which Giddens and others[11] emphasise as a characteristic experience in 'late modern' (urban) society, seems particularly apt as a description of much contemporary rural experience. Many rural people live in localities that are as tightly incorporated into international or global circuits as into national or even regional ones. This may be as a result of the arrival of branch plants of multinational corporations creating and exploiting global divisions of labour, the growth of international tourist networks, the globalisation of the food industry, or the history of previous migration flows that left a residue of kinship and friendship connections between rural areas in Europe and metropolitan centres across the world.

From the point of view of external users of rural places, rural space has acquired many attractions. It is attractive to industries who want to locate branch plants in greenfield sites across Europe, not just because of the greenness of the labour force they hope to find there (the absence of negotiation skills or trade union traditions from rural localities is less and less to be relied on) but because they want access to consumption values associated with the countryside, to improve the lifestyle of their management employees and to enhance their corporate image by associating it with notions of health, nature, freedom, friendliness and being good neighbours. Rural space is attractive to an expanding middle class, whose dependence on the countryside as a place to service its consumption practices is increasing. While this contributes to transforming the countryside into a space for leisure and aesthetic consumption, Irish middle-class consumers of the countryside also try to consume the society that rural Ireland is thought to contain or to symbolise – densely networked, diverse and egalitarian, relaxed and eccentric. It

11 See A. Giddens, *The Consequences of Modernity*, Cambridge: Polity Press, 1990, pp. 17–21; M. O'Brien, S. Penna and C. Hay (eds), *Theorising Modernity*, London: Longman, 1999.

is a sort of society that is increasingly desirable and prestigious to be a part of – but not to be immobilised within.

Actors in late modernity have been described, following Giddens, as skilled and knowledgeable individuals who are experienced and practised at moving *between* social contexts and *using* institutions as resources for sustaining security and stability.[12] Young rural out-migrants who live their working week in an urban centre and return at weekends to the rural area in which they grew up, are not simply people returning home as soon as possible: emotional attachment to the rural locality seems to depend on being away from it for a significant (temporal and social/occupational) part of one's life. However many people who work within their rural locality of origin, but whose working or personal lives constantly re-create relationships with people elsewhere, could be described in similar terms. Both illustrate how a 'glocal' identity is achieved out of a combination of access to rural 'rootedness' and the capacity to escape and integrate into wider social networks.

It is not so much that space gets compressed in late modernity, but that the capacity to move across space can become a source of social status and prestige. Moving between social settings, and combining them in novel ways to develop identities and interactions that are essentially trans-spatial, is a basis for new claims to distinction made by certain rural groups – younger against older generations, women against men or the more modern and progressive against the poor, socially marginalised and 'traditional' actors who are often represented as the stereotypical rural inhabitant. Changes in the distribution of populations across space might be explained simply as a response to economic imperatives; but trans-spatial mobility seems to require an explanation which includes a 'project of the self'

---

12 M. O'Brien, 'Theorising Modernity. Reflexivity, Identity and Environment in Giddens' Social Theory', in M. O'Brien et al., ibid., p. 20.

to construct a new identity and legitimate autobiography. Prestigious personal identities emerge, which are based not on urban establishment or on establishment within a rural world, but on mobility in to and out of both, or a combination of local rural roots with engagement in cosmopolitan networks.

Urbanisation and the autonomy of the rural field

At least two of the three processes picked out above – the emergence of heretical farmers and the rise of heterodox knowledges – suggest that the rural field lacks what Bourdieu calls autonomy, the capacity to defend itself against external influences and to maintain its own criteria of value. If urbanisation does not mean a simple replacement of rural by urban, it does point us towards identifying forces that tend to dissolve the specificity of the rural world in contemporary society. However, Bourdieu sees fields as battlefields, as sites of struggle and contestation, so we should also be looking for processes working in the opposite direction.

Uneven spatial development in late capitalism heightens the significance of location as a source of identity and as a basis for collective mobilisation; thus alongside tendencies to trans-spatiality, tendencies towards 'closures of space' also seem likely to persist as a significant feature of late modernity. And if rural out-migrants claim a new identity, which is neither rural nor urban but combines the two in transcendent ways, incomers into rural localities still often arrive with the expectation of finding a local 'community', which has its own culturally specific hierarchies of distinction and standards of evaluation. Incomers often want to be community activists; assuming their new locality to be an autonomously structured terrain of action, they engage in practices that reconfirm it as such.

If the main development processes among successful farmers have tended to detach them from an agrarian identity and incorporate them into the mainstream of Irish

social class formation, others are pushed towards reproducing a segmented collective identity by the spread of
'movements' for rural or regional development, although
these perhaps are better described as institutionalised
interventions enjoying more or less authoritative status as
nominated agents for the state. Ranging from LEADER
groups to local authorities, from opposition community
development campaigns seeking local control over the use of
local resources for development to community groups incorporated into partnership with state agencies in order to
deliver local resources to the state for national development
purposes, they share a common interest in seeking a
competitive edge in marketing their locality or region and
its produce through strategies for socio-symbolic closure.
For example, they try to establish a brand identity for local
produce, by drawing on whatever elements are available, or
can be imaginatively reconstructed, of a distinctive local
culture, terrain, landscape or history.

These examples might challenge overconfident predic-
tions about the 'disembedding' of social relations from time
and space in late modernity and might indicate the
reproduction of the symbolic significance of the local. The
problem is that they do not necessarily tend towards the
reproduction of the rural. The rural can exist as a separate
field only in a pre-interpreted social world, in which ideas
are already formulated about rural–urban differences and
relationships and where such ideas shape practices. The
reproduction of the rural field may depend particularly
critically on collective social action in the form of new social
movements. These are important carriers of new understandings of social reality that may support or undermine
belief in the autonomy and distinctiveness of the rural
world. They can lodge in the public domain new understandings of the rural, as the site of unique and specific
ways of life, or belief systems, or forms of knowledge and
skills, or as the opposite of all those things.

The dominant social movement in Irish society during
the second half of the twentieth century was a movement

183

for economic modernity, which engaged in a battle to reconfigure all economic activity in line with an industrial production model and an urban consumption one and to represent this as social and cultural progress. However new movements are emerging, particularly out of environmentalism, to challenge this. One is emerging around the growing concern about 'sustainable development', which of course can mean very different things depending on who articulates it. As a social movement it is still inchoate, but it is beginning to provide an arena in which alliances can be formed between urban, middle-class consumers concerned about the safety and the edibility of their food, and small, rural producers trying to find ways of producing food that are both economically and ecologically sustainable. This suggests that there might be a rather different interpretation of the impact of the rise of environmental knowledge elites and related interest groups to the one given earlier. Certain types of ecological movement (such as the organic food movement, which experienced a revitalisation across Europe during the 1990s; the slow food movement, which tries to maintain regionally distinctive forms of artisanal food production through practices of food consciousness-raising among affluent urban consumers; or movements around animal rights, for example Compassion in World Farming) may contribute to the re-skilling of rural producers, or revaluing of the experience-derived skills and knowledges involved in the processes of growing vegetables or raising animals for food, rather than constituting them as marginal and irrelevant. But the claim of such movements to be legitimate, ecological movements is itself diversely made and frequently contested.

The symbolic capital owned or created by such movements, which has the capacity to re-shape rural people's understandings of their lives and social positions, comes from outside the rural field. In this it is no different from the anti-ruralist values and beliefs imported by heretical groups such as entrepreneurial farmers. Perhaps it has always been the case that the right to determine what 'the rural' means, and what value rural practices have, has been claimed by elite social groups detached from everyday agrarian life. Williams argued that the rural–urban contrast, or the country versus city schema, is ultimately best understood as an 'expressive order' that gives English culture ways of talking and thinking about alternative ways of living.[13] The contrast is embedded in Irish culture and history in a very different way, yet here too it may underpin possibilities for utopian thinking. To see what they might be, we need to shift our focus of vision away from 'from rural to urban' and towards 'rural and urban' – that is, to rethink urbanisation as an interactive process of reconstitution and change born out of struggle and contestation over legitimacy, identity and symbolic power.

---

13 R. Williams, *The Country and the City*, London: Chatto and Windus, 1973.

CHAPTER 12

Nation-state, Capitalism and the Right to Work of Asylum Seekers

STEVE LOYAL

O n 26 July 1999, John O'Donoghue, Minister for Justice, Equality and Law Reform in the Fianna Fáil-led coalition government, announced that those asylum seekers who had been in Ireland for more than twelve months and who were still awaiting a determination of their application for refugee status could seek work. This right was also to be extended to those who had sought asylum in Ireland up to 26 July 1999, as soon as they crossed the twelve-month threshold. On this basis, an initial group of some 2,100 asylum seekers were immediately given permission to seek work. By 27 July 2000 – the closing date of the right-to-work amnesty – this figure had risen to almost 3,600.

In this chapter it will be argued that the case of asylum seekers and their right to work illuminates a fundamental contradiction that has emerged in contemporary Ireland between some forms of nationalism and the imperatives of market economics. Ireland's rapid movement in the 1990s from a relatively homogenous ethnic profile to a more multicultural one has brought into sharp relief the divergence between ideologies of nationalism and capitalism. These are relational phenomena, which take on meaning in the wider concrete social relations within which they exist, and may overlap, reinforce or run at odds with each other depending on the specific social and historical context. In the contemporary Irish case, nationalism has tended to promulgate a backward-looking, atavistic vision of Ireland and Irishness. While market economics, premised on the creed of the mobility of labour and capital, preaches the gospel of flexibility and inclusiveness. The case of asylum seekers and the right to work brings into focus the collision between two contradictory visions of contemporary Ireland, and the pragmatic attempts by both politicians and entrepreneurs to forge a compromise between them.

Nationalism

Nationalism, in Ireland as elsewhere, is not a unitary phenomenon. Rather, it consists of a multiplicity of strands and dimensions. Concerns relating to borders, sovereignty, unique peoples, culture, ethnicity, shared language, beliefs and values, common descent and so forth may all be found in nationalist discourses. Rather than speaking of nationalism, therefore, we should speak of 'nationalisms', which shift historically and in response to changing power relations. These nationalisms need to be analysed empirically and on a case-by-case basis.[1] Nevertheless, there are some generic characteristics common to many forms of nationalism and, broadly speaking, nationalist discourses attempt to regulate the ways in which individuals within a given society represent themselves and others.

---

1 In common with many latecomers to nationhood, the Irish state pursued a thoroughgoing nationalistic strategy from its inception in 1922 onward. Part of this strategy involved normalising and regulating human subjectivity in terms of citizenship and nationhood. Irish nationalism predated the existence of the state and was founded and developed largely in opposition to British colonial rule. However, the assumption of statehood enabled the dissemination of a nationalist discourse that permeated all social institutions including politics, economics and culture.

The central piece of legislation that regulated entry into the Irish state was the 1935 Aliens Act. This drew heavily on earlier British legislation, namely the 1914 Aliens Restriction Act, which was drafted on the eve of World War I in order to give unrestricted powers to the British home secretary to decide who could enter, and who could be barred from entering, Britain. Underpinning this legislation was a draconian approach to state security, which was accounted for by the context of its implementation: war. Nevertheless, this approach was adapted and sustained by the Irish state after independence and in subsequent decades.

The Aliens Act, and subsequently the Irish Nationality and Citizenship Act, 1956, are both based on an explicit binary distinction between Irish citizens and 'aliens'. They adhere to a particular notion of homogeneity that often forms a central part of many nationalistic state discourses.[2] Furthermore, they reveal the ideological nature of the concepts of rights and citizenship. As Lentin rightly argues, citizenship in Ireland presupposed a specifically restricted notion of gender and ethnicity.[3] The Constitution, for example, conceptualises the nation in a gendered and ethnically specific way. It assumes that most Irish citizens are sedentary Catholics, and that a woman's place is in the home.

In the formative decades of the state, the nationalist programme of successive governments was overlain by an authoritarian Catholicism rooted in the influence of the church and a ruralist vision of the Irish economy. The compound effect of the operation of these forces was the imposition of a number of reactionary and censorious social principles as a form of social and moral regulation. Catholic

---

2   C. Calhoun, *Nationalism,* Oxford: Blackwell, 1997.
3   R. Lentin, 'Irishness, the 1937 Constitution and Citizenship: A Gender and Ethnicity View', *Irish Journal of Sociology*, vol. 8, 1998, pp. 5–24.

social conservatism and populist nationalism was exemplified by the administrations headed by Eamonn de Valera,
who developed a systematic connection between economic
autarky based on agriculture, and a national identity rooted
in the traditional values of rural society. Irish nationalism
developed on the basis of an inward-looking orientation to
'blood and soil'. However, the moral hegemony forged by the
forces of nationalism and Catholicism was increasingly
challenged: first, on the basis of economic considerations in
the 1960s under Lemass's leadership, later on normative
and cultural grounds by the media, and again more recently
by the development of the 'Celtic tiger' economy.

In light of the changing context of migration in Ireland
(see below), earlier forms of restrictive legislation appeared
increasingly anachronistic. The Refugee Act, 1996 and the
Immigration Act, 1999 superseded earlier legislation. The
Refugee Act, not fully implemented until November 2000, is
the act of law used by the Irish government to guide its
asylum procedures and to interpret the 1951 UN Geneva
Convention. According to the UN Convention, any person
from any country in the world has the right to invoke the
asylum procedure and to seek recognition as a refugee. The
Refugee Act defines an asylum seeker as:

> A person who, owing to a well-founded fear of being
> persecuted for reasons of race, religion, nationality,
> membership of a particular social group or political
> opinion, is outside the country of his or her nationality
> or, owing to such fear, is unwilling to avail himself or
> herself of the protection of that country.

The legislation sets out clearly the procedures governing an
application by an asylum seeker in Ireland, including a
right of appeal against the refusal of refugee status. It also
makes provision for a work permit system that is complex
and cumbersome to negotiate. At present, these are the sole
routes into the country for non-nationals from outside the
EU.

Migration

The arrival of a number of asylum seekers into Ireland during the 1990s has gone some way towards shifting the picture of migration that had hitherto prevailed. Prior to the 1990s, Ireland was the exception among its EU partners: the only country where net emigration exceeded net immigration. The 1990s saw a dramatic turnabout in Ireland's migratory profile: the numbers of people leaving the country declined consistently, while the numbers entering (including a high proportion of returning emigrants) rose dramatically. The growth in the number of asylum seekers has been significant, though not over-whelming. In 1992 Ireland received only 39 applications for asylum. This figure had risen to over 10,938 by the end of 2000. The main countries of origin for asylum seekers arriving in Ireland are Nigeria, Romania, Democratic Republic of Congo and Czech Republic.

However, contemporary asylum seekers are not the first group to seek incorporation into an otherwise homogenous Irish society. The presence of Travellers and Protestants in Ireland indicates that Irish society, though relatively homogenous in terms of whiteness and Christianity, was always more diverse than nationalist discourses claimed it to be. Moreover, the presence of Jews and the arrival, after the 1950s, of a number of programme refugees, including Hungarians, Chileans, Vietnamese and Bosnians, meant that immigrants were present in Ireland throughout the twentieth century. Many of these groups experienced some degree of racism, particularly the Jewish community.[4]

Since arriving in Ireland, many recent asylum seekers have also experienced forms of racism, both directly and institutionally.[5] Through state discourses, particularly legislation and political rhetoric, asylum seekers have been

---

4   D. Keogh, *Jews in Twentieth Century Ireland*, Cork: Cork University Press, 1998.

5   B. Fanning, S. Loyal and C. Staunton, *Asylum Seekers and the Right to Work in Ireland*, Dublin: Irish Refugee Council, 2000.

variously portrayed as illegal, criminal, bogus or as fraudsters who have flooded into Ireland as economic migrants in order to exploit its generous welfare system. They have been represented as a drain on resources and as responsible for the housing crisis, continuing unemployment and the lack of social facilities. The state's disinclination towards the construction of an intercultural society has led to the emergence of pervasive forms of institutional racism.[6] Further, the media, as the social institution with the most graphic and immediate power of representation, has reinforced these discourses through the use of sensationalist banner headlines.[7]

Asylum seekers and the right to work

Immigration is rooted in a new prosperity brought about by the emergence of the 'Celtic tiger' economy. The Republic of Ireland has experienced rapid economic growth in recent years, though, crucially, a profoundly unequal one.[8] The emergence of the 'Celtic tiger' signifies an emphatic shift in the social, political, cultural and economic context for understanding the reception and integration of would-be immigrants. Within this economy, although localised long-term unemployment is still a problem, labour shortages are being experienced in the low-paid services sector, and in the science, technology, software and computing sectors.[9] The

6 E. O'Mahony, S. Loyal and A. Mulcahy, *Racism in Ireland: The Views of Black and Ethnic Minorities*, Dublin: Amnesty International, 2001.
7 For example 'Floodgates Open as New Army of Poor Swamp the Country', *Sunday World*, 25 May 1997. See also A. Pollak, 'An Invitation to Racism? Irish Daily Newspaper Coverage of the Refugee Issue', in D. Kiberd (ed.), *Media in Ireland: The Search for Ethical Journalism*, Dublin: Open Air, 1999.
8 See K. Allen, *The Celtic Tiger,* Manchester: Manchester University Press, 2000.
9 J. Williams, S. Blackwell and G. Hughes, *National Survey of Vacancies in the Private Non-agricultural Sector,* Dublin: ESRI, 1999.

increasing number of work permits issued by the Department of Enterprise, Trade and Employment reflects such labour deficits. In 1993, 1,103 work permits were issued. By the end of 2000 this figure had risen to 18,017. It was in the context of this changed economic milieu that the current scheme for providing asylum seekers in Ireland with the right to work was drawn up.

The decision to allow a limited number of asylum seekers to work followed a sustained period of lobbying by a number of interest groups working under an umbrella organisation entitled the Asylum Rights Alliance (ARA). According to the ARA, long delays in processing applications for asylum – some taking up to three years – force idleness on asylum seekers and leave untapped their potential as a resource. The ARA was formed in November 1998 and comprised about one hundred organisations, including church groups, voluntary groups, trade unions and business organisations. The co-operation between all such organisations in arguing the case for the right to work, however, was based on two distinct sets of concerns.

On the one hand, non-governmental organisations (NGOs) such as Comhlamh, Association of Refugees and Asylum Seekers in Ireland and The Irish Refugee Council, as well as a number of church organisations, argued for the right to work predominantly in terms of a human rights agenda. The general argument put forward by these groups was that the right to work provides asylum seekers with the means to develop a sense of dignity and promotes their integration into Irish society. The provision of a right to work is one method of creating the necessary conditions for more balanced participation in Irish society.[10] The argument put forward by Comhlamh and other like-minded NGOs focused largely on the right to work as a civic right that drew on, and was embedded in, the political sphere.

---

10 M. Peillon, 'Strangers in our Midst', in E. Slater and M. Peillon (eds), *Memories of the Present*, Dublin: IPA, 2000, p. 114.

Essentially, the right to work was conceptualised as an extension of the political rights of citizenship, predicated on Article 23 of the Universal Declaration of Human Rights: 'Everyone has the right to work . . . Everyone has the right to form and to join unions'.

On the other hand, there existed an alternative case for a more relaxed immigration policy that emphasised the right to work solely as an economic imperative, as distinct from a humanitarian or social right.[11] Thus, groups such as the Irish Business and Employers Confederation and the Irish Small and Medium Enterprises Association (ISME) focused principally on the needs of the economy and of employers. Their campaign was supported by members of the Progressive Democrats, such as Tánaiste and Minister for Enterprise, Trade and Employment, Mary Harney TD, and Minister of State in the Department of Foreign Affairs, Liz O'Donnell TD. For these groups, integration and social rights were secondary factors in the acceptance of asylum seekers – though the Progressive Democrats had drawn on the humanitarian discourse for political purposes – rather, they were ostensibly concerned with the right of individuals to sell their labour power freely as a commodity on the market. The argument put forward by the business lobby referred simply to the economic sphere and the need for labour. As ISME states:

> The basic question needs to be put, are we the Irish prepared for and ready to share this Island with a large influx of immigrants of various ethnic backgrounds from low wage economies in order to address the manpower shortage? It is a mystery to ISME, why many high quality African, Indian and Pakistani high tech graduates are refused permission to take up work in both foreign and Irish owned businesses. No such

---

11 B. Fanning, S. Loyal and C. Staunton, *Asylum Seekers and the Right to Work in Ireland*, Dublin: Irish Refugee Council, 2000.

reluctance is evident when it comes to the medical professions.[12]

In the more general context of the immigration of non-nationals, the business lobby tended to advocate a selective immigration policy aimed at preventing a general inflow of low-skilled people.[13] The Small Firms Association, ISME and Goodbody Stockbrokers, for example, advocated the establishment of a quota system based on the skills needs of the Irish economy – an immigration policy similar to the somewhat corporatist models of Australia and Canada.

These two arguments – the right to work as a civic/political right on the one hand, and as a pragmatic response to labour market shortages on the other – jointly under-pinned the case for asylum seekers to be granted the right to work. It is important to note that the various groups involved did not treat these two concerns or principles as mutually exclusive and many linked the economic and humanitarian arguments for allowing asylum seekers to work. However, as an analytical distinction, the question concerning which of these principles the respective groups prioritised and, importantly, which was recognised by the Irish state, is crucial.

The rift between these concerns also represents a division over the meaning of rights and citizenship. As noted earlier, the concept of citizenship is a contested one. Generally speaking, citizenship defines an individual's legal status within a nation-state in terms of rights and duties. However, the content of, and the question of access to, these rights is a contentious issue. For both NGOs and employers' groups, citizenship is largely tied to the notion of civic and political rights. However, NGOs tend to stress dignity, fairness and respect for other cultures; drawing upon the UN Charter of Human Rights, they emphasise cultural rights as a central

---

12 F. Mulcahy, *Manpower Shortages: What needs to be done?*, Dublin: ISME, 1999.
13 Mulcahy, ibid.

criterion in the determination of citizenship. While for employers, the civic right of freedom, particularly the freedom to sell one's labour power, is more important in defining the notion of citizenship. Both views of citizenship are open to criticism. The preoccupation with the freedom of the individual and with cultural rights tends to ignore issues of material equality. According to this argument, the capacity to enjoy freedom, construed in terms of self-determination and cultural recognition, is based only on the initial satisfaction of specific material needs.

In Ireland, the extension of the right to work to a limited number of asylum seekers arose as a compromise between the coalition partners in government. Fianna Fáil is a party that has moved historically from a populist to a corporatist orientation, but it still embodies tenets of social and conservative nationalism.[14] The Progressive Democrats (PDs), established in 1985, retain a strong ideological link to the Irish business community. The basis for the coalition of these parties was a shared liberal economic programme, despite the divergence in their broader social policies. The policy of denying asylum seekers the right to work was based on a belief, held by the Minister for Justice, Equality and Law Reform, that this right would attract more asylum seekers. This view was commensurate with the Department of Justice's historically, and institutionally, sedimented purview of national security. A compromise was reached when the PDs implicitly threatened to withdraw their support from the government over the issue, and explicitly criticised the minister in the media.[15] The result was a right to work that was limited in scope and in supporting rights.[16]

---

14 K. Allen, *Fianna Fáil and Irish Labour: 1926 to the Present,* London: Pluto, 1997.

15 See Liz O'Donnell's reference to the government's immigration policy as a 'shambles', *The Irish Times,* 29 June 1999.

16 These forms of support include employment training programmes, community employment schemes and forms of access to full-time education, language training and resettlement programmes.

The concession of this right was based on an economic imperative rather than on humanitarian principles, hence the continued lack of social and cultural support for asylum seekers.

At the end of the right-to-work amnesty, about half of the eligible asylum seekers were still unable to find a job. Figures from the Department of Social, Community and Family Affairs show that by 27 July 2001, 787 asylum seekers (out of the 3,535 entitled to work) had either found work or had ceased to claim social welfare payments for other reasons. Moreover, those who had found work tended to move into low-paid, insecure types of employment for which many were overqualified. Within this circumscribed horizon, the other major form of entry into the state, the work permit and work visa system, also became racialised.

Work permits – which are available for up to one year and thereafter are renewable annually – are only issued if employers can demonstrate that it has not been possible to fill the vacancy in question with indigenous labour. In the first six months of 2001, the largest numbers of work permits issued by the Department of Enterprise, Trade and Employment went to citizens of Latvia (2,362), Lithuania (1,287), Poland (1,202), Philippines (1,193), South Africa (1,014), Czech Republic (752), Romania (733) and Russian Federation (730).[17] The allocation of these work permits to countries of primarily white ethnic stock, suggests that whiteness carries with it considerable advantages within the application process and confers a kind of 'race privilege'.[18] It is probable that such individuals were perceived as more likely to assimilate with ease into Irish society (similar arguments were made in the past in support

---

17 'New Work Permits Aim to Prevent Exploitation', *The Irish Times*, 7 July 2001.
18 R. Frankenberg, *White Women, Race Matters: The Social Construction of Whiteness*, Minneapolis: University of Minnesota Press, 1993, p. 1.

of more generous visa allocations for Irish people wishing to work in the US). The one country which does not fit this profile is the Philippines, though it should be noted that between 80 and 90 per cent of Filipinos are Catholic.

Work visas and authorisations, which were specifically introduced to facilitate the recruitment of suitably qualified individuals in various sectors of employment, were less visibly racialised. The top five countries in receipt of the 991 work visas issued in 2000 were the Philippines, India, Russian Federation, Slovakia and Yugoslavia. It is noteworthy that this figure represents only about 5 per cent of the total number of work permits (18,017) issued the same year. Significantly, the top five countries for work authorisations, of which 396 were issued, were South Africa, Australia, US, Canada and New Zealand.

Conclusion

The contemporary political context concerning the right to work of asylum seekers reflects a new economic and social situation. It represents a struggle between acute economic needs and attempts to maintain a specific type of nation and national identity that presupposes a restricted notion of citizenship and ethnicity.[19] The Irish government finds itself in the contradictory position of having to maintain an economy which, by 2006, will require an estimated 336,000 skilled economic or labour migrants to meet its expanding needs, while at the same time, regulating the admission of individuals across its borders by deporting asylum seekers as 'bogus' and refusing the majority of them refugee status. Thus, although the number of asylum seekers applying for refugee status is continually rising, the numbers who

---

19 However, this should not be seen as an either/or situation, but merely as a shifting tendency within power contexts. For it would be fatuous to say that Fianna Fáil were not also pursuing business interests. Rather, it is the case that social conservatism plays a stronger role in their party ideology.

actually gain refugee status is rapidly declining. In 1999 Ireland received 7,724 applications for asylum and recognised 74; in 2000 it had received 9,080 applications by the end of October and recognised 34.[20] Moreover, non-nationals from outside the EU who were granted entry into the state through the work permit system were screened not only in terms of their skills, for purposes of meeting economic needs, but, more importantly, according to their physiological, ethnic and cultural similarity to Irish citizens.

Thus nationalism, compounded by Catholicism, operated as such a strong cementing force in the early years of the state that it has even managed to shape the economy in a determinate way. While the connection between nationalism and the economy was broken in the 1960s to some extent, concepts of Irishness remained inward looking, even as the economy began to follow its own independent logic, namely, the logic of capital. Capital, for Marx, is global, expansionary and profit-seeking. A contradiction is developing between the tradition of Irish nationalism – closed, insular, selective, discriminating and particular – and capitalism – open, expansionary, indiscriminate, global and universal.

Nonetheless, the Irish state has remained stringent in relation to the entry of non-nationals, as is witnessed by the low number of asylum seekers who have been granted refugee status and the ethnic profile of those who have been given work permits. Here notions of nationalism come into play. What does it mean to be Irish? Who may be accepted into Ireland? Since the foundation of the state, Irishness and citizenship have been correlated with whiteness and Catholicism. However, the increasing presence of people of colour and of different ethnicities and religions – whether through the asylum route or as part of the need for labour within the 'Celtic tiger' economy – has thrown this restricted view of Irishness into question. The response of the Irish

---

20 See L. Almirral and N. Lawton, *Asylum in Ireland: A Report on the Fairness and Sustainability of Asylum Determinations at First Instance*, Dublin: Refugee Council, 2000.

government to these transformations is not to celebrate diversity and multiculturalism – which is rare for any state anyway – but, rather, is one of restriction and closure.

CHAPTER 13

On the Waterfront

MARY P. CORCORAN*

C ities are in a constant state of formation, and nowhere is that more apparent than in Dublin at the turn of the twenty-first century. Building and rebuilding activities dissolve and recreate different areas as sites of activity and use. Whether it is the refurbishment of City Hall or the development of a public plaza at Smithfield, the road works necessitated by the building of LUAS or the re-invention of the Guinness plant as a state-of-the-art digital media hub, Dubliners have become accustomed to living in a city that is somewhat chaotically in the making.

The building and rebuilding processes, however, raise important questions about the nature of the city itself. Of primary importance to a city's sense of place are the often intangible and always unique qualities associated with the city's character, the meaning and integrity imbued in the vernacular of streetscapes, building design, boundary vistas and neighbourhood configuration. A sense of place in Dublin has historically derived from a complex of factors, including an architectural tradition, history and memory, literary narrative and lively sociability. But in the context of a

*I am grateful to the *Culture of Cities* project which provided a forum for the development of the ideas expressed in this chapter.

system of competing international cities, Dublin has of late been attempting to re-position itself as an attractive location for the global investor on the one hand, and the tourist gaze on the other. This has necessitated a makeover, in terms of the architecture and function of key urban landscapes. How is the 'aura' of the city to be defined in the twenty-first century – by the quality of its buildings, by its scale and design, by its ambience or by the diversity of its citizenry? These are questions to which Dubliners (and urban dwellers throughout Ireland) will increasingly be required to turn.

Any exploration of the character of a city inevitably leads us into the neighbourhood, for it is the mosaic of neighbourhoods that ultimately constitute the urban form. My concern in this chapter is to explicate how the re-making of the city is experienced and responded to at the level of the neighbourhood. An examination of local response in the Dublin docklands to the proposed development of Spencer Dock provides an insight into how place is socially constructed, how a place-bound identity is elaborated and how attachment to locality is reproduced and represented in wider discourses about the future of the city. Docklanders engage in a defence of place, as a source of security and identity, against the perceived threat posed by the 'placelessness' of the proposed development. In reality, their construction of a place-bound identity is driven, at least in part, by that fact that their particular place is already changing through the process of gentrification, which is largely beyond their control.

Developing Spencer Dock

Following the perceived success of the International Financial Services Centre and the Temple Bar renewal scheme in Dublin, a new docklands regeneration scheme was put in place by the government. As with the previous schemes, development is to be carried out in the context of a comprehensive master plan and under the guidance of a government-appointed supervisory body, in this case the

Dublin Docklands Development Authority (DDDA). The rhetoric of urban renewal is familiar in the stated aim of the DDDA: 'to provide homes for 25,000 people, create 40,000 new jobs and provide a menu of mammoth commercial schemes – a whole new thriving town in the heart of Dublin'.[1]

In 1998, the first proposal submitted for the development of fifty-one acres of the brown-field site emerged from a property consortium led by Treasury Holdings. An American-based architect designed a complex of twenty-six buildings for the site, including a national conference centre, apartment blocks, office buildings, hotels, parkland and the refurbishment and change of use of several listed buildings and structures. Partial planning permission was granted by Dublin Corporation, but this decision was appealed by a range of parties, including the local residents, the DDDA and the development consortium. In Spring 2000, as a result of the unprecedented scale of the scheme and the interest it had generated, An Bord Pleanála conducted an oral hearing. In July 2000, An Bord Pleanála rejected the bulk of the scheme, granting planning permission for the national conference centre only.[2]

The hearing on the Spencer Dock development project provides some insight into how the idea of the city, its future and its past, can become the focus of contested claims. Conflicts between commercial interests (Spencer Dock Development Company) and community values (local residents' associations) were largely grounded in arguments over the significance of place. The proponents of the scheme argued that the development would represent the most comprehensive urban project in the history of the state. It would be a landmark development that was, in the

---

1 *Sunday Tribune,* 19 October 1997.
2 For a discussion on the conference centre see M. Horgan, 'The Development of Dublin's Docklands', in P. Moore and M. Risk (eds), *Culture of Cities,* Toronto: Mosaic Press, 2001, pp. 138–45.

words of one architect, 'timely and reasonable'.[3] Another architectural critic defended the development on economic grounds, suggesting that since Dublin was already part of the global information economy it could capitalise on growth in that area by providing commercial buildings such as those proposed in the Spencer Dock scheme. He described the high-rise office towers featured in the development as 'perfect machines for working in', and argued that the scheme was daring and adventurous, creating a new quarter that would constitute 'an aesthetic as well as an economic breakthrough for a city too long held back by its own past'.[4] The developers insisted that, subject to minor alterations, the planned project would be acceptable in terms of architectural/urban design, traffic safety and convenience and would not adversely affect either the amenities in the area or property in the vicinity.

The residents (and a variety of other interested parties and groups) opposed the development on the basis of its architectural inappropriateness, excessive scale, environmental impact, disregard for the past, and social implications for the community. Different normative visions of the city were presented at the hearing, providing us with a rare opportunity to analyse how the urban form is read and interpreted by its various constituencies. In particular, oral testimonies by docklanders give us an insight into the importance of place in the everyday, taken-for-granted life of the city's historic neighbourhoods.

The docklands then, constitute a contested site, animated by the power relations and struggles between developers on the one hand, and conservationists and local residents' associations, on the other. The entire debate surrounding the Spencer Dock development brings into sharp relief the problem facing many contemporary cities that seek to regenerate themselves. That is, how to negotiate between the imperatives of the economy and marketplace, and the

---

3   *The Irish Times*, 15 March 2000.
4   *The Irish Times*, 7 March 2000.

city's role as a repository of culture, history and memory. The building of the Spencer Dock scheme on a brown-field site would not have directly involved the large-scale displacement of existing local communities, however, given its contiguity to the existing neighbourhood, local residents believe that the development would have had very real consequences for them. In the absence of an area action plan, which might have formed part of a planning-led approach to the development of the Spencer Dock site, the docklands residents' associations (along with the DDDA and other interested parties) were required to devise and articulate critiques of the project.

For the residents of the docklands, this meant political mobilisation through a network of representative groups, and fundraising in order to assemble legal and environmental experts who could present the technicalities of their case at the hearing. Individual residents submitted testimonies, as did all of the local residents' associations in the area. Critiques of the proposed development drew on a number of different discourses, ranging from the quality of life at home and in the street, extending out to the configuration of the neighbourhood and ultimately to issues about the kind of metropolis Dublin is to become. Here I will focus attention on the oppositional discourses emanating from those groups representing residents and their supporters, and in particular, the ways in which locality is deployed as a 'background scheme of interpretation' for social action.[5]

The urban villages of the docklands

Relph has argued that the potential for people to develop a sense of place in technologically advanced cultures has been undermined by the possibility of increased spatial mobility

---

5   H. Garfinkel, *Studies in Ethnomethodology,* Cambridge: Polity Press, 1967.

and by a weakening of the symbolic quality of places.[6] Cities in late modernity run the risk of losing their intrinsic character and identity, as spatial transformation renders them, more or less, like any other city. This same reasoning has been employed by the residents' groups, whose opposition to the reconfiguration of their neighbourhood is premised on the potential disruptive impact on the place-bound identity of the docklands.

A key argument mounted by the local residents' associations was that their neighbourhood retains a powerful sense of place, grounded in history, working-class culture and a web of familial ties. In terms of class composition, the docklands area is substantially different to the Greater Dublin region. For Much higher percentages of the population in the docklands are employed in the manual categories. However, the population profile is changing. Between 1991 and 1996, the rate of growth of the numbers employed in the professional, managerial and technical categories was substantially ahead of that of Dublin City and County as a whole. At the same time, there has been an increase in the number of households made up of two or more persons who are not related, and a decline in family households.[7] This evidence suggests that the social composition of the neighbourhood is already undergoing change; change that may be perceived, at least by the long-term residents, as potentially bad for the cohesiveness of the community as a whole. The Spencer Dock development, if granted permission, would in all likelihood have speeded up this change. Hence, the residents' associations sought to anchor their opposition in the past, presenting the community as a series of urban villages linked through collective memory, the historic relationship to the river and

6   E. Relph, *Place and Placelessness,* London: Pion, 1976, p. 66.
7   J. Williams and M. O'Connor, *The Employment and Socio-Demographic Profile of the Dublin Docklands Area,* Dublin: Economic and Social Research Institute, 2000.

the current attempts to defend the communities in the face of developer-led urban change.

Residents testified to their strong kinship ties, their rootedness in the neighbourhood and their orientation toward their own locale. One resident noted: 'My husband's family have lived in this house since 1847 and worked on the railways. We feel cheated . . . it is ironic to see CIÉ now part of a consortium attempting to get rid of former railway workers' housing'.[8] Another resident defined the neighbourhood as constituting 'a community of extended and integrated families, a close knit community, a parish, a village'.[9] Residents' groups argued that the reconfiguration of the neighbourhood would have a deleterious effect on community life: 'There are feelings of fear, isolation and domination resulting from these plans and this would be community genocide if this went ahead. There is life in our community, it's precious, warm and vibrant. Destroy this and you destroy it at your peril'.[10] Other similar statements on behalf of the residents' associations presuppose the existence of a coherent, homogeneous community – an assumption that is partly challenged by the available demographic evidence.

Traditionally, inner-city neighbourhood life is synonymous with a high degree of social interaction, a norm of reciprocity and a shared sense of the past. Everyday life is lived at eye level, whether on the balconies of low-rise flats or on the streets. The proposed development was viewed as a threat to the viability of neighbourhood so defined. All of the opponents of the scheme expressed their distaste for the overwhelming bulk, density and scale of the development. Residents spoke of being swamped and overwhelmed. They feared that the contiguity of the proposed development would have a disembedding effect on the neighbourhood,

8 *Sunday Business Post*, 20 February 2000.
9 Submission 22 to Spencer Dock Oral Hearing, 10 February to 14 March 2000.
10 *Irish Independent*, 25 February 2000.

exacerbating a process already underway through gentrification. The proposed buildings would be a daily reminder of their residual role in the revamped riverside neighbourhood. Social interaction would not be enhanced at street level, since most of the newcomers would be living in highrise blocks. Furthermore, the development threatened to fracture an important aspect of the flow of everyday life by cutting off the lower parish from the upper parish of the historic St Lawrence O'Toole's church.

In affirming the sense of a place-bound identity in the urban villages of the docklands, residents quite self-consciously reject the aestheticisation of place. For them, the significance of place is in the experiencing, creating and maintaining of that place, across the life course. Hence, the assertion that 'contrary to what people think North Wapping Street, Major Street and Abercorn Road are not part of some Jim Sheridan film set. They are homes where people were born, parents died, brothers and sisters emigrated to America and Australia and some have come back in their retirement'.[11] In a world of diminishing spatial barriers, where cultural products circulate in global space, differentiating between cultural representation and lived experience of place becomes problematic. In fact, in defence of the docklands and its sense of place, residents themselves must rely heavily on the cultural and symbolic content of the locale, since the materiality of the place (in the sense of its industrial past centred on the river) is disappearing.

Locals expressed fears of being cut adrift from the place, both real and imagined, that defines their identity. The residents, and their representative groups and supporters, frequently deploy metaphors to convey the pervasive sense of being under siege from the developers. For example, a local priest described the development as a massive mountain in the middle of his parish: 'if this is to be built it will be like living at the foot of the Grand Canyon or the

---

11 Submission 16 to Spencer Dock Oral Hearing, 10 February to 14 March 2000.

Cliffs of Moher with windows'.[12] It was also suggested that the proposed development would make Liberty Hall look like a phone box.[13] It was likened to a Trojan horse by Councillor Ciaran Cuffe and the Towers of Babel by Councillor Gerry Breen.[14] In the weeks before the hearing began, the Taoiseach, Bertie Ahern TD, went on record describing the development as 'a monstrosity'.[15]

A key element of the residents' defence was to portray their communities as urban villages, and cohesive communities embedded in the locality. This was contrasted with the impersonality and gigantism of a development anchored not in the street but in the sky. There is a denial here of the reality that the neighbourhood is already beginning to change; there is evidence of some fragmentation of the traditional working-class communities and intra-neighbourhood transformations are changing the composition of both the north and south docklands areas.

Place attachment

A second theme that resonates in the residents' submissions is the strong sense of place attachment, which tells us much about the meanings imputed by local people to their physical and cultural surroundings. Riley argues that place attachment implies an affective relationship between people and the ordinary landscape of everyday life, which can operate at scales from neighbourhood to entire regional, even national, landscapes. Such attachment is not only a source of satisfaction in and of itself, 'but the stuff of an ever-changing interior drama within the human psyche', wherein the attachment is elaborated through fantasy and

---

12 *The Irish Times*, 25 February 2000.
13 Inspector's Report, Volume 3: Oral Hearing, Ref. PL29N.112850, Dublin: An Bord Pleanála, 2000, p. 76.
14 Submission 3 and Submission 1 respectively, to Spencer Dock Oral Hearing, 10 February to 14 March 2000.
15 *Sunday Business Post*, 5 March 2000.

memory.[16] Crucially, place attachment comes from social interaction with other people and lived experience. The landscape provides the setting. Place as concretely experienced becomes internally reconfigured in the social imaginary. Indeed, Riley suggests that the power of place may lie not so much in inhabiting it, but in remembering it. A threat is thus posed to our individual and collective sense of place when confronted with the potential destruction or disruption of 'place experiences [that] are necessarily time-deepened and memory-qualified'.[17] For the docklanders, neighbourhood is defined not just in terms of its social reality, but also its spatiality, derived from the geography, history and memory of the locality.

Residents attempted to show the impact that the development would have in terms of the ordinary landscape of everyday life. They argued that it would cast shadows over the existing homes and streets denying them access to natural light and adversely affecting their quality of life. Docklands' Communities Against High Rise expressed concern at the prospect of residents losing natural light as early as 6.00 p.m. in mid-summer and 2.00 p.m. or 3.00 p.m. in the winter. If the development were to go ahead, one resident predicted that 'Living on Mayor Street would be like solitary confinement' and his hobby of gardening would be pointless if his property was to be permanently overshadowed.[18]

The combined residents' associations argued that the proposed development would 'remove the context of the quays and the vista of the bay from the indigenous

---

16 R. B. Riley, 'Attachment to the Ordinary Landscape', in S. M. Low and I. Altman (eds), *Place Attachment*, London: Plenum Press, 1992, p. 19.
17 Heidegger quoted in D. Harvey, 'From Space to Place and Back Again: Reflections on the Condition of Postmodernity', in J. Bird et al. (eds), *Mapping the Future: Local Cultures, and Global Change*, London: Routledge, 1993, p. 11.
18 Inspector's Report, ibid., p. 72.

population'.[19] Furthermore, an urban design assessment, commissioned by the residents' associations, submitted that the development would 'intrude on the distant backdrop and breach the distant silhouette of the Dublin mountains from key locations'.[20] Apart from the aesthetic appeal of access to a panoramic skyline, the point was made that this skyline was part of the neighbourhood's heritage because it was referred to in the writings of Brendan Behan and Sean O'Casey, who lived in the area. The attachment to place, as represented at the oral hearing, is conditioned by the background landscape, which, over time, has taken on a particular meaning for residents.

Apart from presenting the docklands as a geographically distinct place with a particular relationship to the city and the skyline, for the purpose of the hearing, residents' groups also constructed their neighbourhood as a repository of Dublin's literary and historical heritage. The meaning of the neighbourhoods can be symbolically represented by the various heroes and characters who have claimed (or have had claims advanced on their behalf) to have an association with the docklands. Tony Gregory TD recalls that he swam and fished in Spencer dock: 'the railway tracks there were my playground'.[21] James Joyce and his brother Stan mitched from school and made their way to the Wharf Swimming Slip in East Wall. Sean O'Casey was a resident for years, as was the renowned folk singer, Luke Kelly. The Sheridan brothers were born on Abercorn Road.[22]

Here the residents' defence focused on the docklands as a special kind of place, which, because of its particular spatial

---

19 Inspector's Report, Volume 2, Ref. PL29N.112850, Dublin: An Bord Pleanála, 2000, Appendix 8.6.
20 Inspector's Report, ibid., Appendix 6.12.
21 Submission 115 to An Bord Pleanála regarding Spencer Dock development, 13 March 2000.
22 Submission 50 to Spencer Dock Oral Hearing, 10 February to 14 March 2000.

relationship to the rest of the city and its role as the repository of part of the city's cultural heritage and memory, should not be violated.

Manhattan on the Liffey

A third theme that emerged in the oppositional discourses was the view that the proposed development represented a kind of battering ram of globalisation, which would inevitably level all semblance of the local in Dublin. The Spencer Dock development plan was described as 'A piece of Manhattan transposed to Dublin which exemplifies the worst excesses of American corporate planning. It looks back to the mistakes of the 1960s rather than the potential of the 21st Century'.[23] This theme was elaborated by Michael Smith, the chairman of An Taisce, when he argued that the 1990s were probably among the worst years in the aesthetic evolution of the city of Dublin: 'Every time I see the visuals for the Spencer Dock Development Scheme the theme music to the soap opera Dallas plays in my head because it is so clearly 1980s or earlier American. It's vulgar and anodyne in architectural character . . . it's all about blocks rather than the European model'.[24]

One councillor went further in criticising the Americanisation of Dublin and suggested that Spencer Dock would result in the 'ethnic cleansing' of the docklands area of the city, a statement that echoed that of the resident who spoke of community genocide.[25] International financier, Dermot Desmond, argued that the 'the design of the individual buildings is inspired by American corporate architecture, and is inappropriate in the context of an historical European city'.[26] The Irish Georgian Society said that the buildings

23 *The Irish Times*, 10 February 2000.
24 *The Irish Times,* 27 May 2000.
25 *The Irish Times,* 27 May 2000.
26 Inspector's Report, ibid., Appendix 8.4.

would add nothing to the site other than 'a déjà vu of some uninteresting downtown US city'.[27] Residents' groups echoed this critique, suggesting that 'an American-style city would be created, and Major Street would be a canyon-like wind-blown street' and that the proposal amounted to 'an anti-social intrusion and an Americanised type of development that would be to the detriment of this vibrant community'.[28] One residents' association leader contended that the 'development is about lots of money and Americanised tycoons with big buildings and big money – all to the detriment of the little people, insignificant people like me. I don't have money but I have a sense of something bigger than money or arrogance'.[29]

The concerns expressed point to a rejection of 'placelessness', which is seen by all critics of the scheme as synonymous with corporate, American-inspired architecture.

Conclusion

In the wake of An Bord Pleanála's decision against the Spencer Dock Development Company, it is unclear whether or not any part of the proposed development will go ahead. The developers had warned that the national conference centre could not be built or funded without revenue from six million square feet of apartments, offices and hotels. While it is inevitable that the docklands will be re-developed, there is considerable uncertainty about what shape development will take. The Spencer Dock episode, however, has provided some useful insights into how local responses to changes from above are constructed and represented.

The structures of the DDDA allowed for considerable representation of dockland communities. This departed

---

27 *Irish Independent*, 25 February 2000.
28 Inspector's Report, Volume 3: Oral Hearing, Ref. PL29N.112850, Dublin: An Bord Pleanála, 2000, pp. 72, 75.
29 *Irish Independent*, 25 February 2000.

from the practice of earlier renewal schemes in which the voices of the indigenous communities were largely sidelined. As a party to the docklands master plan, local community residents and their representatives were given a sense of themselves as stakeholders in the future redevelopment of their neighbourhoods. Nevertheless, this co-optation did not ultimately protect the interests of the residents. When the Spencer Dock Development Company launched its campaign with the backing of CIÉ, the residents' associations had to scramble to create a cohesive front and to develop their own oppositional discourse, outside of the DDDA and alongside the much bigger and slicker guns of Dermot Desmond. The proceedings were dominated by expert witnesses on all sides, and to a large extent the residents remained marginalised.

The residents' representatives employed a territorial, place-based identity as a basis for their political mobilisation. Their commitment to constructing the docklands as a particular kind of place in the mosaic of Dublin's inner-city neighbourhoods owed more to its representational and symbolic qualities than its material base in reality. The docklands are already changing. The community is rapidly losing touch with its industrial past. Dublin's affluent classes are infiltrating the neighbourhood, posing a secular threat to the parish and a cultural threat to the community. The communities chose to represent themselves symbolically as a cluster of urban villages linked through a powerful sense of place attachment to the locality. To some extent, their defence can be read as a form of reactionary and exclusionary politics that harks backward to the past.

The interrogation of the proposed development may also be interpreted as a questioning of the whole globalisation process neatly summed up in the term 'the Manhattanisation of Dublin'. There appears to be a growing awareness that unfettered development, which does not take account of the vernacular of the city, can only lead to a Dublin that is much the same as anywhere else and, therefore, a nowhere place. Furthermore, there was a clear sense that if Dublin was to look for models of development it was not to America but to Europe that it should orient itself.

Nevertheless, a clear vision of the kind of development that would be deemed appropriate for the neighbourhood did not emerge from the proceedings. While residents and their supporters contend that they are not opposed to development per se, they fail to specify what the nature of a place-specific and place-sensitive development would be.

Communities, planners and developers must now seek to identify a form of development that is consensual across a broader spectrum of the citizenry and that is closer in its design, scale and aesthetic to the city vernacular. How do we find a way to express our modernity – that reaches out to the global, while respecting the local? Evidence presented to the oral hearing on the Spencer Dock scheme points to the struggle to define and sustain the individuality of Dublin amidst all those forces that threaten to render the city indistinct. The very openness of a city like Dublin to change and to global influences also limits its capacity to sustain and cultivate its distinctiveness as a meaningful local place.

PART 4

RESILIENT BOUNDARIES

CHAPTER 14

Big Boats: The Transformation of Irish Offshore Fishing

PETER COLLIER

In July 2000, Kevin McHugh launched his €63.5m vessel, *Atlantic Dawn*. This Irish flag vessel is one of the biggest of its type in the world. Large factory vessels such as the *Atlantic Dawn,* although fishing outside European fisheries' waters, dwarf smaller native boats. Owned by catching entrepreneurs and fishing conglomerates, they are heralded with great pomp and ceremony. The success of the catching entrepreneur is marked by the financial opportunities offered to loyal crewmen and by an increased stake in the hunt for fish. The boat is much more than a hunting machine; it is the symbol of its owner's power to influence fishermen and fishing politics and the bigger the vessel, the greater the capacity to attract new crew. *Atlantic Dawn* and the new 'big boats' have an awe-inspiring effect on fishermen's mentalities: they announce the end of the conventional fishing practices.

The share-fishing convention

Irish fishing crewmen[1] do not benefit from a professional career regulated by institutional norms. They need not

---

1   There are an estimated 1,800 active crewmen on 396 Irish-registered fishing vessels. Offshore fishing is defined as fishing trips

undergo any statutory sea training for entry to the fishing hunt. Irish vessel owners have not been obliged to provide a minimum wage and insurance since 1986. Government solutions, under jurisprudence principles, allow crewmen to choose either self-employed or employee status upon joining a fishing expedition. Irish crewmen (deckies) participate in the fishing hunt in the absence of a clear statutory code of rights and responsibilities for either party.[2] Native offshore fishing operates according to conventional relations, which are particular to each harbour. Historical 'dispositions' and technical changes led to the organisation of locally specific work strategies. Deeply inculcated in the group, these dispositions become a second nature, a 'habitus' – that persists over time and changes slowly, according to conditions.[3]

This conventional fishing habitus remains conditioned by a hunter mentality. The fishing expedition is learned as a gamble by individuals to seek their fortune. The successful catching entrepreneur enjoys high prestige and this sea quest for status occurs within a local economy of honour.

---

1 (contd).

   of more than 72 hours away from the home port. *Task Force Report on Training and Employment in the Irish Seafood Industry,* Dublin: European Social Fund, Pesca and the National Development Plan, 2001. The task force was composed of representatives from 14 companies engaged in the seafood industry.

2 National jurisprudence defined the work status of crew fishermen as 'co-adventurers with the boat owner'. Every fishing adventure is considered as a unique event and thus an individual investment in hunting risks. Contingent national strategy, post-CFP (Common Fisheries Policy) entry in 1983, was to adopt a self-employment policy as found in the UK and the US and not other European fishery states. See the report of the government-appointed Sectoral Consultative Committee on the Common Fisheries Policy and its Effects in the Republic of Ireland, *The Development of the Fishing Industry,* Dublin: Government Publications, 1984, p. 72. This committee included 21 representatives of the fishing industry.

3 See, for instance, Pierre Bourdieu, *In Other Words. Essays Towards a Reflexive Sociology*, Cambridge: Polity Press, 1990.

This individualism is sustained by the drive to attain the autonomy of boat ownership. Such individualism is contained by a close working solidarity, the 'we-ness' of the hunting group that develops out of the sheer physical harshness of the task. While working relations may lack statutory rules and are regulated by the share-fishing convention, the habitus upholds rules of fairness demanded by harbour fishermen. These rules are changing. Local fishing economies are subject to greater social and technical control. Fishing strategies are guided by the transfer of the conventional fishing habitus into a field governed by European fishing policy and global sector demand. This dynamic is signalled by increased commercial organisation, along with new modes of crew discipline. In particular, the launching of the 'big boats' flying the national flag threatens to subsume smaller coastal fishing identities. This is illustrated by tracing fishermen's careers over three generations in the south-eastern port of Kilmore Quay, County Wexford.

Genesis of a local fishing habitus

The institutionalisation of commercial fishing in the Republic of Ireland dates from only the 1960s. Prior to this, exceptional fishing entrepreneurs took risks and mobilised younger kin to venture beyond local horizons to seek the 'big lift'.[4] They fished the 'silver gold' of herring, emulating the practices of the hundred or so foreign boats fishing the Dunmore Fishery off Hook Head. The family dispositions of these modern fishing pioneers dominate the pelagic catching order of Killybegs, Galway, Dingle, Castletownbere, Dunmore East and, to a lesser extent, Kilmore Quay.

---

4   The quotations presented throughout this chapter give a glimpse of the different standpoints in a local fishing harbour; they are drawn from a number of interviews conducted for the following study: Peter Collier, *A Monograph Study of Offshore Fishing and Social Change in Kilmore Quay*, Dublin: Marine Institute, Marine Resources Series, no. 15, 2001, available online at www.marine.ie.

The fishing pioneers in the Wexford coastal area, and specifically Kilmore Quay, came from a sea-going tradition of coasting schooners-colliers and deep-sea crewing from Liverpool. World War II brought the more energetic into the merchant navy and monies earned saw fishing return as a realistic opportunity after 1945. Regular inshore catching became a way of life for Kilmore Quay families at the end of the 1950s.

Through his risk-taking and charisma, Willie Bates (1910–94) established fishing as a 'real family thing' in the village of Kilmore Quay. His hard work and forward-looking ideas propelled the Bates family into the boat-owning hierarchy. Bates had worked on schooners and was a skipper of a salvage vessel during the 1930s. After World War II he bought the *Mystical Rose*, which became the unofficial training ship for his five sons and other young men of the Quay. Two other boat-owning families, the Scallans and the Powers, mobilised kin in the same way. It was the lucrative economy of herring fishing that brought these family boats and about sixty fishermen into the early 1960s.

New entrants were nominated by a combination of blood links to boat-ownership, bank credit guarantees and individual will to take risks when contingencies (such as the early death of a father) struck a family. A feeling of restlessness during school days spent 'on the back bench' made fishing attractive as an early exit strategy from school and an alternative to emigration. 'Going fishing' was considered by an agrarian society as non-conformist and 'for those who didn't like the books'. In the local schools no mention was made of either the sea or its work possibilities. Opinion held that 'only poor men fish'.

Pre-selection of the young men who would go fishing and those who would not was heavily influenced by local social divisions. Artisan fishing could sustain young kinsmen provided its founding peers sanctioned selection and exercised discipline over the fishing life. Fishing, as one pioneer skipper put it, 'is the only thing we have here, other than the farmers'. The ambition to become independent fishermen had its origin in the division between those owning viable farms and a labouring cohort whose ownership of small holdings provided bank collateral for a fishing boat.

The first fishermen's co-operative in the Republic of Ireland was founded in 1956 in Kilmore Quay. The co-op developed activities around the core fishing families, intent on controlling fish prices locally. Founders were highly individualistic and co-operative action was a strategy to service their catching units. Abundant and regular fish supply to the co-op attracted fish processing plants into the harbour zone at the end of the 1970s.[5] The arrival of 'fish business' entrepreneurs increased the demand for quality product, prompting local fishermen to invest in a processing plant, 'to cut out the middleman'. However this venture failed and was taken over by private interests in 1981. While not commercially successful, the Kilmore Quay Fishermen's Co-operative helped diffuse rules of 'fairness' into the early organisation of fishing crews. Fishermen judge successful fishing locales to be 'fair' when boat owners are perceived as reasonable in their management of work and openness about payments.

However, working practices also produced intergenerational conflict. A new, brash style of fishing entrepreneur emerged from those young men who had been initiated into the wheelhouse. They made no secret of their determination to break away from the 'posse' and to beat the 'old men at their game'. The most important of them was JK who was recognised by the local fishing families as the inheritor of Willie Bates' charisma and prestige because 'you knew he had the trait, he had the energy and this . . . strange go'.

---

5   Estimated annual turnover from fish landings at Kilmore Quay increased from €317,435 in 1975 to €4.44m in 1996, while the number of offshore fishing vessels increased from 12 to 25, with 15 full-time inshore vessels during the same period.

Pathway of a catching entrepreneur

This second generation of fishing entrepreneurs innovated a 'more calculated' catching style, dependent on local knowledge for navigation and sonar technology for catching.[6] In 1978, JK purchased a large, Irish-built vessel with finance raised from BIM (Bord Iascaigh Mhara – the Irish sea fisheries board) 'unaware that at the time there were banks available to put the money up' (interest rates moved from an initial 8 per cent per annum to a crippling 21 per cent by 1980). It took JK 'seventeen years to climb out of the mess' he had committed himself to. He considers that out of the sixteen young Irish skippers who committed their energies to similar national contracts 'only two or three of us have come through'. To 'come through', JK put in one fishing year of 263 days at sea, 'keeping the head down'. JK never considered abandoning Kilmore Quay, which he describes as 'his home and his base', even though he had to pay a high price to stay there.

JK is viewed by his colleagues as 'one of the most successful catching entrepreneurs of his generation'. The question of whether he should have moved his operation to a more lucrative fishing locale is part of his daily confrontation with self-doubt. Skipper-owners, like JK, must trust their intuition to succeed, 'to know where to fish just trust whatever is coming into you'. Highly motivated by 'the fishing buzz', JK likes nothing 'better than to be on my own when hunting'. He uses the collective 'we' when he describes his boat and its crew as his catching unit. He does not listen to world news when at sea and he does 'not talk as there is so much happening right around us and it needs full concentration'. He considers 'knowing what you want' as being essential to the catching plan as 'how in the name of God can He give me what I want when I don't know myself'.

---

6   Satellite global positioning systems (GPS) and sonar instruments can pinpoint mackerel shoals to a 3 km radius of precision.

JK is a believer in divine providence and in his own ability to continue to catch more fish. He has the reputation of driving his men to the limit. However, he is judged as fair in his dealings with others, and being fair remains a key factor in retaining a crew. He is 'very conscious of the situation of the man working on the deck', and the fact that he 'must come back and put up a decent week's wages for the lads'. His professional standpoint is: 'Once they are looked after then I am definitely OK'. At the same time, he baulks at taking responsibility for his crew's health insurance and tax affairs. In total they only spend 'twenty weeks at sea', and he does not know why 'they should be looked after' by him as 'they earn more than most onshore workers'.

Like JK, the majority of the second-generation, Irish skipper-owners who survived the 1980s are conservative in their investment strategies today. Their experience of market fluctuations and financial instability, increasing surveillance by Common Fisheries Policy policing, combined with the perils of the sea, do not encourage them to increase the size of their catching units or to take bigger financial risks. For many, their vessel and its official fishing tonnage are their sole patrimonial assets; they must decide whether to pass it on to the next generation or to quit the fishing game.

A fishing partnership

A recent development in Irish offshore fishing is multi-vessel ownership. In 1988, four of the O'Flaherty brothers came together in an effort to set up a business in their native village of Kilmore Quay.[7] They established a 'loose partnership of honour' and obtained one of the last sea fishery licences from the Department of the Marine. Pooling

---

7   The father of the O'Flaherty brothers, a retired tillage farmer, had no immediate connection with the local fishing families. However, storm records going back to the late 1880s show that along with other land-owning families who lost boats there was an O'Flaherty family recorded.

their capital, they borrowed from the bank (not availing of BIM grant assistance) and assembled a fleet of second-hand fishing vessels. Their drive towards fishing autonomy was built on dispositions embedded in Kilmore Quay's fishing habitus. The share-fishing convention was transposed to the new working arrangements by inserting a new figure in the crew: the supervisory skipper.

The O'Flaherty partnership has gone from strength to strength. Today, there are more than sixty people working around them and their enterprise enjoys prestige among the other fishermen. The O'Flaherty 'star is rising now in Kilmore Quay, just as Willie Bates's did, because they saw what other people saw centuries ago. Keep the steam up and the nets down. They took it a step forward by making it socially a wee bit better'.

The common sense approach of the brothers was to 'keep the boat fishing all the time', as it 'was the only way to get into' the catching sector from the outside. The working arrangements of the catching units were changed, with the introduction of a '10 days on/10 days off' roster. The O'Flaherty crews are each composed of seven men, four of whom go to sea at a time. Every fifth trip is a back-to-back double sortie that assures continuity and crew commitment to their fishing unit's success. The majority of the group's vessels work on a percentage system of 60:40, whereby 40 per cent of residual profits (less fuel and food costs) of every expedition are divided across seven and a half shares (the skipper receives an extra half share). In this way, men resting at home know that their colleagues at sea are 'working for them':

> What attracted me to the O'Flaherty boat was the time off. Now you know that you will get at least four days at home with your family. Even that is a lot for a man with a big family as he can go and do something. The old system meant that if you wanted to do something you had to take off time for which you did not get paid. Now when you are out there you have to make it pay for

everyone. You are paid now for your time off. Where would you get that anywhere? . . . That's what I find attractive about the job: time off with pay.

Each crew has autonomy regarding decisions taken on where and how the vessel operates and, to a lesser extent, who may join the crew in the event of defection or what is still commonly called 'jumping ship'.

A risk-taking orientation and a commitment to keep boats at sea have given the group wider margins of freedom over local artisan boat-owners. 'They have passed the risk barrier' is the general opinion acknowledging the group's fishing success. The partnership owns the regulatory tonnage that allows them direct access to the Spanish market for quality fresh fish. They run four large container lorries to Spain at the height of the fishing season. Higher quality standards increase demand on crewmen to handle the fish with care on board and transport it directly upon landing. The O'Flahertys delegate to their supervisory skipper the authority to supervise his catching unit's strategy at sea in order to motivate the crew. The reality is that the fish no longer command the hunt, but the market.

Individual crews negotiate their own informal agreements on how they work together at sea and hunt fish. 'What happens on the boat, stays on the boat', is the universal rule of all fishing crews. Transparency is sought at the pay-off after each trip and experienced crews know what their overall catch is worth on the market. 'If a deckie does not know to within a tenner what his boat has caught then he shouldn't be fishing'. In this transforming sea-fishery environment, experienced crewmen evaluate money-making opportunities in the context of: the sea practices of the catching units and fairness amongst the crewmen overseen by a supervisory skipper; and the legitimacy of the boat owner's authority and the transparency of shares from the fish sale profits.

There is no formal contract of employment, but informal share agreements that attract crewmen towards the more powerful catching units. Boat owners must constantly ensure that trust prevails. 'He works for us', said one owner, while another countered, 'no he works with us'. This ambiguity surrounding a crewman's professional status reflects the convention of share fishing with its invisible ties to possible boat ownership. The preferred designation of crewmen who may have inheritance chances, however distant, is self-employed. However, the majority of men working on fishing decks with which they have no blood-ties consider themselves as employees.

'Fishing is all about money' and the dominant opinion of bigger boat owners is that freedom of movement for crewmen labour is the only way to motivate men to go to sea for ten-day trips. With market demands as close to fishing crews as their mobile phones, a new commercial regime increasingly adapts conventional share-fishing practices to keep boats at sea. The strategic goal of 'big boat' ownership is to introduce a new fishing regime to allow for greater risk control of financial investment and salaried deck-factory work. The effects of this on an unregulated labour market is that it is difficult for smaller artisan units to retain ambitious and experienced crewmen. Tightening profit margins force crewmen to compare fishing with onshore labour opportunities. To increase their individual returns from share-fishing, catching units must reduce the number of expedition shares (that is the number of crewmen on board), thus increasing work at sea and, with fatigue, safety risks.

Social effects of a new fishing regime

At the bottom of this seafood hierarchy is the native deckhand and his family, many of whom remain outside social and fiscal regulation, and are thus dominated by an increasingly arbitrary labour market. Irish crewmen are unsure of their statutory rights as few have the time 'to read up on things like that'. They consider themselves to be 'mavericks', 'pirates' or 'outsiders', dependent on informal network ties to stay in the 'fishing gamble'.

During the 1980s, 'going fishing' attracted younger men without school qualifications, while a second generation of skipper-owners negotiated alliances to increase catching opportunities. During the 1990s, Irish offshore fishing became more rationalised, driven by better catching technology and monopolising fishing tonnage on the open market. This provided experienced crewmen with a stronger sense of security. However, as competitive forces and diminishing fish stocks demand more time at sea to earn equivalent returns, the onshore lives of deckhands and their dependants becomes subject to increasing uncertainty.

The social and cultural patterns of life for these men are characterised by a closed, loosely bound fraternity, based on the fact that they share a hard working-life. Distinctive body signs such as razed head, earrings and fanciful arm tattoos identify crewmen. Fishing life at sea is 'forgetful' of onshore events and problems, despite mobile phone connection with partners and friends. A fishing life is a constant sequence of trips into the unknown challenge of the hunt. When skippers leave the harbour, they often do not know their ultimate fishery destination. They decide as the hunting expedition unfolds, relying on experienced insight, tracking technology and gaming tactics. Radio and telephone conversations are screened constantly, as information about fish whereabouts is monitored. Conversation among different fishing crews is influenced constantly by 'finding out something about another boat or back-stabbing other men'.

This dual configuration, of at-sea boat secrecy and onshore alienation from normal social life, structures the fisherman's world as latently schizophrenic. During moments of withdrawal from the hunt's drive to *fortuna,* (during illness or regular failure to land sufficient fish), fishermen have difficulty articulating a coherent meaning for life onshore. Depression is common among those who consider themselves, or are considered by opinion, to be no longer 'winning in the fishing game'. Given the high profile of the successful catching entrepreneur and his spanking new 'big boat', those who are positioned on the margins must motivate themselves before every trip back to sea. While the prize of success in offshore fishing can be very rewarding, the psychological fallout of failure can be fatal.[8]

Between high moments of hauling the 'big lift' are long months of repetitive deck work. Offshore fishing is an 'anti-social and macho-thing' of physical endurance, a performance orchestrated inside a small habitat: the sea-home and workplace of the boat. The shared conditions of men with the 'fishing buzz' produce strong crew ties with their boat home, which distance many from family households onshore.

'Big boat' awe as symbolic force

Irish fishing locales were organised around strong kinship ties that engendered an egalitarian discourse in the close competition between boat-owning families. During this stage of modern fishing's development, the community provided the dominant symbol of identification and constraint. Fishing was structured by patriarchal control. The drive towards fishing autonomies, in the case of Kilmore Quay, was family-oriented rather than organised as a co-operative effort. Capital accumulation and higher risk-taking saw the emergence of powerful individual catching entrepreneurs. The losers of this high-risk game had their boats repossessed (a juridical act perceived as symbolic violence) during the 1980s, most of these men became relief skippers for the successful entrepreneurs. Despite the harshness of this selection, there remained a sense of the identification with the harbour locale. This identification

---

8   Suicide is not uncommon in the fisherman's world. Its presence haunts every fishing harbour in Ireland. There is a common saying that when a man has had enough of the sea, he 'must walk away with his back to the harbour and never look back'. 'You mustn't let fishing get to you, if it gets to you then you are dead', said one older fisherman.

has been increasingly challenged, however, by the commercial transformation of the fishing order during the 1990s.[9]

The accumulation of a fleet of more powerful vessels by the O'Flaherty brothers helped to treble the cumulative fishing effort of Kilmore Quay over a period of fifteen years. The transfer of conventional practices into new organisational structures of crewing was the key to this success. In the process, the local symbol of a 'fishing community' was weakened as the symbol of the new regime: 'big boat' fishing, came to the fore.[10]

This effected a transformation of local fishing dispositions. The powerful attraction exercised by a bigger fishing group alters traditional practices in relation to recruitment choices and norms of fairness.

It is not just the economic force of this new regime of fishing organisation that attracts men, but the symbolic force of the 'big boat'. This force is closer to sheer awe when related to the general state of the Irish fishing fleet. Many of the second generation fishing elite, whose life's work was to secure autonomy for family fishing patrimonies, can no longer see a future framed by a local fishing habitus. Many declare that 'fishing is finished', when the reality is that 'fishing has finished with them'. The harshness of this

9   Out of a total of 130 men working on offshore fishing boats (staying at sea for an average of five days per trip) only 37 are related to the original Kilmore fishing family core, while 93 men have no kinship ties to these families. See Peter Collier, *A Monograph Study of Offshore Fishing and Social Change in Kilmore Quay*, Dublin: Marine Institute, Marine Resources Series, no. 15, 2001, available online at www.marine.ie.

10 Symbolic embodiment of patrimonial ties during the second generation of fishing was given to the naming of boats after daughters or wives. In 1977, ten of the 32 boats from Kilmore Quay carried the names of wives or daughters. New boat names reflect the change from kinship alliances with boat ownership to the drive toward corporate identities for boats. The naming of a new O'Flaherty beam trawler *The Quay Fisher* in 1999 is an example of this change in local fishing symbols of identification.

realisation is that many distance themselves from any collective project to reproduce their harbour locale as a historic fishing community or knowledge-based identity.[11] They wait, sitting on their fishing spoils, as one of the more successful second-generation entrepreneurs put it, 'for something to happen, preferably a hurricane!'.

---

11 This is significant regarding the new sea fishery proposals contained in *Towards Innovation and Sustainability in the Fisheries Sector – Supporting Measures for Sea Fisheries Development*, Policy Guidelines, Dublin: Department of the Marine and Natural Resources, 2001. Unless this elder elite can be induced back to invest their time and knowledge into the local management of small coastal fisheries, then the future is bleak.

CHAPTER 15

The Gendered Field of Irish Sport

KATIE LISTON*

Football is all very well as a game for Rough Girls, but it is hardly suitable for Delicate Boys.

Oscar Wilde

There can be no doubt that sport is important in Irish society. Think, for example, of the reception awarded to the Irish men's soccer team on their return from the 1990 World Cup; the attention regularly devoted to sport in the mass media; the importance of sport activities in terms of employment, tourism, travel and the Irish economy (sport accounted for 2 per cent of Ireland's GDP in 1994 and the 1.4 per cent share of consumer spending on sport that year ranked Ireland third in a list of seven European countries);[1] the numbers who take part in sport as participants or spectators (in 1995, 74 per cent of a representative sample of Irish men and women stated that they regularly participated in sport);[2] the impact in 2001 of the Foot and

---

* My thanks to A. Feldman and A. Mulcahy for their comments on this chapter.
1 *The Economic Impact of Sport in Ireland,* Dublin: Department of Education, 1994.
2 *A National Survey of Involvement in Sport and Physical Activity,* Dublin: Department of Education and the Health Promotion Unit, 1996.

Mouth virus on the sporting timetable (Gaelic football, hurling, soccer, rugby, camogie, athletics and so forth), which served to highlight the diversity and importance of sport to many; and the 'household name' status accorded to successful sportsmen and women, for example Sonia O'Sullivan, Michelle Smith, Roy Keane and Brian O'Driscoll. As a former minister of state notes:

> Irish people love their sport and either play or follow a wide range of sporting activities ... The value of participation in sport and active leisure pursuits in the physical, psychological and social development of individuals is well documented and accepted.[3]

Not only is sport a popular activity, it is also deeply embedded in the social fabric of society. The idea that sport is good for one's physical and mental health reflects an increasing awareness of health and lifestyle choices. Sport also enshrines the value of achievement in upholding a standard of excellence and serves to build an achievement-oriented national character. It crystallises collective identities, whether it be at parish, club, team, county, national or international level. It unites against the 'enemy', but also pits one group against another. Sport generates excitement and helps release tension in our everyday lives. It teaches us the value of fair play, of being magnanimous in defeat and gracious in victory.

Sports have varied in form throughout history (contrast gladiatorial combat to synchronised swimming) but generally modern sports are best defined as: 'institutionalised competitive activities that involve vigorous physical exertion or the use of relatively complex physical skills'.[4] Sports,

---

3 Bernard Allen TD, in *Targeting Sporting Change in Ireland: Sport in Ireland 1997–2003 and Beyond,* Dublin: Department of Education, 1997, p. iii.

4 J. J. Coakley, *Sport in Society: Issues and Controversies,* New York: McGraw-Hill, 1998, p. 19.

defined in this way, are distinguished from play/spectacle and exercise (structured, regular and rhythmic movements designed to maintain physical fitness). This is not to suggest, however, that sports do not include these aspects. In fact, sport combines intrinsic enjoyment, the desire to display physical skills and physical fitness, but it is the balance between these factors that distinguish it from either dramatic spectacle or play. This definition also covers individual and team sports and while the dynamics may vary between the two, the actual forms of the sport do not change. This chapter focuses on high-profile team sports such as rugby, Gaelic games and soccer, with only brief references to individual sports such as tennis and athletics. While positive functional aspects of sport have been previously identified, the following analysis takes a more critical look at how sport generates its own practices and ways of looking at the world, particularly as a gendered 'habitus'.

Sporting capital and the gendered value of sporting achievement

Sporting capital can be defined as the forms of power held by athletes such as achievement, ability, 'sportsmanship' and competitiveness, and its value is ultimately determined by its capacity to be translated into monetary reward, jobs, general status, star status, political influence and so forth. This concept is adapted from Bourdieu's analysis of social life, how it is constituted through the interaction of people in, and between, different 'fields', for example the economic field, the cultural field and the political field. The sporting field could be seen as having its own practices or ways of being (laws). 'It is constituted through a struggle for different stakes between challengers and established dominant actors'.[5] The dominant positions in the sporting

---

5   P. Bourdieu, *Sociology in Question*, London: Sage, 1993, p. 72.

field depend on the resources or capital that athletes accumulate through sports and through interaction with other fields, for example translating sporting success into financial reward through product endorsements or into celebrity status as a sports commentator on television. The accumulation of sporting capital, importantly, determines a person's or group's ability to contribute to and change the dominant discourse on sport.

It can be contended, for instance, that the successful participation of men in the game of rugby generates a sporting capital which enjoys a high value and can be converted into various social rewards. For one, its membership draws from a relatively privileged class background and attracts strong economic investment. The game is entering a professional era and recent international successes have reinforced its popularity and marketability. More importantly, the close association between rugby and masculinity accounts for its broad base of support throughout Ireland. Men's rugby exemplifies the structuring principles of sporting capital, in that it is characterised by a high level of physical contact, strength, competitiveness, aggression, risk of injury and the 'will to win'.

The code of play for women's rugby is exactly that of their male counterparts, yet while it requires the same physical and mental traits as the male game, the profile and acceptance of women's rugby is low. Women who participate in rugby are often regarded as 'she devils', unfeminine and, more often than not, lesbian.[6] In other words, despite their achievement of notable physical fitness and sporting ability, the more masculinised bodies of female athletes cannot be used as a form of capital in the positions they occupy or aspire to occupy. It is the main goal of this chapter to explain why sporting capital is granted a far lower value for women than for men.

---

6   The RTÉ television series *The Grip* highlights this in series 3, programme 2, entitled 'Women in Sport'.

The emphasis on achievement, character formation, teamwork and fair play could be applied to most sports but, in reality, these qualities relate more specifically to male sports. This is because the field of sport, in its modern Irish form, is a site for the demarcation of dominant forms of masculinity and femininity, generating gendered practices and ways of looking at the world. It is also shaped by the economic, cultural, political and ideological conditions in which it takes form.

Modern sport is a site where the link between biology, gender and sex is most evident; this is clearly revealed in gender verification tests. Pentathlete, Mary Peters, recalled lining up in the 1970s, dressed in only a towel, before a major championship race to have her genitals examined as part of 'femininity control', a procedure that ensured only women competed in women's events.[7] Since then, femininity control testing has evolved to sex chromatin analysis, which is required today by most international sporting federations. Gender verification in sport is criticised because 'it says nothing about the sex of an individual from an anatomical, physiological and psychosocial standpoint'.[8] Irrespective of arguments about the biological basis for 'tomboyism' and what is 'naturally' masculine or feminine, developments in our understanding of the physiology of the body do not address the idea that Irish women should not use their muscles or, when they do, for example through sport, that they should do so in an 'appropriate' way.

A male preserve

On 4 May 2001 a World Spirit of Rugby Banquet was held in Limerick, as a national salute to the game of rugby. The importance of rugby was summarised as follows:

---

7   M. Peters and I. Wooldridge, *Mary P*, London: Arrow, 1974.
8   M. A. Hall, *Feminism and Sporting Bodies*, Champaign, IL: Human Kinetics, 1996, p. 17.

The game of rugby encourages a spirit that brings forth the very best of human endeavour – personal achievement; physical and mental fitness; teamwork; fair competition – and above all the ability to accept the outcome and deal with the circumstances with dignity and grace.[9]

One month previously, the final episode of RTÉ's *True Lives* television series documented the path of Clongowes Wood College in the 2000/2001 Leinster Schools Rugby Senior Cup. The documentary incorporated the above musings on rugby: physically demanding training in difficult weather conditions, the need for mental and physical fitness and strength, pre-match exhortations in the dressing room and on the pitch, footage of the game itself, cheer practice, elevation of team members to honorary status at school assembly before and after a match, the crucial role that a Clongowes connection has in a young Irishman's future and the role that rugby plays in the formation of identity, particularly a masculine identity.

International sociological research shows that modern sport is a male preserve. It is best understood as 'having come to represent what is for large numbers of males a principal locus for the inculcation and public expression of traditional standards of masculinity'.[10] The importance of Gaelic games to nineteenth-century Irish society was emphasised by Archbishop Croke in his letter to the Gaelic Athletic Association (GAA) accepting patronage of the association (18 December 1884). He described a male athlete as 'a modern young man . . . arrayed in light attire, with parti-coloured cap on and racket in hand'. He went on to express his preference for:

---

9   *The Irish Times*, 4 April 2001.
10 E. Dunning, *Sport Matters: Sociological Studies of Sport, Violence and Civilization,* London: Routledge, 1999, p. 236.

... the youthful athletes whom I used to see in my early days at fair and pattern, bereft of shoes and coat ... prepared to play at hand-ball, to fly over any number of horses, to throw the 'sledge' or 'winding-stone', and to test each other's mettle and activity by the trying ordeal of 'three leaps', or a hop, step and jump. [He believed that] if we continue ... condemning the sports that were practiced by our forefathers, effacing our national features as though we were ashamed of them, and putting on, with England's stuffs and broadcloths, her 'masher' habits and such other effeminate follies as she may recommend, we had better at once, and publicly, adjure our nationality, clap hands for joy at sight of the Union Jack, and place 'England's bloody red' evultingly above 'the green'.[11]

While Croke's words highlight the relationship between sport and Irish cultural nationalism, they are also a striking example of how Gaelic sports were seen as the embodiment of manhood, with effeminate sports less valued.[12] Within the field of Irish sport, the social position of a male athlete is determined by the volume and composition of his sporting capital, which represents a recognition of his achievement, athleticism, sportsmanship and competitiveness. This sporting capital is highly valued and is easily transformed into social rewards of various kinds. Brian O'Driscoll's climb to fame rests on his clean-cut, heterosexual and sporting image. Not only is he a recognised rugby talent in Ireland and abroad, but he is also rapidly becoming a household name through product endorsements. In other words, he is

---

11 P. Griffin, *The Politics of Irish Athletics 1850–1990*, Leitrim: Marathon Publications, 1990, p. 16.

12 For a further exploration of the role of Gaelic sports in the construction of Irish masculinity see P. Ryan, 'Gaelic Sports and the Construction of Irish Masculinity', paper presented at the Sociological Association of Ireland Annual Conference, Westport, County Mayo, 1997.

able to translate his sporting capital into star status and financial reward.

In most aspects of Irish society, particularly in all-male environments such as Clongowes Wood College, those males that deviate from culturally appropriate sporting interests and participation are liable to be categorised as effeminate or sometimes homosexual. Accusations of homosexuality that emerge in the sporting field indicate not only the social sanctioning of 'inappropriate' gender behaviour, but also the existence of a culturally acceptable form of sexuality – heterosexuality. Sport, as a cultural practice, not only reinforces appropriate forms of masculinity and femininity, but can also act to police boundaries around the proper expression of sexuality. Paul O'Connor's disclosure of his homosexuality after his rugby career had ended highlights the role of sport in the creation and maintenance of a dominant form of masculinity, based on sporting participation in a high physical-contact game and on an appropriate form of sexuality.[13] In O'Connor's case, his sporting prowess could not be traded for other forms of social reward, as his sexuality challenged dominant ideas upon which the conversion of sporting capital is founded. Rugged team sports (such as rugby) are important arenas in which male touch generally does not denote homosexuality but enhances a male heterosexual and virile image.[14] Therefore, the entry of women into these sports challenges the myth of female frailty and suggests that sport could, in some way, cease to masculinise men.

Sport is not feminine?

Women are, from the outset, participating in what is traditionally regarded as a male preserve. The importance of sport, particularly team sports, in the formation of

---

13 *Sunday Tribune*, 13 May 2001.
14 E. Dunning, 'Sport as a Male Preserve', in N. Elias and E. Dunning (eds), *Quest for Excitement,* Oxford: Basil Blackwell, 1986.

masculine identity has meant that women's sports are often ignored or regarded as being a fairer version (sometimes implied as inferior) of the male equivalent. Apart from 'female-appropriate' sports such as synchronised swimming and netball, femininity and sport do not sit comfortably with each other, while masculinity and sport have an almost instinctive relationship.[15]

Irish women who participate in sport are challenged in social and personal perceptions of their femininity, particularly those women who participate in traditionally male-associated sports such as rugby, soccer, hurling (camogie being the female equivalent) and Gaelic football. In contrast to the relative ease with which men's sporting capital can be translated into monetary reward and status, female athletes in these sports experience severe limitations in doing so. One example is the difficulties experienced by Irish lesbian soccer players who were not considered for further/future international selection.[16] The reason, cited by the manager, was not their lack of ability, fitness, achievements or will to win. Rather, that they were lesbian and the manager was trying 'to get rid of the element' – the lesbian reputation of, and participation in, women's soccer in Ireland – in order to promote the image of the game and build a wider playing base. These female athletes transgressed standards of femininity and breached norms of acceptable sexuality. This had a direct impact on their ability to translate their sporting capital into monetary reward, general status and the possibility of future professional careers in sport.

Other examples of limitations on women to trade their sporting capital include: the low numbers of, and quantitative differences in, third-level athletic scholarships available to women in Ireland; the reliance, in the past, of

---

15 For details of ongoing research on gender stereotyping and gender associations in sport see K. Liston, 'Sport, Gender and Commercialisation', *Studies*, vol. 90, no. 359, 2001, pp. 251–5.
16 This example is taken from ongoing doctoral research.

international female rugby players on their own financial resources to purchase their sports clothing and travel to play in international games; and the amateur status of most elite female athletes, which means that annual holiday leave is mostly taken up with training and competition.

Female sporting participation is not valued for the kind of aggressive and physical action that is associated with sportsmen, but, on the contrary, for its low physical contact and aesthetic qualities. This is typified in the bogus Joe Rabbitte call to RTÉ Radio 1, where the caller described camogie players as 'unhealthy, unfeminine and unlady-like'.[17] He went on to say: 'We don't mind girls playing tennis, you know, we don't mind them playing golf, but certainly not camogie or Gaelic football or soccer . . . Anyway, it's not healthy for girls to be playing this type of game'.

The 'slur' about the lack of femininity of camogie players was more clearly expressed by Kilkenny captain, Tracy Millea, when she said: 'they seem to think camogie is only for half-men, half-women, that the players are all very butch . . . we can take the knocks as well as the men'.[18] Camogie players are not the only sportswomen to highlight the implications of sporting participation on their femininity. Clare Scanlan, a semi-professional, Irish international soccer player, referred to the 'tomboy' issue when she said: 'every young girl in this country has to deal with being called a tomboy just because they play soccer . . . sometimes it even goes as far as saying that all soccer players are lesbians'.[19]

The gendered differentiation of sports has impacted on the formation, organisation and subsequent participation

---

17 This hoax call was made on 31 August 2000 to presenter Maura O'Neill on the Marian Finucane show on RTÉ Radio 1. The caller claimed to be the then Galway hurling captain, Joe Rabbitte.

18 *Irish Independent*, 5 September 1999.

19 K. Liston, 'Playing the Masculine/Feminine Game . . . So He Plays Harder and She Plays Softer', *PaGes*, vol. 6, Dublin: University College Dublin, Faculty of Arts, 1999.

levels of women's sports. Slurs regarding the unfemininity of sports (which imply the adoption of a more masculine quality) can act as a deterrent to sports participation by all women. This process is reinforced throughout the lifecycle of Irish men and women, particularly through the Irish second and third-level education system where certain schools build their reputation on male and female sporting success. Clongowes Wood College and Blackrock College are associated with men's rugby and Loreto with women's hockey. In fact, Irish research (with second-level education students) has shown that girls are significantly more unhappy with their bodies than boys. Within the second-level sports curriculum, rhythm and placidness were traits associated with girls, whilst endurance and aggression were commonly associated male traits.[20] Irish sports and physical activities are subject to gender stereotyping and gender associations.[21]

The Ladies' Gaelic Football Association of Ireland has approximately 80,000 officially registered members in various clubs, leagues, schools and universities throughout Ireland. While this sport has grown enormously in terms of participation and broader interest levels and is the fastest-growing female sport in Ireland today, it is relatively under-funded, receives little media coverage and has low membership levels in comparison to the GAA. Females make up 16 per cent of the total membership of the GAA and 10 per cent of the playing membership. Female non-playing membership is higher (20 per cent), with female non-playing involvement predominantly in social committees and administration.[22] It is not unrealistic therefore to argue that women's Gaelic football is the poor relation of the 'real'

20 Physical Education Association of Ireland, *Girls and Boys Come Out to Play*, Limerick: PEAI, 1999.

21 For a more detailed outline of this research see K. Liston, 'Sport, Gender and Commercialisation', *Studies*, vol. 90, no. 359, 2001.

22 *Nationwide Survey of 509 Gaelic Football and Hurling Clubs*, Dublin: Increased Participation Committee of the GAA, 1997.

game – men's Gaelic football – despite its huge popularity with Irish women and, increasingly, with Irish society at large. However men's rugby has a relatively small membership base, and yet has well-recognised status and media coverage within the broader parameters of sport and sports coverage in Ireland. A 1996 national survey showed that 6 per cent of a representative sample of Irish men and women stated they had participated in Gaelic football compared to a 1 per cent participation rate in rugby. It might come as a surprise to note that judo, karate, sailing and volleyball had similar participation rates to rugby.[23] Why then has men's rugby a higher social, economic and media profile?

Despite the social constraints highlighted previously, women have participated in sports for as long as men and they continue to participate in sports. Interviews with elite female athletes (from ongoing doctoral research) reveal that their main motivations for participation in sports such as rugby, Gaelic football, camogie and soccer are: the expression of female physicality, which is limited or even forbidden in everyday interaction; 'the camaraderie and everything around it . . . you'll go out and put your body on the line for your other team-mates'; the release of stress; the addictive feeling of mind/body unity when an athlete performs to her peak; and the maintenance of physical fitness and strength. These motivations closely correspond to those of men: women emphasise the same qualities and abilities in their participation in sport and they are pursuing the same rewards. Yet, these qualities and abilities are perceived as being of lower value because they do not uphold the standards of conventional femininity.

The love of female athletes for their particular sport transcends their awareness that their participation in it raises questions about their heterosexuality. However they tend to compensate for that perception by behaving in ways

---

23 *A National Survey of Involvement in Sport and Physical Activity*, Dublin: Department of Education and the Health Promotion Unit, 1996.

that are considered conventionally feminine, for example wearing make-up after a match or having long hair. These athletes also point out the importance of their participation to future women's sports, to the role of sport as an expression of freedom and physicality for women, to the resources it provides, and to the possibility that their participation and actions could bring about a change in attitudes towards women's sports, and to the field of sport in general.

The low value of sporting capital for women engaged in team sports does not necessarily extend to more individualised sports, such as running, swimming or even tennis. This is because the emphasis on strength, aggressiveness and physical contact is removed, and features that conform more to conventional perceptions of femininity are highlighted. Their publicised or assumed heterosexuality allows them to be acceptably attractive and feminine athletes. The sporting capital of women who are successful in such sports can be more easily traded. For instance, Sonia O'Sullivan's feminine and heterosexual (now motherhood) status has facilitated her successful trading of athletic ability and achievement with sponsorship deals, product endorsements and recent documentary and photographic publications. Similarly, Michelle Smith's celebrity status and subsequent product endorsements (for example advertisements for shampoo) after the 1996 Olympics were also supported by her appropriately feminine, heterosexual and marital status.[24]

However, such individualised sports cannot fully escape the requirements of physicality. A prime example can be seen in print media coverage of international women's tennis, with headlines such as 'Frills in jeopardy as power

---

24 *The Irish Times*, 22 July 1996, front-page report describes her 'face wreathed in happiness and rivulets of water streaming down her body, . . . [in] the arms of her husband and coach Erik de Bruin . . . [having] already felt the crush of an embrace from the Minister of State for Sport, Mr Bernard Allen'.

replaces grace and panache' (*The Irish Times*, 24 May 1999), 'Thigh Breakers: Biceps not backhands, ferocity not finesse. Has women's tennis gone too far?' (*The Examiner*, 12 May 1999) and 'Women muscle the girls out of the way' (*Evening Herald*, 26 June 2001). These articles allude not only to broader cultural perceptions of female muscularity, but also to the alarm of some female tennis players

> . . . at the arrival in their midst of what appears to be a new breed of power women, who are compromising the unique selling points of grace and skill. Venus and Serena Williams, the American sisters built like rugby lock forwards, have been closely followed by French teenager Amelie Mauresmo, a woman with shoulders so broad she is rumoured to enter the locker room sideways.[25]

Anna Kournikova receives substantially more media coverage for her 'feminine attributes' than her tennis achievements. She has sponsorship deals (one of the most well-known being her 'Only the Balls Should Bounce' promotion of a sports bra) that far outstrip her relative strength as a player. It is her culturally acceptable femininity and sexuality, rather than her sporting achievements, which facilitate her acceptance as a sportswoman. In fact, female sporting achievement is often undermined by a fascination with the female body and its appropriate gendered and sexual form.[26] This reflects the primacy given to heterosexual appeal in any context in which female performance is evaluated.

---

25 *The Irish Times*, 24 May 1999.
26 For example: 'Until her comfortable victory in yesterday's round, her [Jennifer Capriati's] physique had been spared the forensic attention devoted to so many other female players simply because her life story was more interesting than her muscle mass', *Evening Herald*, 26 June 2001.

Conclusion

Studies indicate that overall rates of Irish participation in sport and physical activity are increasing. Recent successes by the Camogie and Women's Gaelic Football Associations in obtaining RTÉ television coverage of their All-Ireland finals and semi-finals respectively, and the affiliation of the Irish Women's Rugby Football Union to the Irish Rugby Football Union, indicate a growing involvement, interest in, and acceptance of, women's sports in Ireland.

While women have gradually improved their position in Irish society over time (for example increased labour force participation and greater involvement in the public sphere generally), sport remains a relatively unchallenged area in which an Irish male can develop his identity in opposition to a rigid and narrow perception of what an ideal Irish woman should be. Socially constructed forms of gender and sexuality determine the value of sporting capital, structure sporting practices and shape our views of the sports world.

But women's deployment of the resources that sport provides can change the fields of sport and gender in Ireland. The growth of women's Gaelic football since 1974 is an example of this. Initially the subject of social derision, the association has now established itself as a leading proponent of women's sport in the face of, what is perhaps historically, the most traditionally male-associated sport in Ireland.

Sport is not just a physical activity that is good for your health. It is part of wider social processes that construct male and female bodies as moving, active, physical, passive, aesthetic, skilful and graceful and which, as a result, have particular consequences for sportspeople. Women's participation in sports, particularly those regarded as appropriately and traditionally male, challenges the historical association between sport and masculinity in Irish society and positively suggests that sporting participation and interest can be socially rewarding for both men and women. Oscar Wilde's words were, perhaps, more indicative of the social context of his time! While football is all very well as a game for rough girls, our socially constructed perceptions of gender and sexuality convey a logic to gendered sporting practices and ultimately shape our consideration of 'roughness' and 'delicacy' in sport.

CHAPTER 16

The Drama of Childbirth

JANE GRAY

In 1999, Cuidiú – The Irish Childbirth Trust, with the assistance of the Department of Health and Children, published the third edition of its consumer guide to maternity services.[1] One of the principal trends Cuidiú identified was an increase in the percentage of births by caesarean section. In this respect, Ireland appears to be 'catching up' with many other European states. Some commentators suggest that patient preference has contributed to the increasing number of caesarean sections in Ireland. In the view of Cuidiú's President, Sue Jameson, women's expectations for a 'perfect, pain-free birth' have increased the likelihood of intervention.[2] The Master of the Rotunda Hospital, Dr Peter McKenna, stated in his *1997 Annual Clinical Report* that: 'There seems little doubt to me that, part of the rise in our caesarean section rate is meeting the patient request and, against a background of good results and proven safety procedure, it is difficult not to accede to these requests'.[3] The Master of the National Maternity

1 Cuidiú – The Irish Childbirth Trust, *Preparing Together for Birth and Beyond: A Consumer Guide to the Maternity Services in Ireland*, Dublin: Health Promotion Unit, 1999.
2 Sylvia Thompson, 'The Rise of the "Perfect, Pain-free" Childbirth', *The Irish Times*, 31 January 2000.
3 Rotunda Hospital, Dublin, *1997 Annual Clinical Report*, available online at www.rotunda.ie/publications/report97.html.

Hospital, Dr Declan Keane, claimed that the 'close alliance' between a country's GNP and its caesarean section rate indicated 'a direct relationship with patient demand and expectations'.[4]

In this representation of Irish maternity care, obstetricians respond to the actions and choices of childbearing women, who are identified as consumers. However, the image of women as active participants in the growth of medical intervention does not stand up to minimal scrutiny. In this chapter, I argue that childbirth in Ireland continues to be structured by the exercise of power in ways that limit the extent to which women can take an active part in their own labour and delivery. The pattern of increased surgical intervention has thus emerged in the context of institutional practices that deny women choice and agency.

Ireland's childbirth regime

To give birth in an Irish maternity hospital is to be transformed from an active, childbearing person, into the appendage of a recalcitrant body from which a child is delivered by medical technology and personnel. This is because childbirth in Ireland is governed by an institutionalised set of formal and informal practices and ideas that serve to perpetuate what I will call the Irish childbirth regime (ICR). I use the term 'regime' to emphasise the extent to which these practices and ideas *appear* to be uncontested within certain boundaries of time and space – that is, they have a character peculiar to modern Ireland. Of course the 'medicalisation' of childbirth is not unique to Irish maternity hospitals. However, the absence of any significant public challenge to the process is extraordinary. In this chapter I will suggest three reasons why the ICR is so powerful: the status of 'active management of labour' as

---

4   Colin Kerr, 'Management of First Labour Can Reduce the Need for C Sections', *Irish Medical Times*, vol. 34, no. 42, 2000.

an Irish modernisation project; the relative, and para-doxical, success of the home birth movement in Ireland; and the reproduction of the regime in the everyday drama of hospital-based maternity care. In my view, the ICR seriously disempowers women by ensuring that childbirth is experienced as something that happens to their bodies, rather than as an active individual accomplishment. However, in that case, why is there so little public resistance to the regime?

Scott has argued that, under oppressive regimes, the appearance of consent is accomplished by public displays of compliance, agreement and deference.[5] Most of the time childbearing women, and other subordinate players in the ICR, especially midwives, have a strategic interest in observing its rules, and thus appear to affirm the values of its dominant players, mainly obstetricians. As Scott observed, this does not mean that what women say and do 'offstage' is necessarily more truthful than their 'onstage' performance in the consulting room. It is possible that if Irish women had real choices about how they wanted to give birth, most of them would opt for a medicalised experience anyway. The important point is that under the current regime, which denies choice, it is illegitimate to infer that the trend towards more medical intervention is a reflection of women's preferences.

Active management of labour as a modernisation project

The package of maternity care known as 'active manage-ment of labour' was introduced in the National Maternity Hospital (NMH) at Holles Street, Dublin in the late 1960s, under the direction of the then Master, Dr Kieran O'Driscoll. By employing strict diagnostic criteria for 'true' labour, and by the routine use of amniotomy (breaking of the waters)

---

5   James C. Scott, *Domination and the Arts of Resistance: Hidden Transcripts*, Yale: Yale University Press, 1990, p. 5.

and synthetic oxytocin (the hormone that stimulates labour), practitioners of active management ensure that no labour lasts longer than twelve hours. The NMH also includes 'continuous professional support' as an essential component. A chart called a partogram is used to monitor progress in labour by plotting the rate of cervical dilation. Under active management, 'normal' labour is depicted as a straight line, because a woman's cervix is supposed to dilate at the rate of one centimetre per hour.[6]

The purpose of active management, according to O'Driscoll, is to 'enhance the experience of childbirth for mothers, particularly first-time mothers'.[7] In the article that introduced active management to the medical community, O'Driscoll and Meagher notoriously described prolonged labour as a 'harrowing experience' liable to cause 'permanent revulsion' to childbirth on the woman's part.[8] However, prolonged labour in first-time mothers is not unusual according to the criteria of the NMH, which reported that 50 per cent had their labour accelerated in 1998.[9] More recently, active management has been promoted on the grounds that it reduces the rate of caesarean sections. The best evidence for this claim is the low (but increasing) rate of caesarean sections at the NMH. However, systematic research does not support the contention that active management reduces the risk of caesarean section.[10]

---

6 See Kieran O'Driscoll, Declan Meagher and Peter Boylan, *Active Management of Labour: The Dublin Experience*, London: Mosby, 1993.

7 Kieran O'Driscoll, 'Active Management of Labour', *British Medical Journal*, vol. 309, 1994, available online at www.bmj.com/cgi/content/full/309/6960/1015.

8 Kieran O' Driscoll et al., 'Prevention of Prolonged Labour', *British Medical Journal*, vol. 2, 1969, pp. 477–80.

9 Cuidiú – The Irish Childbirth Trust, *Preparing Together for Birth and Beyond: A Consumer Guide to the Maternity Services in Ireland*, Dublin: Health Promotion Unit, 1999, p. 30.

Active management has been enthusiastically adopted by obstetricians throughout the English-speaking world. According to Thornton and Lilford: 'An important factor in this process was the personality, and vigorous prose style, of active management's foremost advocate, Kieran O'Driscoll of Dublin, who managed to convince even the most cautious clinicians'.[11] The *British Medical Journal*'s reviewer of O'Driscoll and Meagher's first book-length publication on active management (1980) wrote that: 'Our era will be seen as one in which there occurred a revolution in intrapartum care centring on Dublin'.[12] For a postcolonial country still mired in socio-economic underdevelopment, this represented an extraordinary achievement of modernisation. In his history of the NMH, Farmar explicitly invoked the Irish modernisation project by linking O'Driscoll's name to those of Whitaker and Lemass in the first sentence of his chapter on active management.[13] O'Malley has argued that, with respect to industrialisation, Ireland suffers from the problems of a 'latecomer'.[14] With respect to maternity care, Ireland clearly suffers from the problems of an 'innovator': because innovators achieve extraordinary initial success, they invest heavily (both materially and psychologically) in the techniques they have pioneered; this makes it difficult

---

10 W. Fraser et al., 'Effects of Early Augmentation of Labour with Amniotomy and Oxytocin in Nulliparous Women: A Meta-Analysis', *British Journal of Obstetrics and Gynaecology*, vol. 105, 1998, pp. 189–94.

11 J. G. Thornton and R. J. Lilford, 'Active Management of Labour: Current Knowledge and Research Issues', *British Medical Journal*, vol. 309, 1994, pp. 366–9, available online at www.bmj.com/cgi/content/full/309/6951/366.

12 Cited in J. G. Thornton and R. J. Lilford, ibid.

13 Quoted in J. G. Thornton and R. J. Lilford, 'Active Management', in Tony Farmar, *Holles Street: The National Maternity Hospital 1894–1994*, Dublin: A & A Farmar, 1994, p. 150.

14 Eoin O'Malley, *Industry and Economic Development: The Challenge for the Latecomer*, Dublin: Gill and Macmillan, 1989.

for them to adapt to new information or changing circumstances.

It is difficult to obtain precise information on just how routinely Irish maternity units other than the NMH practice active management. Cuidiú's report tells us only that: 'Many hospitals set time limits for each stage of labour (Active Management of Labour)'. Of the eight hospitals that reported the percentage of first-time mothers who had their labour accelerated, four, including the NMH, gave a figure of 35 per cent or more. If those hospitals that did not distinguish between first-time mothers and all others are included, seven out of fourteen reported average acceleration rates that matched or exceeded that of the NMH (30.5 per cent). Seven hospitals did not provide any information. These data are obviously unsatisfactory, but it is reasonable to infer that the practice of active management is widespread. More importantly, however, the cultural salience of active management means that the woman-centred idea of active *birth* is alien to Irish obstetrical thinking. It is an integral part of the 'assembly-line' model of maternity care that I describe below.[15]

The paradoxical success of the Irish home birth movement

It may seem perverse to argue that the home birth movement has been successful in Ireland, given the vehemence of opposition to it, especially on the part of general practitioners, and the difficulties women continue to experience in obtaining state funding for the services of domiciliary midwives. However, my contention is that the high public profile of the home birth debate has deflected attention from the problem of medical intervention in childbirth. It has done so by establishing the perception that women who want to give birth actively are also women who

---

15 Cuidiú – The Irish Childbirth Trust, *Preparing Together for Birth and Beyond: A Consumer Guide to the Maternity Services in Ireland*, Dublin: Health Promotion Unit, 1999, p. 9 and *passim*.

want home births and therefore that such women are a small and eccentric minority. This argument is not intended as a criticism of home birth advocates, whose courageous efforts to increase the choices available to Irish women must be applauded. Rather, my point is that if the ICR is to be transformed, the challenge must go further than a demand for home births.

According to Maire O'Regan, the successful centralisation of Irish births in hospital maternity units by the 1970s created a 'greenfield scenario' for home births in the 1980s. 'The opportunity to establish truly autonomous woman-centred midwifery care, from first principles, uninfluenced by the prevailing straitjacket of Irish labour management protocols, existed for one relatively short window of time'.[16] The problem was that such care was only available to women who could afford to pay for the services of an independent midwife. In 1994, the Maternity and Infant Care Scheme Review Group acknowledged that under the 1970 Health Act women who chose to give birth at home were entitled to free maternity care.[17] The publication of their report in 1997 resulted in the introduction of domiciliary pilot schemes based at University College Hospital, Galway and at the NMH in Dublin. Home birth advocates are already concerned that these projects represent the medicalisation of home births – their incorporation into the ICR – as they include strict criteria for admission to the schemes, and for when transfer to hospital is deemed necessary.[18]

16 Maire O'Regan, 'The Ann Kelly Case: the Final Regulation of Irish Midwives', *AIMS Journal*, Summer, 1999, available online at www.aims.org.uk/jnlsum99b.htm.

17 Department of Health, *Report of the Maternity and Infant Care Scheme Review Group*, Dublin: Department of Health, 1997, pp. 20–3.

18 Marie O'Connor, 'Fundamental Rights the Issue at Stake', *The Irish Times*, 11 April 2000.

Childbirth as a respectable performance

Above, I have suggested two reasons why the ICR is so powerful. However – as the demand for home births shows – no regime is ever entirely uncontested. Scott argued that any system of domination requires daily maintenance by means of small, routine dramatisations of power. These displays serve to conceal the true character of the relationship between dominant and subordinate groups, and to affirm the authority of those in power. The success of the drama depends on the appearance of unanimity and consent, so that it is essential to marginalise those who do not conform.

In this section, I will argue that a pregnant woman who seeks care at one of Ireland's maternity hospitals is swept up in a scripted performance that reproduces both the dominant model of childbirth, and her own subordination within the regime. If she steps outside the script, she is marginalised and made to feel like a troublemaker. The performance works by inducing – and reinforcing – feelings of isolation, fear and helplessness in childbearing women. It is important to note that my argument does not imply an active conspiracy on the part of the obstetrical establishment to demean women. Indeed, as Scott observed, in dramatisations of power, the leading actors form a more important part of the audience than the bit players do.[19]

In the absence of much research, most of the argument below is necessarily based on my own experience. I cannot claim that other women experience the ICR in the same way or that my experience would not have been different had I attended other maternity units. However, the Maternity Review Group reported that, according to submissions it received, 'the mother's voice is sometimes lost in the

---

19 James C. Scott, *Domination and the Arts of Resistance: Hidden Transcripts*, Yale: Yale University Press, 1990, pp. 45–69.

organised hospital situation'.[20] I think mothers' voices are not so much lost as silenced.

When I tried to choose where to give birth to my first child, I was astounded by how difficult it was to obtain information on which to base a choice. Irish maternity hospitals simply do not make public any policies about the ways of giving birth they support or allow. The publication of successive editions of the *Consumer Guide to Maternity Services in Ireland* has clearly led to greater openness about such subjects as rates of caesarean sections, assisted deliveries and so on. Just by asking questions about whether birth plans are facilitated or if women are free to choose their own position during delivery, Cuidiú and their predecessors in the Irish Association for Improvements in Maternity Services (IAIMS) have made vital dents in the armour of the ICR. However, much of the information in the consumer guide remains singularly uninformative. For example, 21 out of 24 hospitals report that birth plans are 'facilitated' – but what does that mean? How will the obstetricians in charge react if your birth plan includes practices they disapprove of or refuses interventions they consider necessary? Thus while Cuidiú aims to 'provide information which will assist [women] to make choices about childbirth', there is a very limited sense in which their publication can succeed in this goal, since the ICR is premised on women not making choices.

The concealment of this effective denial of choice is a delicate business – if it were openly stated as a policy, it would risk violating the principle of informed consent. The Maternity Review Group recommended that: 'there should be an acceptance by professionals of the right of a woman to refuse an intervention'.[21] However, most of the time, the

---

20 Department of Health, *Report of the Maternity and Infant Care Scheme Review Group*, Dublin: Department of Health, 1997.
21 Department of Health, ibid., p. 65.

routine practices surrounding antenatal care and childbirth ensure that there is very little danger of a woman refusing an intervention in the delivery suite. When you attend an antenatal clinic in an Irish hospital, you find that you are expected to play your part as the object of an assembly line of routine tests, examinations and, in the delivery room, interventions. To stretch the dramaturgical analogy, the script is so taken-for-granted that you are never even given your lines! You get extremely restricted opportunities to ask questions, and the staff never volunteer information about why a particular test or intervention is being carried out. Moreover, the routines dramatise the hierarchy of authority as you proceed upwards from receptionist to nurse, midwife and doctor. If you are a public patient you will probably rarely encounter the obstetrician, who's absent power thus inspires even greater awe than it does in the private clinic.

Given the large numbers of women who must be cared for, it is understandable that the system is somewhat impersonal. However, in my view the assembly-line model of care serves purposes other than mere efficiency. Most importantly, it dramatises the process of childbirth as a set of standardised practices carried out by professionals on interchangeable women. It functions as a display that continuously reaffirms both the power of obstetricians and the apparent acquiescence of pregnant women within the childbirth regime. The parade of buzzing medical personnel and the mass of anonymous, undifferentiated pregnant bodies in the waiting room are both actors and audience in this drama. As an individual woman caught up in it you feel strangely at a disadvantage, since your participation is never invited, it is simply taken for granted. If you are secretly a confused or unwilling performer you feel isolated, since everybody else appears to play their part unquestioningly. As Scott observed, such displays of power also serve to demonstrate that, for subordinates, the only significant relationships in the drama are vertical, with those above them in the hierarchy.[22] Midwives sometimes openly enlist pregnant women as fellow subordinates within the structure of command, for example by referring to the obstetrician as 'the boss'.

The assembly-line script guarantees the appearance of consent because it places the onus on each individual woman to object, instead of including her in the decision-making process from the beginning. A woman is unlikely to object very strenuously, as she has an obvious incentive to retain the good will of her caregivers, especially if she is a first-time mother with a natural fear of the unknown. If she does voice an objection (or an unacceptable preference), it does not take much to induce a feeling of marginalisation that will almost certainly bring her back into line. Feigned amazement at her desire to adopt a position other than semi-reclining for delivery, a soft sneer at her wish to cope without painkillers or to avoid an episiotomy and, if all else fails, the suggestion that she might be putting her baby at risk – all of these stratagems undermine a woman's confidence in her ability to give birth actively, and increase her fear. Moreover, a woman becomes more vulnerable as the birth approaches and her ability to resist diminishes progressively. Who wants the delivery room to be a battlefield?

When a woman is fighting *for* or *against*, she is not free to attend to herself. Nor, despite the information she absorbs, can she ever foresee all of the possibilities that may arise. Encouraged to develop offensive or defensive strategies, or a combination of both, mothers find themselves in the insupportable position of having to depend on the people they are strategising against. A woman seeking a 'natural' birth feels tense because she is under assault, having to prove herself – to produce a perfect experience out of the choices she has made. Often she has to give up her autonomy bit by bit. No wonder that she gives in to the

---

22. James C. Scott, *Domination and the Arts of Resistance: Hidden Transcripts*, Yale: Yale University Press, 1990, p. 62.

imperatives of the medical machine. No wonder, her thoughts teeming with 'should haves', that she blames herself when she 'fails'.[23]

It is so much easier to follow the script.

But things could be different. An alternative model of care would be less like an assembly line and more like a branching tree in which every encounter between a woman and her professional caregivers represents an opportunity for both parties to come to an agreement about which branch to follow. Instead of a system in which women can exercise choice only through refusal, we could have one in which women participate in the decision-making process throughout. It is important to emphasise that the idea of woman-centred maternity care does not necessarily imply that every woman will choose so-called natural childbirth – it means only that the woman's part is active and central throughout. Midwives and obstetricians could be partners in helping women to achieve the kinds of births they want. If women were confident that their goals were understood and respected, they could accept those births that did not work out as they had hoped, knowing that they, and their professional partners, had done their best.

Conclusion

I have been very critical in this chapter of the system of maternity care in Ireland, describing it as a power regime with obstetricians as the leading players. Any sociologist will tell you that people with power do not give it up voluntarily. It is thus encouraging to hear from Professor Bonnar, Chairman of the Institute of Obstetricians and Gynaecologists, that: 'I don't want to see different camps – one for home confinement, one for a midwifery-led unit and for a specialist service. We should all be working together and agreeing the principles . . . Clearly the voice of women

---

23 Jane Pincus, 'Childbirth Advice Literature As It Relates To Two Childbearing Ideologies', *Birth*, vol. 27, 2000, p. 211.

has to be listened to. We can't go on telling them what they ought to be doing'.[24] It is essential, however, that the integration of services envisioned by Professor Bonnar does not mean their incorporation to a power regime in which the parameters for giving birth are dictated by a small, medical elite.

In this chapter I have identified a number of reasons to be sceptical that the ICR will topple of its own accord. These include: institutional and psychological rigidity arising from the modernisation project of active management; the marginalisation of women's desire for active birth through its association with home birth; and the reproduction of women's subordination in the everyday performance of antenatal care and birth. Women's voices remain largely unheard because the drama of childbirth continues to be performed within a script that disempowers and isolates them, while reassuring obstetricians that – with the exception of a small and eccentric minority – most women are content with the service they provide. Women themselves must therefore ensure that they are included as active partners in the dismantling of the Irish childbirth regime, and its replacement with woman-centred ways of giving birth. In order to break the charmed circle of obstetrical power we must have the courage to speak more openly about the fear, anger and dreams that make up women's hidden experience of the drama of childbirth.

---

24 Niamh Connolly, 'All Midwifery Services Should Be Integrated Including Home Births', *Irish Medical Times*, vol. 33, 1999, available online at www.imt.ie/news/imt_old/news/1999/vol33no40/feature/4.php3.

CHAPTER 17

The Great Reversal
Nationalism and Unionism,
1950–2000

LIAM O'DOWD

The ideologies of nationalism and unionism have dominated Irish political life for over a century. Both are highly complex, but also rather different and asymmetrical. They give different answers to the so-called national question in Ireland – namely within what state, and what type of state, should political activity be pursued.

My aim here is not to outline a general historical account of the development of both ideologies. Rather I want to examine a major reversal or transition within each ideology between the 1950s and the late 1990s. In the case of nationalism it is a perceived movement from the politics of failure to the politics of success; in the case of unionism, the movement is in the opposite direction from perceived success to failure. In the 1950s, nationalist ideologies were contemplating the failure of the whole nationalist project, while unionists were celebrating the consolidation and relative success of Northern Ireland as a political entity. By the mid-1990s, the roles had been reversed.

What follows falls into three parts: a brief description of the nature and scale of the two ideological shifts, an examination of some of the reasons for the reversal in the perceived fortunes of nationalism and unionism in a changing material and global context, and some tentative conclusions and an evaluation of the possible consequences of these changes for each ideological framework and the relationship between them.

The rescuing of the nationalist project

The reversal in nationalist ideology has been dramatic. In the 1950s, after almost forty years of independence, the nationalist project was in deep crisis. The independent Irish state had failed to realise any of the major objectives set for it by its founders: the ending of partition, the revival of the Irish language and, most significantly of all, it had failed to develop sustainable economic development or halt emigration and population decline. By the end of the twentieth century, however, independent Ireland was being represented as a national success story, a model for other states and nations in eastern Europe and for developing countries. Its success was being presented most succinctly, if not comprehensively, by the metaphor, the 'Celtic tiger'.

Contemporary Irish historiography has typically reconstructed the 1950s as the great watershed in the history of the Irish state. When de Valera was replaced by Lemass as Taoiseach in 1958, the latter was confronted in the words of Joe Lee with:

> Pervasive mediocrity which gave the Irish, after nearly forty years of independence, the lowest living standard, the highest emigration rates, the worst unemployment rates, and the most intellectually stultifying society in Northern Europe. [1]

Closer examination does reveal, of course, that the seeds of economic and social transformation were being sown in the

---

1   J. J. Lee (ed.), *Ireland, 1945–70*, Dublin: Gill and Macmillan, 1979, p. 24.

1950s. However, the social commentary of Irish intellectuals since partition does confirm the sense of deep crisis that pervaded nationalist Ireland in the 1950s at all levels, economic, political and cultural.[2]

Since partition, Catholic clergy had promulgated a comprehensive social programme to combat the perceived threats of socialism, liberalism and communism. Catholic social thinking sought to prescribe a Catholic social order for independent Ireland which drew on the social encyclicals of the papacy and on the Catholic social movement in continental Europe. Its defining features were an emphasis on the family, the limiting of state intervention in everyday life, the superiority of rural over urban living, the belief in small property, the replacement of the political party system by a system of vocational organisation, and the centrality of the clergy as the moral guides of the people and their intellectuals. This ideology was idealist in the philosophical sense. It gave priority to ideas, spirituality and principles rather than to material factors. It lacked any viable economic analysis of the Irish Republic's dependent relationship with the British economy. In fact, constructing a Catholic social order in the Ireland of the time was at least as difficult as building socialism in one country in Stalin's USSR.

Literary intellectuals within the nationalist tradition reached a peak of disaffection in the 1950s. They consistently lambasted church-inspired censorship, petty materialism, puritanism and the romanticised myths in the nationalist and clerical ideologies. The Ireland of the 1950s was represented as a cultural desert where large groups of people were forced to escape family life into permanent celibacy or escape from the country altogether via emigration. The cultural climate of the time was seen to mirror the climate of economic stagnation, high unemployment and

---

2   L. O'Dowd, *The Image of the City in Irish Social Commentary and Urban Planning*, unpublished PhD, Department of Sociology, Southern Illinois University, 1974.

mass emigration. Mervyn Wall's *Leaves for the Burning*, described by Thomas Kilroy as the saga of post-Treaty rural Ireland, captures the time well.[3] One of Wall's characters periodically reads aloud from newspaper headlines capturing the cultural mediocrity and repression of the time. The headlines include: 'De Valera condemns new Government', 'Bishop denounces mixed bathing', 'Irishman tries to hang his mother', 'Plumbers want justice not charity', 'Clergy denounce dance hall menace' and 'Farmer threatens to cut off tinker's head'. The failure of nationalist Ireland glares through all the fiction and social commentary of the period. Ireland is a place from which people need to escape in one way or another.

Politically, the 1950s was also a time of short-lived governments with precarious majorities. Ireland lagged behind the rest of western Europe, which was caught up in the post-war boom. Most palpable of all was the abject failure of the language restoration policy. While the social fabric of rural Ireland was withering away with late marriages, high rates of permanent celibacy and the large-scale flight of women from the rural areas to the cities in Ireland and beyond. Indeed, it seemed that in the national ideology of the time, failure was manifested at all three levels: economic, political and cultural.

The subsequent economic modernisation programme, and the return of optimism, rising marriage rates and lower levels of emigration in the 1960s have been well rehearsed by historians. The latter, in conjunction with other commentators, subsequently reconstructed the period between independence and 1960 in highly negative terms; in Fallon's words, these decades were 'demonised'.[4] This helped legitimise the shift in nationalist ideology to new concerns,

---

3   M. Wall, *Leaves for the Burning,* Dublin: Millington, 1973 (first published 1952); T. Kilroy, 'Mervyn Wall: The Demands of Satire', *Studies,* vol. 47, 1958.

4   B. Fallon, *The Age of Innocence: Irish Culture 1930–1960*, Dublin: Gill and Macmillan, 1999, p. 3.

notably around economic modernisation, membership of the EEC, and dealing with unfinished, and unwelcome, business connected with the Northern conflict.

The demise of unionist confidence

The experience of unionism has been the reverse. In the 1950s, unionist ideologists proclaimed the unionist project a success, frequently contrasting it to the spectacular failure of its nationalist opponent. Unionists had stood by the Allies in a victorious war effort. Northern Ireland's economy was benefiting from post-war economic reconstruction and the extension to the region of Britain's developing welfare state. The prosperity gap with the south was at an all-time high. Political nationalism was in disarray: the anti-partition campaign far from undermining partition had copper-fastened it. Within Northern Ireland, neither a moribund nationalist party nor the ineffectual IRA campaign of 1956 to 1962 had come remotely near to unsettling the unionist administration. The Ulster Unionist Party, in firm alliance with the ruling British Conservatives, had monopolised power since partition.

By the late 1990s, however, unionists were surveying an entirely different scenario. After thirty years of conflict, unionism had fragmented; and nationalists, even republicans, were sharing power with unionists in a new assembly at Stormont. The demographic balance between the two Northern Ireland communities had shifted substantially in favour of nationalists. Perhaps even more significantly, the prosperity gap between north and south had disappeared; the Irish economy was noticeably more dynamic than its Northern Irish counterpart. As the British and Irish governments jointly oversaw the implementation of the Belfast Agreement, it was clear that the economic and political case for partition was much weaker than it had been in the 1950s.

Unionist ideology in the 1950s was largely, if not entirely, a celebration of supremacy and success. Although even then it contained a kind of apocalyptic undercurrent, which has endured in northern Protestant thinking – a 'siege mentality', constantly looking for enemies without and traitors within. Paisley had begun his evangelising campaigns with the founding of his Free Presbyterian Church in 1951. His successive campaigns against liberal Protestant clergy and unionist politicians were being waged in the gospel halls of working-class Belfast and rural Northern Ireland. Over the next fifty years his influence was to grow dramatically as more and more unionists came to interpret the Northern Ireland conflict and the various attempts to resolve it as a succession of defeats, concessions and betrayals.

In the 1950s, however, the dominant voice of unionism was confident that Northern Ireland had succeeded and that it was superior in all respects to the Republic of Ireland. Unionists typically contrasted the levels of economic and social development in the north with the stagnation and periodic crisis in the south. They continually highlighted instances of discrimination against Protestants and the threats posed by the Catholic Church to freedom of conscience. 'Hypocritical' attitudes of the Irish government to language revival and the IRA were also mooted.[5] Liberal unionists argued that unionism was synonymous with modernity and individual freedom:

> In Éire they pondered over history, and nursed sores which should have been long healed, and the memory of ancient wrongs . . . We belong not to ourselves but to a much wider area, and we serve a much higher purpose than could be achieved within the borders of Northern Ireland.[6]

5 W. A. Carson, *Ulster and the Irish Republic*, Belfast: Cleland, 1957.
6 B. Maginness, a Stormont minister, quoted in the *Belfast Newsletter*, 5 March 1955.

This contrast, between the modern, outward and forward-looking north and the inward-looking south preoccupied with the wrongs of the past, pervaded unionist political commentary. The benefits of the Union were so self-evident to unionists that they spent little time elaborating a unionist or Protestant culture and even less at legitimising Northern Ireland as a political entity for all its inhabitants.

The cultural case for a separate Northern Ireland had never received much attention in any case. Unionist Ireland, unlike nationalist Ireland, did not look so much to public intellectuals for cultural legitimacy as to its popular support, which saw Northern Ireland as a bulwark against Rome rule and nationalist domination. The six-county unit was a pragmatic compromise, not the realisation of a cultural ideal. It was designed to protect the economic and political interests of the unionist elite and, to a lesser extent, unionist workers. Unlike nationalism, unionism lacked an intellectual elite interested in constructing a 'national past', in restoring a lost language, or in correcting the effects of foreign oppression.[7] As Bell has noted, there was no Hyde or Pearse on the streets of Portadown.[8] Nor did the Protestant clergy, divided among several denominations, advocate anything as remotely ambitious (or as utopian) as the Catholic social order with its emphasis on a third way between capitalism and socialism. In other words, in unionist Ireland in the 1950s, unlike its nationalist counterpart, there was no sense of grand projects unrealised or expectations disappointed.

The great reversal

If the clock is moved forward to the contemporary period since the mid-1990s, the contrast with the 1950s is striking.

7   L. O'Dowd, 'Intellectuals and Political Culture: A Unionist–Nationalist Comparison', in E. Hughes (ed.), *Culture and Politics in Northern Ireland,* Milton Keynes: Open University Press, 1991.
8   D. Bell, 'Contemporary Cultural Studies in Ireland and the 'Problem' of Protestant Ideology', *The Crane Bag*, vol. 9, no. 2, 1985.

Irish nationalism seems to have moved from the politics of failure to the politics of success, while unionism has travelled in the opposite direction. All the great nationalist problems, which seemed to question the viability of a separate Irish state in the 1950s, now appear to be resolved, redefined or have vanished from the national agenda. The Irish economy has enjoyed phenomenal growth rates for a number of years. On some common economic indicators such as GDP per capita, it now outranks not only Northern Ireland, but also the UK, Germany, France, Sweden and Japan.

From the mid-1990s onwards, it appeared that the failures of nationalist Ireland had been reversed. Economic growth brought an apparent resolution of two critical national problems of the pre-1960 period – a declining population had been replaced by an expanding one, and emigration had been replaced by net immigration. Most previous national policy and ideology had been stood on its head. Doctrines of self-sufficiency and economic autonomy had been replaced by an apparently successful policy heavily based on foreign (largely American) direct investment. Irish nationalists had embraced membership of the European Community enthusiastically and successfully, even if it seemed to undermine elements of political and economic independence. Irish culture, for example art, literature, music and dance, was a highly successful commodity in global markets. The Irish language revival issue had slipped almost silently off the national agenda. Above all, however, after 1998, the most glaring failure of Irish nationalism – the partition of the country – had been reframed in ways that allowed nationalists, north and south, a much greater role in the running of Northern Ireland.

Of course, the nationalist ideological framework has thrown up a new set of pressing public issues: massive social inequality in class and gender terms, the collapse of traditional Catholic values, immigration, multiculturalism, political and business corruption and questions of economic competitiveness. But in many respects these are problems of success, of relative affluence, rather than problems of failure. Moreover, these issues are easily perceived as problems that face all western states in varying degrees rather than as distinctively and intractably Irish. The issues confronting Irish nationalism and debated by nationalists are different from what they were in the 1950s, and in many respects they are the by-products of widely perceived success.

By the 1990s, however, unionists represented themselves as coping with the politics of decline and failure; with a fragmentation and lack of strategic direction within unionist politics and a growth in the cohesiveness and power of their nationalist opponents with whom they have been forced to share power. The Union was a self-evident good in the 1950s, and beyond intellectual scrutiny except as a mantra for mobilising the vote at elections. By the 1990s, this was not only a matter of debate with non-unionists, but also a matter of negotiation and compromise. Indeed, some unionist intellectuals were suggesting that the Union was being redefined in ways that undermined the unionist position. In other words, as Aughey has suggested, the Union is being used against unionists; it is no longer solely on unionist terms and may produce a political framework that is 'substantially Irish and residually British'.[9]

After 1960, whereas nationalist ideology was re-invented and even reversed to meet changing conditions, much of the unionist response to change and the Northern Ireland conflict in particular comprised calls for the restoration of law and order, for a return to 'normality'. As the prospect of a return to pre-1968 normality receded, unionists began to reconstruct the history of the 'troubles' as a long list of successive defeats and concessions to their nationalist

---

9   A. Aughey, 'The Constitutional Challenge', in J. W. Foster (ed.), *The Idea of the Union: Statements and Critiques in Support of the Union of Great Britain and Northern Ireland*, Vancouver: Belcouver Press, 1995, pp. 26–52.

opponents. Unionist response to the Belfast Agreement was not to welcome it as a 'victory for unionism' – which might have been tactically effective. Rather it was to get embroiled in an intra-unionist debate over whether it represented yet another set of concessions or whether it had the potential to underpin the Union in the long term. It is unclear as yet which view will prevail.

The economic merits of the Union as opposed to closer links with the Republic can no longer be taken for granted. Just as some of the more apocalyptic commentators were forecasting the extinction of nationalist Ireland in the 1950s, others were contemplating a similar fate for unionism at the end of the twentieth century. Demographic change threatens the majority at regional level and in several important localities including Belfast. There is a sense of retreat to a smaller Northern Ireland, made up of consolidated Protestant areas in the Lagan Valley and the suburbs of Belfast. The strong strain of apocalyptic thinking in northern Protestantism and the significance of the myth of siege in unionist ideology feed an underlying political and cultural pessimism that a strengthened enemy is about to overwhelm the defences.

Unionism and the myth of state

It is important not to take at face value the ideological representations of success and failure outlined above. As with all ideologies, unionism and nationalism obscure as well as reveal. A detailed socio-historical analysis of Ireland in the last half of the twentieth century would uncover much contrary evidence to the ideological viewpoints outlined. The success celebrated in nationalist ideology is of relatively recent origins, dating from the early to mid-1990s and it may be precarious. The late 1970s and 1980s were marked by economic downturn and high emigration rates. Nevertheless, over the whole period, it is possible to detect a growth in the confidence of the political class in the Irish Republic arising from the long-term economic modernisation

269

programme, involvement in the EU, and the growing partnership with the UK government in the management of Northern Ireland. While nationalists in Northern Ireland can point to steady advance in terms of socio-economic and political reforms and in terms of their capacity to build external alliances, nationalist communities in many parts of Northern Ireland remain highly vulnerable to loyalist intimidation and violence. While the Republican narrative of advance through struggle can be persuasive, it serves to hide their failure to force a British withdrawal and their acceptance, at least in the short term, of partition.

Unionist narratives of decline, fragmentation, concession and defeat can also be questioned. It is worth asking what have unionists lost in the last twenty years. There is little evidence, for example, of a decline in the material circumstances of the unionist community, or of any weakening in the British commitment to maintaining Northern Ireland within the UK as long as a majority so wishes. Unionist political losses arguably have been relative; they have lost their monopoly of political power and have to share power with nationalists. The sectarian headcount also suggests their relative decline. As Anderson and Shuttleworth have argued, much unionist ideological rhetoric arises from a 'deflated superiority complex' relative to the northern nationalists and the Irish Republic.[10] One further powerful reason for unionists' sense of loss arises from their perception that nationalist and republican leadership has become more effective and united as unionist leadership has become more fragmented and ineffectual.

It is not my intention here to use some objective measuring rod to determine the validity of the ideological reverses outlined. Nor is it possible in a brief discussion to analyse the changing social basis of nationalism and unionism and the changing composition of their political

---

10 J. Anderson and I. Shuttleworth, 'Sectarian Readings of Sectarianism: Interpreting the Northern Irish Census', *Irish Review*, vol. 16, 1994, p. 87.

classes. A complete analysis would take into account these changes and would examine the underlying material changes in the relative economic and political position of nationalists and unionists. But here I want to probe two related reasons for the different trajectories of nationalism and unionism: the different characteristics of the ideologies themselves and their differential capacity to adjust to the changing international context in which Ireland is located.

There is a fundamental asymmetry in the nature of Irish nationalist and Ulster unionist ideology. The former is primarily based on the myth of the nation, and has historically been based on the cultural construction of nationhood as a means of establishing claims for an independent Irish state. Intellectuals have played a key role in developing a narrative of a 'diasporic' nation in search of a state. Thus the ideological narrative of Irish nationalism has been that of a nation seeking a state, based on recognition that no Irish state, even an all-Ireland one, could incorporate all those who see themselves as Irish.

The central myth in unionism is a myth of the state rather than a myth of nation. In some senses, unionism is about a state seeking a nation although this is a more accurate description of contemporary British nationalism. Ulster unionists may differ internally on which nation they belong to – Ulster Scots, British and even Irish. Where there is overwhelming consensus, however, is that they 'belong' to the British state – a state which has given them, in a commonly used phrase, their 'civil and religious liberty'. There is a strong and weak version of this state myth. The strong version emphasises the myth of the archaic British constitution, the trappings of monarchy and the 'Crown in Parliament', British war memories and allegiance to the British army, the Union flag, and the 'banal nationalism' of British state rituals. The weaker version emphasises the merits of British citizenship, the benefits of belonging to a modern, multinational, multicultural welfare state. This version is willing to lay claim to particular aspects of Irish culture, to what Kennedy terms 'non-political Irishness', while prioritising identification with the British state and British citizenship.[11]

Unionists' sense of political decline is part of a wider transition from British imperialism to a contemporary form of British nationalism. They share in what Taylor has called 'the post-hegemonic trauma' of an imperial state readjusting to a lesser position as a member state of the EU.[12] Since the 1950s, the disappearance of empire and the shrinking of the global role of the British state have made the tacit, universalistic connotations of 'Britishness' harder to sustain. This, in turn, has affected unionist ideology in Northern Ireland, where Britishness was contested from the outset by a large minority.

Today, Britishness is even contested in Britain and has led to the development of a more strident form of British nationalism associated with the right wing of the Tory party. This form of nationalism claims to be anti-nationalist seeing nationalism as a form of disease affecting the peripheries of the British Isles and countries abroad. These sentiments are echoed precisely in the Ulster Unionist Party's (UUP) official website. Despite sharing power with Irish nationalists, the UUP's official policy is that: 'it is opposed to any form of nationalism which it views as exclusive and confrontational'. It goes on to point out that: the 'effects of nationalism are still evident in parts of Europe today' and that 'it remains a threat to the peaceful co-existence of people in Northern Ireland'.[13] According to the UUP, the UK is a multicultural entity and as such British citizenship safeguards the civil liberties of all its peoples. As David

---

11 D. Kennedy, 'The Realism of the Union', in J. W. Foster (ed.), *The Idea of the Union: Statements and Critiques in Support of the Union of Great Britain and Northern Ireland*, Vancouver: Belcouver Press, 1995, p. 35.

12 P. J. Taylor, 'The English and their Englishness: A Curiously Mysterious, Elusive and Little Understood People', *Scottish Geographical Magazine*, vol. 107, no. 3, 1991, pp. 146–61.

13 See www.uup.org.

Trimble put it at a party conference: 'it is only unionism which can be genuinely multinational and multi-cultural, a better vision than anything sectarian Irish nationalism has to offer'.[14] It is tempting to regard such sentiments as a somewhat plaintive and unconvincing echo of 1950s unionism.

Popular Orange and loyalist narratives also fuse with narratives of British national decline, but supplement them with memories of plantation, of settlers under siege from threatening natives, an enduring anti-Catholicism and specific collective memories of involvement in British wars old and new. While small parts of this ideological framework might incorporate some Catholics and nationalists in Northern Ireland, for the most part, it is at once too exclusive and too general, to form a legitimating ideology for the region as a separate political unit.

Porter has identified the myth of state as the central element that holds all types of unionism together: the conviction that the Union is an end in itself, or 'better the end to which all other ends are subservient'.[15] In the context of Northern Ireland, this means identifying the survival of unionists, or more specifically Protestants, as a community with continued membership of the British state.

The failures of Irish nationalist ideology in the 1950s gave key members of the political class, including intellectuals, the tools to critique it. The perceived success of unionism in the same decade was a disincentive for such criticism. Indeed, more to the point, the ideological priority given to the Union, or to the myth of the state, largely precluded the emergence of such a critique and illuminated resistance to reform. When the Stormont system collapsed under pressure from the civil rights movement, the British government and the IRA campaign, the dominant

---

14 D. Trimble, 'Address to Ulster Unionist Party Annual Conference', *The Irish Times*, 21 October 1996.

15 N. Porter, *Rethinking Unionism: An Alternative Vision for Northern Ireland*, Belfast: Blackstaff Press, 1996, p. 169.

ideological response was firstly to re-establish Stormont, then to take ever-harsher methods to restore law and order and ensure a return to 'normality'. All the major socio-economic reforms introduced by the British government were opposed by mainstream unionism. All were seen as concessions to those whose aim was to weaken a Union that was deemed to be non-negotiable.

Nationalism and the myth of nation

In the south, nationalist ideology was successfully re-invented and renewed as part of an economic modernisation programme and entry into the European Community. The resurrection of the national question in the north posed more severe problems. For many in the south, it was an unwelcome distraction from the business of modernisation, a reminder of the failure of Irish nationalism over partition. The northern conflict provoked an intense and long-running debate over the assumptions, record and methods of Irish nationalism and republicanism. This debate and the exigencies of responding to the Northern Ireland conflict produced at one level a greater awareness of north/south differences and the necessity for new policies to deal with them.

Much of the new nationalist ideology was focused on the 26-county state, seeing Northern Ireland as a problem to be resolved by both the British and Irish governments. This process was carried on through the medium of the New Ireland Forum in the 1980s, the Anglo-Irish Agreement and more recently the Belfast Agreement. It culminated in the changing of Articles 2 and 3 of the Irish Constitution and in the acceptance of Northern Ireland as a bi-national region. As the influence of the British economy on the Republic declined, the nationalist fixation with Britain faded. The sense of being an ex-colonial satellite of the metropolis was exchanged for a self-image of Ireland as a small modern European state with strong links to the US and Britain as well as the rest of the EU.

This redefinition of Irish nationalist ideology did not break from the past in one important respect. It remained philosophically idealist, initially at least, stressing the pre-eminence of ideas, cultural values and above all questions of identity over questions of material change. In the wake of the Cold War, the resurgence of nationalist movements and the prominence of identity politics internationally, Irish nationalist ideology was very much in tune with international developments. The nationalist construction of the Northern Ireland problem as a conflict of identities was easily comprehensible abroad. Unionist ideology, on the other hand, traditionally concerned with the state myth and with political control, was ill-equipped to engage in culture wars over national identity.

While the ideological reversals within unionism and nationalism have much to do with the changing nature of Irish politics, they are also related to the differential capacity of unionists and nationalists to adjust to globalisation. In the 1950s, the internal coherence of the Northern Ireland economy depended on a number of inter-linked industries: shipbuilding, engineering, linen and increasingly commercialised agriculture. These industries were the legacy of nineteenth-century industrialisation and supported a unionist political class dominated by local capitalists, landlords and a professional class biased towards science, engineering and technical occupations. By the 1960s, it was clear that this type of economy was precarious as global restructuring of industry shifted factory production to the third world or greenfield sites in the first world. From the 1960s onwards the Lagan Valley took some of the characteristics of a 'rust belt'.

The Republic of Ireland, on the other hand, was better placed to take advantage of new forms of globalisation such as the restructuring of global industry and the emergence of the so-called weightless economy. Significantly, one of the main features of new forms of global capitalism was the commodification of culture. A major influence on the changing self-perception of Irish nationalists is the successful commodification and marketing of Irish culture. Tony O'Reilly's suggestion that Ireland must be a quality brand has gone much further than perhaps he realises. Ireland is a successful brand in a world of brand capitalism. Its landscape, people, literature, even its cultural neuroses and introspection have benefited from economic globalisation. The global marketing of Irish traditional and popular music, dance and Irish pubs has transformed both the economic and the ideological climate. The Irish diaspora, traditionally a mark of Irish inferiority and the failure of the Irish state, is now a major economic resource. An ideology built around the myth of nation rather than the myth of state is more adaptable in the new global climate.

For unionists, marketing identity is not such an easy option; 'selling' Northern Ireland to foreign investors and tourists is difficult. A course must be steered between British and Irish identities. Irish linen, Irish beef, Irish whiskey co-exist with a virulent anti-Irishness, epitomised in the loyalist mural on Belfast's Newtownards Road which says 'Irish out' and which is flanked by images of Cuchulainn, the legendary defender of Ulster against the rest of Ireland in the old Celtic sagas. The relative scarcity of political and cultural intellectuals committed to unionism is a disadvantage within the new global economy. Indeed, frequently, the most articulate supporters of unionism are intellectual converts from Irish nationalism.

Conclusion

The consequences of the ideological reversals I have described in this chapter are not yet fully apparent. However, it is clear that unionist intellectuals have been forced increasingly to elaborate a case for the Union.[16]

---

16 L. O'Dowd, 'New Unionism, British Nationalism and the Prospects for a Negotiated Settlement in Northern Ireland', in D. Miller (ed.), *Rethinking Northern Ireland, Culture, Ideology and Colonialism*, London: Longman, 1998.

Popular unionist ideology also focuses increasingly on Protestant and loyalist culture. Here there is certain mimicry of traditional nationalist ideology, in the attempts to promote the Ulster-Scots language and to reconstruct the myth of a separate Ulster based on the ancient Pictish people. The conflict has generated loyalist heroes, songs and memorials, echoing the Republicans' politics of memory.

At another level, however, unionist support for practical cross-border co-operation reflects a desire for businesses to be associated with the success of the Irish economy. This is reflected also in the claims of some unionist intellectuals that British nationality and citizenship is compatible with an Irish cultural identity. The onset of devolution in Britain has complicated unionist ideology – it is pulled between identifying with a strident and often reactionary British nationalism promulgated by its close ideological counter-parts in the Conservative party, and arguing for a distinctive Ulster identity within a multinational and multicultural UK. Paisley and the extreme fringes of loyalism are beyond either of these two tendencies and find themselves arguing a case for traditional Ulster Protestant-ism often in the face of material advantages to be gained by agreement with the Irish and British governments. This search for a purified, 'not an inch' unionism is not unlike certain traditional forms of Irish nationalism in its rejection of material and political advantage in favour of protecting a (Protestant) way of life.

The ideological changes described above include a certain transference of traits across the two traditions, a mimicry on the part of some unionists of traditional nationalist practices and greater engagement between the two ideologies than has existed since the nineteenth century. It is difficult to predict how this engagement will develop. However, reviewing the changes in nationalist and unionist ideology over the last fifty years, it is tempting to conclude that nothing succeeds like failure and nothing fails like success.